Avoid the

Harmful
Side Effects

of Today's Commonly
Prescribed Drugs

Medical Director: David Juan, MD

Written by: Amber Toutant

Copy editor: Karolina Rous

Book design: Audrey O'Handley

Cover design: Jay Eckert

Avoid the Harmful Side Effects of Today's Commonly Prescribed Drugs

ISBN# 0-9734765-0-8

Printed in Canada.

Avoid the
Harmful Side Effects
of Today's Commonly Prescribed Drugs

Table of Contents

WHAT YOU NEED TO KNOW ABOUT COMMON HERBAL SUPPLEMENTS AND VITAMINS. 177

BRAND-NAME DRUG INDEX. 197

APPENDICES 215

Avoid the *Harmful Side Effects* of Today's Commonly Prescribed Drugs

PREFACE

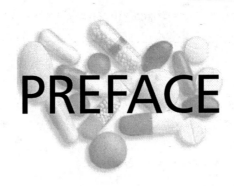

PREFACE

Why Are ADRs Important?

Adverse drug reactions, or ADRs, are becoming a national health problem since more and more new drugs hit the market and the number of elderly in North America is on the rise. Why is ADR an important topic for people who are on more than one prescription or over-the-counter drug plus dietary supplements? The reasons are listed below:

A Common Problem

In the year 2000, American doctors wrote a total of 2.8 billion prescriptions, on an average of 10 per patient. In the same year, the Institute of Medicine reported that there were about 100,000 deaths due to medical errors, of which 7,000 were attributed to ADRs. The general public is not aware of the fact that after the Food and Drug Administration approves a drug for marketing only about 3,000 individuals (normal subjects and patients) have been exposed to the drug—and only for a short period of time. For this reason, there is no way that the drug companies would know all the ADRs, since some ADRs are uncommon and would appear only after a substantially greater number of patients have been exposed to the drug for a much longer period of time than during clinical trials.

Other scary statistics tell us that:

- ADRs account for 2.9-15.4% of all hospital admissions in the United States.

- Close to 16% of nursing home residents are hospitalized because of an ADR.

- ADRs are believed to be between the fourth to sixth leading cause of death among hospitalized patients.

- Approximately 6.7% of hospitalized patients experience serious ADRs are defined as those requiring or prolonging hospitalization, are permanently disabled, or result in death.

- ADRs in hospitalized HIV patients are close to 20%.

Preventable 80% of the Time

The majority (about 80%) of ADRs are related to the dose. More often than not, ADRs arise because your physician either gives you the wrong (higher) dose than you need and/or he is not aware of some of the drugs (usually over-the-counter) and dietary supplements you are taking that interact with the prescribed drugs. Therefore, it is absolutely necessary for you to let your physician know about all the drugs and dietary supplements you are taking. In fact, I often ask my patients to write down all the names and doses of the drugs and dietary supplements before seeing me in the office.

Unnecessary Worries

When you walk into your doctor's office and he prescribes one or more drugs to you, I am sure you worry whether or not these drugs may cause unintended or adverse side effects in some way. Just remember that all drugs, even the commonly used aspirin, are associated with side effects. It is your job to find out what they are and what to do with the ADRs once they occur from your physician and the local pharmacists instead of worrying about it.

Definition and Classifications

According to the World Health Organization, the definition of an ADR is any response to a drug, (prescribed or over-the-counter) that is noxious and unintended, and that occurs at doses normally used in humans for prophylaxis, diagnosis, or therapy of disease. There are many different classification systems used to address ADRs. It may be helpful to be familiar with other, less commonly used classifications of ADRs, since your physician may use any given classification system. For example, the Physicians' Desk Reference (as well as clinical trials for the development of new drugs) uses the following, less common classifications:

Classification According to Severity

1. Mild—may not be noticed by patient e.g. raised liver function tests with many drugs.

2. Moderate—requires corrective measures but not hospitalization
    (e.g. antibiotic=induced rash).

3. Major—organ damage and hospitalization is likely (e.g. jaundice with chlorpromazine).

4. Life threatening—pulmonary embolus caused by oral contraceptives.

Classification According to Incidence

1. Very common: More than 10% of those exposed (e.g. drowsiness with carbamazepine, an anti-seizure drug).

2. Common: 1-10% of those exposed (e.g. swelling the legs with carbamazepine).

3. Uncommon: 0.1-1% of those exposed (e.g. diarrhea with carbamazepine).

4. Rare: 0.01-0.1% of those exposed.

Common Drug Classes Causing ADRs

To be an educated consumer, you need to know what some of the common ADRs associated with the various classes of drugs your physician may prescribe for you. The following table shows the common ADRs associated with different classes of drugs that are commonly prescribed.

Drug Class	Examples of ADRs
Antibiotics	Diarrhea, rash, itching
Anti-cancer	Nausea, vomiting, losing hair, suppression of bone marrow to produce white blood cells, red blood cells, or platelets
Blood thinners	Bleeding from any organ, bruising
Heart drugs	Swelling in feet, irregular heart beat, heart block
Anti-diabetic	Low blood sugar, diarrhea, gastrointestinal discomfort
NSAIDs	Gastrointestinal ulcer and bleeding, kidney failure
Opiates	Sleepiness, dizziness, constipation
Water pills (diuretic)	Low potassium, high uric acid in blood, high blood sugar in blood
Diagnostic agents	Low blood pressure, kidney failure, allergic reactions
Central Nervous System drugs	Dizziness, drowsiness, headache, hallucination

Organ Systems Commonly Affected by ADRs

The drugs you are on could be causing your the symptoms or disease conditions. The list below is just to illustrate what symptoms or disease states your drugs may cause. Always remember to ask your physician this important question: Could the drug(s) that you prescribe be causing my problem?

Body System	Examples of ADRs
Central nervous system	Anxiety, depression, insomnia, pain, dizziness, fatigue, seizures
Cardiovascular	Angina pain, palpitations, heart failure, fainting spells, irregular heart rhythms
Endocrine	Under active thyroid (hypothyroid), breast enlargement in men
Gastrointestinal and liver	Stomach upset, swallowing difficulty, colitis, jaundice, hepatitis, no appetite
Renal and Urinary	Vaginitis, blood in the urine, protein in urine, painful periods, urinary retention, nephritis
Hematological	Anemia, low platelets count, blood disorders
Dermatological	Itching, losing hair, brushing, rash, red spots on skin, hives
Metabolic	Osteoporosis, low sodium, potassium in blood
Musculoskeletal	Aching muscle and joints, numbness and tingling in arms, fingers, lower legs, and feet
Respiratory	Shortness of breath, coughing up blood, nosebleed, wheezing
Sensory	Impaired vision, hearing noise in ears, double vision, impaired taste or smell

Risk Factors Associated with ADRs

Since we have already mentioned the fact that up to 80% of all ADRs are preventable, therefore it is important that you, the consumer, be aware and understand the potential risk factors of the drugs you are taking. This is a critical step in ADR prevention.

Lack of Patient Education

It is estimated that in an outpatient clinic, the average time of patient-physician contact is less than 10 minutes. Therefore, it is not surprising that little or no patient education occurs during this brief period of time. It is an axiom that an educated consumer is a better consumer. Thus, this book is an attempt of filling in for the knowledge gap, which you, the patient as well as a healthcare consumer, require.

Inappropriate Prescribing or Monitoring of Prescription Drugs

Oftentimes, physicians prescribe drugs without going through the thinking process. A good example is the prescription of penicillin for all sore throat concerns, despite knowing the fact that most sore throats are caused by a virus unresponsive to penicillin. It is known that a new disease-modifying drug for rheumatoid arthritis, Leflutaminde (Arava) requires monthly monitoring of liver function since this drug might cause liver dysfunction. However, either due to ignorance or forgetfulness, physicians who prescribe this drug fail to monitor liver function on a regular basis. Consequently, some patients taking this drug develop liver problems later.

Altered Physiology Due to Aging

With aging, the processing (or metabolism) and excretion of drugs declines. Age-related decline in kidney function is probably the most important. Moreover, the brain in tan elderly person is often more sensitive to central nervous system acting drugs, such as drugs used for the treatment of anxiety or depression (i.e. Elavil, Valium).

End Organ Impairment Due to Disease

The liver and kidney are the two organs that are responsible for either processing (or metabolism) and/or excreting drugs in our body. Liver diseases such as hepatitis, cirrhosis, or kidney disease would impair the ability of these vital organs either to process (metabolize) or eliminate the drugs. Therefore, if you have liver or kidney disease, it is of paramount importance for you to be extra careful with any drug (prescription or over-the-counter), or dietary supplements. Be sure to question your physician and your local pharmacist about the DOSE prescribed.

Previous History of ADR, Including Allergic Reactions

It is known that if you have a previous ADR to a certain drug you are at greater risk of having the same reaction to the same drug or related drugs. Be sure you tell your physician about any previous adverse reaction to any drug, including the over-the-counter drugs, and even dietary supplements.

Hereditary Factors

Genetic differences also influence the likelihood of some ADRs, especially drug interactions. It is wise to ask your parents, siblings, and your relatives about the types of ADRs they have had, and let your physician and pharmacist know about these ADRs in order to avoid possible potential ADRs to the same drug (or same class of drug).

Female Gender

Women are more likely to experience ADRs than men. From data collected over a 10-year period by the Glaxo Wellcom-Sunnybrook Drug Safety Clinic, more than 77% of all ADRs were reported in women. In general, a woman over the age of 19 is 43-69% more likely than her male counterpart to experience an ADR. The exact reason for this gender difference is unknown. However, differences in circulating sex hormones and more frequent use of drugs, which inhibit liver processing, are cited as possible explanations.

Age Factor (Children and Elderly)

Age is an important risk factor for the development of ADRs. Both very young children and the elderly are particularly vulnerable to ADRs. During the development of a drug by pharmaceutical companies, these age groups are often excluded from test groups. Therefore, by the time the drug is marketed, there is often little or no clinical experience in terms of ADRs in these age groups. The reasons for a very young person to experience a great risk of ADRs include immature organ function, for either drug processing or elimination, and differences in drug distribution due to smaller body weight and the amount of muscle/fat ratio.

Dose and Duration of Prescribed Drugs

Drugs with a narrow therapeutic window such as digoxin (for heart failure), blood thinners (warfarin, heparin), theophylline (for asthma), aminoglycosides (for infection), and anticonvulsants (for seizure disorders) most often lead to ADRs. A therapeutic window describes how wide or narrow the drug level in blood, which separates drug toxicity from drug under dosing. Thus, a drug with a narrow therapeutic window simply means that the drug levels that separate drug toxicity from drug ineffectiveness is not wide, thus making the proper dosing by physician so important. Fortunately for physicians, there are many commercial laboratories, which could measure the blood levels of these drugs quite easily. If your physician prescribed any one of these drugs, be sure to remind him/her to monitor your drug levels in your blood in order to avoid unnecessary ADRs down the road.

Multiple Disease States

Diabetes, heart failure, asthma, chronic lung disease, obesity, and high blood pressure are common diseases especially as we get older. Any of these disease would increase our risk of ADRs since these diseases alter the physiology and key drug processing (metabolism) and/or drug eliminating organ functions such as the liver and kidney. If you are elderly, or having muscle wasting, or become malnourished for some reason, you need to be especially careful with any drug prescribed by your physician, since your kidney function is most likely not functioning properly.

Multiple Drugs

It is a well established fact that the more drugs you are on the more likely an ADR may occur—especially if you are on more than five to six drugs. In medicine, this is known as "polypharmacy." The factors that contribute to polypharmacy include multiple physicians, absence of primary care physician, multiple pharmacies, frequent drug regimen changes, self-treatment, multiple disease conditions, over prescribing, and aging.

80% of ADRs are Preventable! Dose, Dose, and Dose!

As previously mentioned, approximately 80% of all ADRs are dose-related and therefore preventable. In an article written by Dr. J. S. Cohen from the University of California in San Diego, published in the *Archives of Internal Medicine* in 2001, entitled "Dose Discrepancies between the Physicians' Desk Reference and the Medical Literature, and Their Possible Relationship to the Incidence of Adverse Drug Events," he cited the effective, lower doses for the 53 top-selling drugs that patients won't find in the *Physician's Desk Reference* as shown below.

Note: This list is for information only. You should consult your physician before changing dose.

DRUG	DRUG COMPANY INITIAL DOSE	EFFECTIVE LOWER INITIAL DOSE
Aldactone (spironolactone)	50-100 mg a day	25 mg
Allegra (fexofenadine)	60 mg twice a day	20 mg three times a day, or 40 mg twice a day
Altace (ramipril)	2.5 mg a day	1.25 mg a day
Ambien (zolpidem)	10 mg before bedtime	5 mg or 7.5 mg before bedtime
Axid (nizatidine)	150 mg twice a day, or 300 mg at bedtime	25-75 mg twice a day, or 100 mg at bedtime
Baycol (cerivastatin)	0.4 mg a day	0.2 or 0.3 mg a day
Calan(verapamil)	120-180 mg a day	90 mg a day
Celebrex (celecoxib)	100 mg twice a day	50 mg twice a day
Cozaar (losartan)	50 mg a day	25 mg a day
Cytotec (misoprostol)	200 µg four times a day	50-100 µg four times a day
Dalmane (flurazepam)	30 mg at bedtime	15 mg at bedtime
Demadex (torsemide)	10 mg a day	5 mg a day
Desyrel (trazodone)	150 mg a day	25-100 mg a day
Dyrenlum (triamterene)	100 mg twice a day	25-100 mg a day
Edecrin (ethacrynic acid)	50 mg a day	25 mg a day
Effexor (venlafaxine)	75 mg a day	37.5-50 mg a day
Elavil (amitriptyline)	50-75 mg a day	10-25 mg a day
Estrace (oral estradiol)	1-2 mg a day	0.5 mg a day
Estraderm (transdermal estradiol)	0.05-0.1 mg a day	0.02-0.025 mg a day
Estratab (esterified estrogens)	1.25 mg a day	0.3-0.625 mg a day
Hydrochlorothiazide (HCTZ)	25 mg a day	12.5 mg a day
Hygroton (chlorthalidone)	15 mg a day	12.5 mg a day
Inderal (propranolol, regular and XL)	80 mg a day	40 mg a day
Isoptin (verapamil)	120-180 mg a day	90 mg a day
Lasix (furosemide)	80 mg a day	40 mg a day
Levatol (penbutolol)	10 mg a day	20 mg a day*

Lipitor (atorvastatin)	10 mg a day	2.5-5 mg a day
Lopressor (metoprolol)	50-100 mg a day	50 mg a day **
Mevacor (lovastatin)	20 mg a day	10 mg a day
Motrin (ibuprofen)	300-400 mg three or four times a day	200 mg three times a day
Norvasc (amlodipine)	5 mg a day	2.5 mg a day***
Pamelor (nortriptyline)	50-75 mg a day	10-25 mg a day
Pepcid (famotidine)	20 mg twice a day or 40 mg at bedtime	10 mg twice a day or 20 mg at bedtime
Plendil (felodipine)	5 mg a day	2.5 mg a day
Pravachol (pravastatin)	10-20 mg a day	5-10 mg a day
Premarin(conjugated estrogens)	0.625 mg a day	0.3 mg a day
Prilosec (omeprazole)	20 mg a day	10 mg a day
Privinil (lisinopril)	10 mg a day	5 mg a day
Prozac (fluoxetine)	20 mg a day	2.5, 5, or 10 mg a day
Sectral (acebutolol)	400 mg a day	200 mg a day
Serzone (nefazodone)	100 mg twice a day	50 mg a day, or twice a day
Sinequan (doxepin)	75 mg a day	10,25,50 mg a day
Tagamet (cimetidine)	800 mg at bedtime	400 mg at bedtime
Tenormin (atenolol)	50 mg a day	25 mg a day
Tofranil (imipramine)	75 mg a day	10-25 mg a day
Verelan (verapamil)	120-180 mg a day	90 mg a day
Voltaren (diclofenac)	50 mg two, three, or four times a day	25 mg three times a day
Wellbutrin (bupropion)	100 mg twice daily	50 mg twice a day
Zantac (ranitidine)	150 mg twice a day, or 300 mg at bedtime	100 twice daily, or 200 mg at bedtime
Zebeta (bisoprolol)	5 mg a day	2.5 mg a day ****
Zestril (lisinopril)	10 mg a day	5 mg a day
Zocor (simvastatin)	10-20 mg a day	2.5, 5. 10 mg a day
Zofran (ondansetron)	8 mg twice a day	1-4 mg three times a day
Zoloft (sertraline)	50 mg a day	25 mg a day

* *The Physicians' Desk Reference* states: "A dose of 10 mg also lowers blood pressure, but the full effect is not seen for four to eight weeks."

** One brand of metoprolol is recommending a starting dose of 100 mg a day, whereas another brand is recommending a starting dose of 50-100 mg a day.

*** *The Physicians Desk Reference* states that the usual starting dose of Norvasc is 5 mg a day, but then it states that 2.5 mg may be enough for small, elderly, or debilitated patients. Experts in this area usually recommend a starting dose of 2.5 mg for all patients.

**** *The Physicians' Desk Reference* usual starting dose of bisoprolol is 5 mg a day, but it states that 2.5 mg a day may be enough for some patients. The sixth report of the Joint National Committee on Prevention, Detection, Evaluation, and Treatment of High Blood Pressure (JNC VI) recommends a starting dose of 2.5 mg for all patients.

How is Avoid the Harmful Side Effects of Today's Commonly Prescribed Drugs *Different?*

More Medically Oriented

Unlike many similar books on the market, which overload the readers with facts as the Physicians' Desk Reference does, this book is written with the layman reader in mind. As I sat down to write this book, the two questions foremost on my mind were:

1. What does my reader want to know about this particular drug?

2. What can I tell my reader that will help him/her avoid an ADR?

Therefore, under each drug, I have included the key information you need to know as the consumer of drugs, namely,

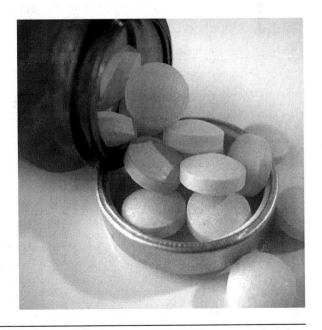

- What is the medical condition that this drug is prescribed for?

- What are some known contraindications or drug interactions associated with this drug?

- What are some common side effects associated with the use of this drug?

- What are some of the long-term side effects?

- What, if any, are some of the toxic, life-threatening side effects?

- What general advice I would give my readers about the proper use of this drug?

Based on my years of clinical experience with patients, I have created a checklist you can follow, entitled *Personal Medication Record*. Remember to use this checklist every time your physician prescribes a new drug to you and you could avoid many unnecessary ADRs.

More User Friendly

As I have already mentioned above, this book is written with you, the reader, in mind. Therefore, the language and medical terminology used are usually followed by an explanation. I have created blank forms for you to jot down questions for your physician the next time you have an appointment to see him/her. Moreover, I have created an *ADR Medication and Side Effects Diary* for you to write down any ADRs you experience. Human beings are forgetful—especially those who are accustomed to the hectic North American way of life. Unless you write down your ADR as soon as it occurs you will definitely forget it the next day. So, I encourage you to write all the ADRs you experience—regardless of whatever drugs you are taking. Show this to your physician and pharmacist and I am sure they will be very impressed.

More Comprehensive

I can say without a shadow of a doubt that *Avoid the Harmful Side Effect of Today's Commonly Prescribed Drugs* is the most comprehensive book of its kind. Most books similar to this one just list the indications, contraindications, side effects, dosage, and toxicity. However, this book goes beyond that because it includes:

- Sound advice about how to avoid ADRs

- A checklist of questions you should ask your physician whenever he or she prescribes you a drug

- A review of common herbs and vitamins, which you should tell your physician and pharmacist how to avoid unintended ADRs

- A special report entitled What Pharmacists Never Tell You

- A list of common food additives and associated ADRs

- A detox/cleansing program

- A *Personal Medication Record* section

More Authoritative

I used to teach the rational use of drugs, including their adverse effects to medical students, residents and practicing physicians while I was at Northwestern Medical School in Chicago. I now practice internal medicine in the San Francisco area, and have daily contact with patients who occasionally complain of ADRs from the drugs I prescribed to them. Therefore, I have had first-hand experience with ADRs for years as a practicing physician, as well as a teacher of clinical medicine. Moreover, I have done clinical research on drugs in the last 20 years, as well as conducted clinical trials on drugs. I have seen and analyzed ADRs in the development of new drugs prior to marketing. It is with this wealth of experience and knowledge that I undertook the writing of this book.

David Juan, MD

Avoid the

Harmful Side Effects

of Today's Commonly Prescribed Drugs

HOW TO AVOID HARMFUL SIDE EFFECTS

NOTES

GETTING EXPERT HELP

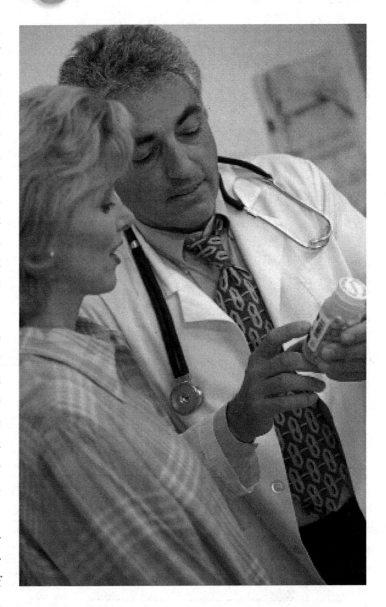

Naturally, your doctor is the person who prescribes the drug. But for various reasons, he or she may not sit down and discuss all the ins and outs of a medication with you. You may never learn all the factors he considered before settling on this particular medication; by the same token, he may choose a prescription without knowing everything about you — such as what supplements you take (see the checklist that follows this chapter, *Questions to Ask your Doctor*).

Meanwhile, another factor to consider is that your doctor may have a great manner and be a whiz at conventional medicine, but he may not be a great fan of alternative therapies. That's fine, you don't have to switch. But you may want to augment his prescription with wisdom from other resources.

The question is, apart from your doctor, whom can you turn to for expert advice? Does the owner of the health food store, for example, have professional training with respect to the supplements he or she sells? Or do you even need high level advice about supplements? Will a good book — or information from the Internet — do the trick?

Here's an overview of the expert resources available and how you can expect these people to help you.

Pharmacists

Pharmacists have got to be one of the most underutilized resources in the medical "industry." Many people don't realize there is so much more to a pharmacist than a person counting pills into bottles.

In reality, the training to become a pharmacist is comparable to a medical program. Of the 81 degree-granting colleges, only a few accept high school graduates. Most insist on one to two years of college-level, "pre-pharmacy" specialist education. Students are expected to come into the program with a solid background in mathematics and the basic sciences — chemistry, biology, and physics — plus some coursework in the humanities. Some colleges also administer an admissions test to applicants.

Once in, the program generally involves six years of study before students receive their Pharm.D. degree. But even then they're not finished their education. To obtain a license to practice candidates must pass a State examination. Afterwards, depending on where they live, they may be required to continue their education in order to maintain their licenses.

Now, with particular respect to consumers, as part of the pharmacy curriculum students study something called "pharmacy practice." This area emphasizes patient care and effective communication both with patients and other health professionals. In other words, pharmacists get taught how to discuss your medication with you — and, when necessary, to take up your concerns with your doctor.

Rx Tip: Buy all your prescriptions from the same pharmacy. That way the pharmacy can keep complete records of the medications you've taken (and possible reactions) in the past, and know everything you're on now — meaning they'll be more likely to pick up on potential interactions, and be better prepared to recommend the optimal supplement program.

When you bring in a new prescription to be filled, your pharmacist reviews the dosage instructions and other important information with you. Some pharmacies distribute detailed instruction sheets with medications, explaining how to take the drug and what to watch out for. But don't just accept what you're handed. This is a golden opportunity to ask all your questions—specifically so you get detailed information on interactions, side effects and supplements.

In fact, you should prepare for your trip to the pharmacy almost as carefully as you do when you go to your doctor. Write out a list of questions about your medication—but don't feel bound by it: If your conversation with your pharmacist brings more questions to mind, make sure you ask them. Take a pen and paper so you can jot down the answers.

Alternative Physicians

The American Association of Naturopathic Physicians, or AANP, explains that naturopathic medicine combines conventional medicine with alternative healing techniques to achieve a more holistic approach. Specifically, the AANP identifies "therapeutic nutrition, botanical medicine, homeopathy, natural childbirth, traditional Chinese medicine, hydrotherapy, naturopathic manipulative therapy, pharmacology, and minor surgery" as skills its members must master.

Licensed, qualified naturopathic physicians—who are entitled to identify themselves as "ND"—are graduates of a four-year graduate-level specialty medical school. Their curriculum includes both conventional medical courses and training in the areas above, plus some others, such as counseling to help their patients choose a more healthy lifestyle. Qualified naturopathic physicians take exams, just as ordinary doctors do, in order to get licensed in their particular jurisdiction.

If you have any trouble locating a licensed practitioner where you live, one of the following organizations should be able to help.

American Association of Naturopathic Physicians (AANP)
3201 New Mexico Avenue, NW Suite 350
Washington, DC 20016
Toll Free: (866) 538-2267
Phone: (202) 895-1392
http://www.naturopathic.org/

National College of Naturopathic Medicine (NCNM)
2220 Porter Street,
Portland, OR 97201
Phone: (503) 552-1515
http://www.ncnm.edu/intro.html

Canadian College of Naturopathic Medicine (CCNM)
1255 Sheppard Ave. E.
Toronto, ON
M2K 1E2 Canada
Phone: (416) 498-1255
Toll Free: (866) 241-2266
http://www.ccnm.edu/

Health Food Retailers

If you felt like it—and had the money—you could open a health food store tomorrow. Call the suppliers, get them to ship the merchandise over, stock the shelves and voilà!—you're in business.

Of course, that wouldn't make you an expert, and therein lies the problem with health food retailers. Some establishments take their business very seriously, study hard, affiliate themselves with naturopathic physicians and are very careful about what they say and sell. Others are more careless: the owner may have some knowledge, but lowly-paid sales clerks have little incentive to learn. Sadly, there's also a third group, in which unscrupulous vendors try to maximize profits on dubious products.

Consequently, the challenge for you, as a consumer, is to find a business in that first group—the stores with the most credibility and highest reputations. Indicators to look for include:

- Many successful years in business

- A dedication that goes beyond retail, such as, seminars, newsletters, and other educational programs

- Ethical practices that extend the concept of "health food," such as environmental, fair trade

- Knowledgeable and committed staff (You see this most often in co-ops)

Understand that even after you find this trusted source, you will still not be getting advice on par with a trained naturopath or pharmacist. Chances are you'll get plenty of anecdotal information—these retailers tend to know their customers well and talk at length with them—and while that can be quite valuable, it cannot replace years of formal, specialist education.

The Internet

It's not the "information highway," but the information trail—wild west style. You "meet" all kinds of "specialists" on the Internet, and just because a site looks professional doesn't mean the advice is worth a dime. A slick, well-designed site is often the visible presentation of a company selling snake oil on-line.

That being said, there are excellent sources of information on-line, if you're prepared to dig. Just be careful about whom you trust. Look for the web sites of trusted university medical centers, medical publications and government health services.

Here's a great example: To find generally accepted information on a drug, start with the Medline Plus database **http://www.nlm.nih.gov/medlineplus/druginformation.html**. Medline brings to the public, information from the National Library of Medicine and the National Institutes of Health, and more. In fact, if health is just generally a subject of interest to you, bookmark this site and check it often—it's updated with new material every day.

CHECKLIST: QUESTIONS TO ASK YOUR DOCTOR

Doctors' offices can be intimidating places, but always remember: This is YOUR body we're talking about, and you have a right to understand what's going on. There's no such thing as a stupid question when it comes to your health. If you don't understand something, say so. Don't worry that asking may take extra time: regardless of how many people are sitting in the waiting room, your doctor is there to provide you with a service.

That said, it's important to use your time with your doctor wisely. Obviously, while the doctor is still conducting his examination you don't want to interrupt, because he needs to concentrate to make his diagnosis. Afterwards though, when he sits down to discuss his findings with you is a good time for you to raise your questions.

As far as possible, make a list beforehand—covering your symptoms, gray areas and concerns. Take pen and paper, so you can make notes. Here are some questions specifically about medications that you may want to use during your consultation:

Feel free to copy the following checklist for your own personal use. We suggest you bring a copy to every doctor's appointment you have.

☐ Name of medication _____

☐ Is this medication for treating symptoms (e.g., pain) or the condition itself?

_____

_____

☐ If symptoms only, what treatment is indicated to deal with the condition?

_____

_____

_____

_____

☐ How effective is this medication? _____

_____

☐ How long do I need to take this medication before I will feel its effects?_____

☐ Are there any alternative treatments available, including no treatment? _____
If so, what are the risks and benefits associated with each?_____

_____

_____

_____

☐ Does the dosage need to be adjusted—for example, due to other medical conditions
or medications taken? _____

_____

_____

_____

_____

☐ Instructions for taking this medication: _____

_____

_____

_____

☐ What are the common side effects of this medication? _____

_____

_____

_____

☐ Is there any way to minimize or prevent the side effects?

_____

_____

_____

☐ What are the known interactions with food, other drugs, and/or supplements?

_____

_____

_____

☐ What supplements can, or should, be taken with this medication, and why?

_____

_____

_____

☐ Is it safe to suddenly discontinue this medicine, or must it be tapered off?

_____

☐ What if the medication doesn't work? _____

_____

_____

_____

NOTES

Avoid the
Harmful Side Effects
of Today's Commonly Prescribed Drugs

WHAT YOU NEED TO KNOW ABOUT SPECIFIC DRUGS

Please Note: While we have tried to include in this book information on as many common prescription drugs as we can in the scope of this book, you may be taking or be prescribed a medication that does not appear here. Try looking it up by brand-name in the index provided.

Even if a drug you are taking is not in this book, however, there is a lot of useful information that appears in the following pages that you should read. Look for the "prescription pad" boxes throughout this book for valuable tips that make any prescription drug you're taking safer, and refer to our NSAIDs, Aspirin, herb, and vitamin entries before you take an over-the-counter pain reliever or supplement.

In addition, everyone who reads this book should take advantage of the medication diary and personal medication record worksheets that appear in the back of this book – keeping this information in a handy place will help you and your doctor determine the best course of action for your particular health concerns and keep you from forgetting important information about the drugs you take.

Your health and safety were our first priority in creating *Avoid the Harmful Side Effects of Today's Commonly Prescribed Drugs*, and we wish you and your family health and happiness in the days and years to come.

NOTES

_____

_____

_____

_____

_____

_____

_____

_____

_____

_____

_____

_____

_____

ACE Inhibitors
(Angiotensin Converting Enzyme Inhibitor Family)

Includes: Benazepril, Captopril, Enalapril, Fosinopril, Lisinopril, Quinapril, Ramipril,

Brand Names: Benazepril: Lotensin, Lotrel

Captopril: Acediur [CD], Alti-Captopril, Apo-Capto, Capoten, Capozide [CD], Novo-Captopril, Nu-Capto, Syn-Captopril

Enalapril: Lexxel [CD], Vaseretic [CD], Vasotec

Fosinopril: Lin-Fosinopril, Monopril

Lisinopril: Prinivil, Prinzide [CD], Zestoretic [CD], Zestril

Quinapril: Accupril, Accuretic

Ramipril: Altace, Ramace

 Used For

- Control of mild to severe hypertension (high blood pressure)

- Treatment of congestive heart failure

- Helps with blood pressure helper in active exercisers

- Other cardiovascular related problems

 Known Contraindications and/or Interactions

- Depending on the type of medication, doses may need to be reduced for those with liver and kidney problems, or for people with diabetic protein loss and with difficulty excerting metabolic waste (creatinine)

- Taking these drugs after the first trimester of pregnancy could be dangerous, also certain kinds like Ramipril, or certain combination drugs are not advised, so be cautious and ask your doctor for assistance

- Interactions may occur when taking ACE inhibitors with Allopurinol, Azathioprine, Capsaicin, Clomipramine, Cyclosporine, Dalfopristin, Erythropoietin, Fluconazole, Iron, Interferons,

R Most online pharmacies — the good ones anyway — will require a brief medical history. In this you should include any illnesses you are suffering from, information of other major diseases in your family, such as cancer or liver diseases, the medications you are taking, be it prescription, non-prescription, herbal or nutritional. Also include your height and weight and any allergies you suffer from, including drug allergies or environmental allergies.

Lithium, loop diuretics, Metformin, Nestiride, Hypoglycemic Drugs taken orally, Pergolide, Phenothiazines, Potassium supplements and diuretics that reserve Potassium, Quinupristin, Rifampin, Saquinavir, Thiazide, Cotrimoxazole, Antacids, COX-II inhibitors, Ibuprofen, Naloxone, Naloxone, Salicylates

 Common Side Effects

- When taking Enalapril, some people experience a loss, or change, in sense of smell

- Burning feeling in mouth

- Neausea, constipation, cough, dizziness, fainting from loss of blood pressure or increased heart rate with Captopril when moving from a sitting or lying to a standing position

 Occasional/Long-Term Side Effects

- Rarely, some people experience allergy, swelling, fever, changes in mouth — including sores or salty or metallic taste, hair loss, pain in joints, blood sugar drop, nightmares, sleep disturbances, bone marrow depletion, anemia, oedema, cardial fluid retention, hallucinations, serious skin conditions, liver or kidney problems, pancreatitis, loss of libido, vaginal itching, sensitive breast tissue in men or impotence

- Long term use may result in a persistent cough or an increase in Potassium levels of blood

 Toxicity/Adverse Reaction (Contact your doctor)

- Signs of overdose: Dizziness, feeling of light-headedness, fainting

 General Advice and Precautions

- Salt intake may need to be altered

- Caffeine and other stimulants like Guarana and Yerba Mate may raise blood pressure, making these drugs less effective. Ginseng, Hawthorn, Saw Palmetto, Goldenseal, and Licorice should similarly be avoided, but Garlic and Calcium may help the effectiveness of ACE inhibitors

- Zinc or Iron may need to be supplemented. Speak with your doctor

- Grapefruit juice and alcohol may affect drug levels. Use with caution

- Smoking, which may increase the cough producing effects of these drugs, is not advised

- The drugs Captopril, Enalapril, Ioexipril, Ramipril and Trandolapril may cause photosenisitivity, so be cautious with sun exposure

- Some drugs can be stopped without sudden withdrawl (Captopril, Lisinopril, Quinapril, Fosinopril, Benazepril) but it is best to talk to your doctor before discontinuation of any drug

Acebutolol

Brand Names: Apo-Acebutolol, Gen-Acebutolol, Med-Acebutolol, Monitan, Rhotral, Sectral

 Used For

- Mild to moderate high blood pressure

- Prevention of heart arrhythmias

- Stabilize angina pectoris

- Help heart attack patients live longer

 Known Contraindications and/or Interactions

- Do not use while breast-feeding

- Drugs with known interactions include other antihypertensive drugs, Reserpine, Alfentanil, alpha-one-adrenergic blockers, Amiodarone, and more. Discuss all your medications with your doctor and pharmacist.

 Common Side Effects

- Lethargy, easily tired, lightheadedness

 Occasional/Long-Term Side Effects

- Cold hands and feet

Toxicity/Adverse Reaction (Contact your doctor)

- Call your doctor if you experience dizziness, falling, hallucinations, confusion or uncharacteristically frequent urination

- Signs of overdose: Slow pulse, low blood pressure, weakness, fainting, cold and sweaty skin; leading to convulsions, coma, congestive heart failure

General Advice and Precautions

- Follow a "heart-friendly" diet

- Herbs and minerals to avoid include Ginseng, Hawthorn, Saw Palmetto, Ma Huang, Guarana, Goldenseal, Yohimbe, Licorice

- Do not smoke Marijuana while on this medication

- May cause drowsiness; be cautious about driving

- Do not skip doses

- Blood pressure should be checked frequently and health condition monitored

- This drug needs to be discontinued gradually over two to three weeks under a doctor's supervision

Acetaminophen

Brand Names: Tylenol with Codeine (Tylenol 2, Tylenol 3, Tylenol 4)

Used For

- Mild to moderate pain
- Cough control

Known Contraindications and/or Interactions

- Do not use in children under two

- Do not use in high doses or for a prolonged period in late-term pregnancy

- Consult physician before use if you are pregnant or breast-feeding

- Do not use or use with caution if you have asthma, chronic bronchitis, respiratory difficulty

- Drugs with known interactions include over-the-counter Acetaminophen (Tylenol), sedatives, MOA inhibitors, Tramadol, Quinidine, Rifabutin, Ritonavir, Naltrexone, atropinelike drugs

- Do not take if you are planning for surgery with general anesthesia

- Do not take if you have impaired liver or kidney function

- Do not use if you have a history of alcoholism or drug addiction

- Do not take after head injury

 ## Common Side Effects

- Drowsiness, lightheadedness

- Dry mouth

- Constipation

- Urinary retention

 ## Occasional/Long-Term Side Effects

- Habit-forming, psychological and physical dependence

- Chronic constipation

- Liver/kidney damage, pancreatitis

 ## Toxicity/Adverse Reaction (Contact your doctor)

- Seizures

- Impaired breathing, allergic reactions

- Dizziness, confusion

- Nausea, vomiting

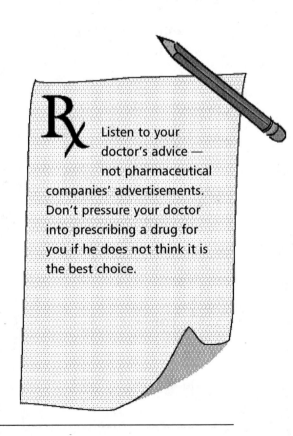

R℞ Listen to your doctor's advice — not pharmaceutical companies' advertisements. Don't pressure your doctor into prescribing a drug for you if he does not think it is the best choice.

General Advice and Precautions

- Do not combine with alcohol

- Smoking tobacco reduces the effectiveness of Tylenol with Codeine

- Smoking Marijuana will impair mental and physical ability, increase drowsiness, and increase pain relief

- Avoid hazardous activities, including driving

- Limit use to short term

- Increased risk of constipation, dizziness, and drowsiness in elderly patients

Acetic Acid

Including Diclofenac, Etodolac, Indomethacin, Ketorolac, Nabumetone, Sulidac, Tolmetin
Brand Names: Apo-Diclo, Arthrotec, Cataflam, Novo-Difenac, Nu-Diclo, Voltaren, Lodine, Apo-Indomethacin, Indameth, Indocid, Novo-methacin, Nu-Indo, Zendole, Acular, Apo-ketorolac, Toradol, Apo-Nabumetone, Gen-Nabumetone, Novo-Nabumetone, Nu-Nabumetone, MS-Nabumetone, Rhoxal-Nabumetone Relafen, Apo-Sulin, Clinoril, Novo-Sundac, Novo-Tolmetin, Tolectin

 Used For

- Pain relief

- Relief of inflammation

- Relief from gastrointestinal problems

 Known Contraindications and/or Interactions

- Do not take this drug if you have had an allergic reaction to it in the past

- Do not take this drug if you have peptic ulcers, you are pregnant, have asthma, nasal polyps, stomach bleeding, liver disease, wear contact lenses, have kidney problems, have narrow veins, have a history of rectal bleeding or porpyria

- Arthrotec should never be taken if you are pregnant or nursing

- Consult your doctor before taking it if you are allergic to Aspirin, have an infection, have a bleeding disorder, ulcers, epilepsy, Parkinson's disease, mental illness, liver or kidney problems, high blood pressure, history of heart failure, take Aspirin, Acetaminophen, or anticoagulants

- Drug interactions may occur with Aminoglycoside antibiotics, anticoagulants, Warfarin, Cyclosporine, Digoxin, Eptifibatide, Lithium, Methotrexate, Phenytoin, Tacrolimus, thrombolytics, Zidovudine, ACE Inhibitors, Bumetanide, Captopril, Ethacrynic Acid, Furosemide, Loop diuretics, Thiazide diuretics, Aspirin, NSAIDs, Clopidogrel, Dicumarol, Diflunisal, Dipyridamole, low molecular weight heparins, Probenecid, Sulfinpyrazone, Valproic Acid, Alendronate, Colestipol, Cholestyramine, Levofloxacin, Ofloxacin, Methotrexate, Ritonavir

 Common Side Effects

- Drowsiness

- Tinnitus

- Fluid retention

- Prolonged bleeding time, inhibited clotting

 Occasional/Long-Term Side Effects

- Eye changes

- Stomach or intestinal irritation

- Vaginal, uterine bleeding

- Breast enlargement in men and women

- Impotence, decreased libido

 Toxicity/Adverse Reaction (Contact your doctor)

- Mild adverse reaction: Skin rash, swelling, headache, dizziness, nausea, indigestion, vomiting, loss of hair, increased need to urinate

- Serious adverse reaction: Difficulty breathing, angioneurotic edema, vision changes, confusion, depression, fever, ulcers, liver damage, kidney damage, bloody urine, bone marrow problems, thrombophlebitis, severe skin irritation, fluid retention, worsening of congestive heart failure, pain in extremities, lung fibrosis, pancreatitis, pneumonitis, aseptic meningitis, seizures

- Signs of overdose: Drowsiness, bleeding, confusion, vomiting, diarrhea, disorientation, seizures, coma

 ## General Advice and Precautions

- Herbs and minerals: Avoid Ginseng, GGinkgo, Alfalfa, Clove Oil, Feverfew, Cinchona Bark, Garlic, White Willow Bark, St. John's Wort, Eucalyptus, Skull Cap, Hay Flower, Mistletoe, White Mustard Seeds

- Speak to your doctor about vitamin supplementation while taking this drug

- Do not drink alchol while taking this drug

- Take this medication with food to avoid stomach irritation

- May cause drowsiness, dizziness, and vision changes. Avoid driving and/or operating machinery until you know how this drug affects you

- Some medications in this category cause photosensitivity, so speak to your doctor

- Do not take over-the-counter pain relief treatments while taking this medication without speaking to your doctor first

- Do not suddenly stop taking this drug. Discontinue gradually under your doctor's supervision

Albuterol

Brand names: Accuneb, Airet, Alti-Salbutamol, Apo-Salvent, Combivent, Diskhaler, Novo-Salmol, PMS-Salbutamol, Proventil (HFA, Inhaler, Repetabs, Tablets) Rotahaler, Salbutamol, Ventodisk Rotacaps, Ventolin (HFA, Inhaler, Nebules, Rotacaps, Syrup, Tablets), Volmax (Sustained Release Tablets, Timed Release Tablets)

 Used For

- Bronchial asthma

- Exercise-induced bronchospasm

 Known Contraindications and/or Interactions

- Do not use while breast-feeding

- If taking this drug as an inhalant with Beclomethasone, use the Albuterol first, 30 minutes earlier

- This drug should not be taken by anyone who is allergic to it, has an irregular heartbeat, has hyperthyroid, or has taken a monoamine oxidase (MAO) type A inhibitor in the preceding two weeks

- This drug may not be suitable for people with heart or circulatory disorders, diabetes, or who take Digitalis or stimulants. Talk to your doctor

 Common Side Effects

- Aerosol format may cause dryness or irritation of the mouth/throat and affect sense of taste

- Tablet may cause nervousness and rapid heart rate

 Occasional/Long-Term Side Effects

- Patients may develop tolerance. However, consult your doctor before increasing your dose

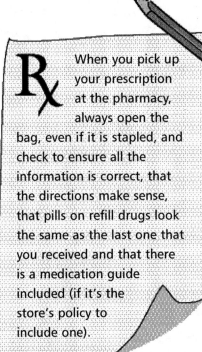

When you pick up your prescription at the pharmacy, always open the bag, even if it is stapled, and check to ensure all the information is correct, that the directions make sense, that pills on refill drugs look the same as the last one that you received and that there is a medication guide included (if it's the store's policy to include one).

Toxicity/Adverse Reaction (Contact your doctor)

- Mild adverse effects include hand tremor, headache, nervousness, insomnia

- Serious adverse effects include decreased blood Potassium, chest pain (angina), abnormal heartbeats

- Irregular heart rhythm and even death by cardiac arrest can result from patients taking too much, too often

 General Advice and Precautions

- Never double a missed dose

- Herbs and minerals: Talk to your doctor before taking St. John's Wort, Ma Huang, Guarana or Kola. In general, asthmatics should avoid Fir or Pine Needle Oil

- You may need to supplement with Potassium. Consult your healthcare provider

- Asthma is often not treated properly because people don't provide a full and accurate description of their symptoms. Talk to your doctor

Alendronate

Brand Names: Fosamax

 Used For

- Treatment and prevention of osteoporosis in postmenopausal women

- Treatment of symptoms in Paget's disease

- Prevention of osteoporosis in patients taking corticosteroids

 Known Contraindications and/or Interactions

- Drugs with known interactions include antacids, Aspirin, NSAIDs, estrogens, Foscarnet, Foscavir, Magnesium, Mesalamine, Olsalazine, Ranitidine, Zantac, Teriparatide, Forteo

- Do not take this medication if you are pregnant or breast-feeding

- Do not take this drug if you have a low level of Calcium in your blood

- Do not take if you have kidney disease

- Do not take if you cannot sit or stand for 30 minutes after taking this drug

- Do not take if you have esophageal disease

- Tell your doctor if you have difficulty swallowing

- Advise your doctor if you have ulcers or a Calcium or vitamin D deficiency

 ## Common Side Effects

- Stomach and esophageal irritation, heartburn

- Fever

 ## Occasional/Long-Term Side Effects

- Increased bone density

 ## Toxicity/Adverse Reaction (Contact your doctor)

- Headache, blurred vision, conjunctivitis

- Flatulence, diarrhea, constipation

- Muscular or skeletal pain

- Ulcers of the esophagus

- Liver toxicity

- Scleritis

- Nausea, vomiting

- Hypocalcemia, hypophosphatemia

 ## General Advice and Precautions

- Take this drug on an empty stomach, at least half an hour before you eat or drink in the morning

- Take this drug with at least eight ounces of water

- Do not lay down for at least 30 minutes to an hour after taking this medication

- Do not take any other medication for at least 30 minutes after taking this medication

- Supplement this treatment with Calcium and vitamin D, but ensure you take the supplements at least 30 minutes after taking this drug

- Herbs and minerals to avoid include soy products, White Willow Bark, or Ipriflavone

- Do not stop taking this medication without advice from your physician

- Heavy exercise is not recommended while taking this drug

- Do not drink alcohol or smoke cigarettes while taking this drug

Alprazolam

Brand Names: Alprazolam Intensol, Apo-Alpraz, Med-Alprazolam, Novo-Alprazol, Nu-Alpraz, Xanax, Xanax XR

 Used For

- Treatment for mild to moderate anxiety disorder

- Treatment of anxiety due to neurosis

- Treatment/prevention of panic disorder

- Treatment for severe PMS symptoms

- Treatment of cancer pain, vomiting from chemotherapy

- Treatment of agoraphobia

- Treatment of alcohol withdrawal

- Treatment of anxiety due to depression

 Known Contraindications and/or Interactions

Drugs with known interactions include: Amprenavir, Itraconazole, Ketoconazole, birth control pills, Cimetidine, Tagamet, Delavirdine, Rescriptor, Disulfiram, Antabuse, Fluconazole, Diflucan, Fluoxetine, Prozac, Fluvoxamine, Luvox, Isoniazid, Rifamate, macrolide antibiotics,

Omeprazole, Prilosec, Paroxetine, Paxil, Propoxyphene, Darvon, Ritonavir, Norvir, Sertraline, Zoloft, Valproic Acid, Depakene, Carbamazepine, Tegretol, Rifampin, Riimactane, Theophylline, Benzodiazepines, Buspirone, antihistamines, antipsychotics, narcotics, Lipitor, Nefazodone, Serzone, Tricyclic antidepressants, other antidepressants

- Do not take this drug during the first trimester of pregnancy

- Do not take this drug if you have glaucoma

- Do not take this drug if you are under 18 years of age

- Smaller doses may be necessary in elderly patients

- Tell your doctor if you have a chronic lung disease or decreased liver/kidney function

- Tell your doctor if you have a history of alcoholism or drug addiction

- Tell your doctor if you have epilepsy

- Tell your doctor if you are breast-feeding, pregnant, or planning pregnancy

- Tell your doctor if you are allergic to Benzodiazepines

- Tell your doctor if you have heart palpitations or tachycardia

- Tell your doctor if you take any other prescription drugs

 ## Common Side Effects

- Drowsiness

- Light-headedness

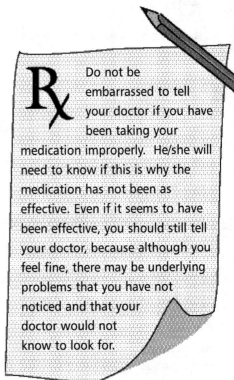

R Do not be embarrassed to tell your doctor if you have been taking your medication improperly. He/she will need to know if this is why the medication has not been as effective. Even if it seems to have been effective, you should still tell your doctor, because although you feel fine, there may be underlying problems that you have not noticed and that your doctor would not know to look for.

 ## Occasional/Long-Term Side Effects

- Psychological/physical dependence

- Loss of libido

Toxicity/Adverse Reaction (Contact your doctor)

- Allergic reactions

- Headache, dizziness, blurred vision

- Nausea, vomiting, salivation

- Confusion, depression, excitement, agitation

- Hallucinations

- Heart palpitations

- Low blood pressure

- Feeling intoxicated

- Deep sleep, coma, stupor

- Tremor

 ## General Advice and Precautions

- Herbs and minerals to avoid include Kava, Danshen, Valerian, Kola Nut, Ginseng, Yerba Mate, Ephedra, Guarana, Ma Huang, St. John's Wort

- Avoid caffeine while taking this drug

- Do not drink alcohol while taking this drug

- Smoking cigarettes will reduce the effectiveness of this medication

- Smoking marijuana while taking this medication will increase sedative properties of the drug

- Do not stop taking this drug without medical supervision

- Withdraw from this drug slowly under medical supervision

- This medication can impair driving ability

- Photosensitivity is rare, but possible

Amantadine

- Brand Names: Antadine, Symadine, Symmetrel

 Used For

- Treatment of Parkinson's disease; other uses include treatment of respiratory tract infections

 Known Contraindications and/or Interactions

- Do not take this drug if you have had an allergic reaction to it in the past

- Consult your doctor before taking if you have a seizure disorder, eczema, angle closure glaucoma; if you have a history of emotional/mental disorder, heart disease, liver or kidney problems, peptic ulcer disease, low white blood cell counts, orthostatic hypotension; or if you take drugs for emotional/mental disorders

- Avoid this drug if you are pregnant or breast-feeding

- Drug interactions may occur with atropine-like drugs, Levodopa, amphetamines and amphetamine-like drugs, Hydrochlorothiazide, Cotrimoxazole, Sulfamethoxazole, Triamterene, Trimethoprim, Zotepine

 Common Side Effects

- Dizziness, weakness, lightheadedness; dry mouth, constipation; skin discoloration on legs

 Occasional/Long-Term Side Effects

- Confusion, delerium, and hallucinations may develop over time in people older than 60 years.

- Congestive heart failure (in susceptible people)

 Toxicity/Adverse Reaction (Contact your doctor)

- Mild adverse reaction: rash, headache, irritability, inability to concentrate, trouble sleeping, slurred speech, difficulty breathing, nausea, vomiting, loss of appetite

- Serious adverse reaction: extreme rash, depression, aggression, hallucinations, seizure (in epileptics or if medication is suddenly stopped), congestive heart failure

- Signs of overdose: hyperactive, confused, hallucinating, aggressive, seizures, heart rhythm changes, drop in blood pressure

 ## General Advice and Precautions

- Herbs and minerals: Avoid Calabar Bean, Betel Nut, Kava Kava. Avoid Echinacea if you have multiple sclerosis

- May cause drowsiness, dizziness, blurred vision. Avoid driving or operating machinery until you know how this drug affects you

- Use caution to prevent excessive exposure to cold

- Do not stop this drug suddenly when using it to treat Parkinson's. Discontinue gradually under your doctor's supervision

Amiodarone

Brand Names: Cordarone, Alti-Amiodarone, Braxan, Gen-Amiodarone, Med-Amiodarone, Novo-Amiodarone, Pacerone

 ## Used For

- Treatment of abnormal heart rhythms

- Treatment of severe congestive heart failure

- Treatment of chest pain, arrhythmia, patients who have survived sudden heart attack

 ## Known Contraindications and/or Interactions

- Drugs with known interactions include antihypertensive drugs, atropine-like drugs, Cyclosporine, Digoxin, Lanoxin, Procainamide, Warfarin, Coumadin, Procan, Amprenavir, Indinavir, Ritonavir, protease inhibitors, beta-blockers, calcium channel blockers, Cimetidine, Tagamet, Cisapride, Propulsid, Clonazepam, Klonopin, Disopyramide, Norpace, Dofetilide, Tikosyn, Dolasetron, Anzemet, Fentanyl, Actiq, Duragesic, Flecainide, Gat floxacin, Levofloxacin, Sparfloxacin, Quinolone Antibiotics, Halofantrine, Ibutilide, Halfan, Indinavir, Insulin, Oral Antidiabetic drugs, Lidocaine, Methotrexate,

Mexiletine, Moxifloxacin, Avelox, Nelfinavir, Viracept, Phenytoin, Propafenone, Quinidine, Ritonavir, Norvir, Sotalol, Betapace, Verapamil, Ziprasidone, Cholestyramine

- Do not take if you are pregnant or breast-feeding

- Tell your doctor if you have a history of heart attack, low blood pressure, decreased liver function, vision impairment, low blood platelets, lung disease, blocked ventricles or if you have a pacemaker

- Tell your doctor if you are planning on traveling or moving

- Tell your doctor if the functioning of your left heart ventricle is compromised

- Tell your doctor if you have thyroid problems

- Tell your doctor if you cannot avoid exposure to the sun

 ## Common Side Effects

- Inflammation of the veins

 ## Occasional/Long-Term Side Effects

- Microdeposits in the cornea of the eye

 ## Toxicity/Adverse Reaction (Contact your doctor)

- Allergic reactions

- Blue-grey skin color

- Hair loss

- Headache, tiredness, dizziness

- Insomnia, nightmares

- Low blood pressure

- Changes in your cholesterol levels

- Loss of appetite, nausea, vomiting

- Thyroid functioning changes

- Abnormal heart rhythm

- Lung toxicity

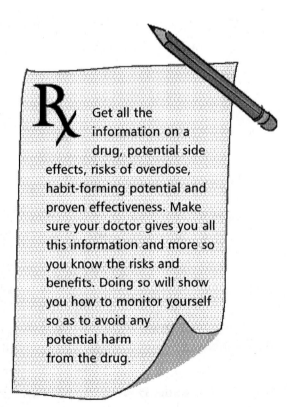

Rx Get all the information on a drug, potential side effects, risks of overdose, habit-forming potential and proven effectiveness. Make sure your doctor gives you all this information and more so you know the risks and benefits. Doing so will show you how to monitor yourself so as to avoid any potential harm from the drug.

- High blood sugar

- Abnormal movements

- Jaundice

- Extremely slow heart rate

 ## General Advice and Precautions

- Herbs and minerals to avoid include St. John's Wort, Ma Huang, Ephedra, Guarana, Kola, Belladonna, Henbane, Scopolia, Pheasant's Eye Extract, Lily-of-the-Valley, Eucalyptus, Skullcap, Pyridoxine

- Reduce your intake of caffeine

- Avoid alcohol and smoking cigarettes while taking this medication

- Do not stop taking this medication without medical advice

- You may need to limit driving, as blurred vision is possible

- Increased risk of heatstroke

- This drug does cause photosensitivity

- Elderly patients should be monitored closely while taking this medication

- This drug should be taken on a full stomach or with food

Amlodipine

Brand Names: Lotrel [CD], Norvasc

 ## Used For

- Lowering blood pressure (anti-hypertensive)

- Prevention of the two major forms of angina

 ## Known Contraindications and/or Interactions

- Interactions may occur when taking with other anti-hypertensives such as beta-blockers or Digitalis, or other drugs like Adenosine, Ritonavir (and other protease inhibitors),

Rifampin, Quinupristin, Dalfopristin, NSAIDS, Warfarin, Amiodarone, Azole Antifungals, Imidazoles, Cyclosporine, Delavirdine, Dofetilide, or Cimetidine (Tagamet)

- Lower doses should be taken if you have liver problems or suffer from bulimia, anorexia, starvation, or consume little protein (due to the protein albumin that carries Amlodipine around the body)

- It is best to avoid this drug during pregnancy, but if necessary use during the last six months, and only under the guidance of the physician. It's also best to avoid taking the drug while breast-feeding, as effects are unknown

 ## Common Side Effects

- Increase in sensation of body heat, looking flushed, swelling of ankles and feet, problems or changes with sense of smell. People over 60 years of age are more prone to feel dizzy, faint and weak, and may fall or injure themselves easily

 ## And Occasional/Long-Term Side Effects

- Some rare side effects may be allergy, headache, cough, fatigue, dizziness, nausea, constipation, increased heart rate from high doses, eye pain, double vision, ringing sound inside ears, muscle pain, urge to urinate is increased, gums become enlarged/overgrown, swelling, skin problems, trouble breathing

- Long term use seems safe, but watch for development of any adverse reactions or complications with your liver

 ## Toxicity/Adverse Reaction (Contact your doctor)

- Signs of overdose: seizure, heart attack, sinus arrest, low blood pressure, weakness, fainting, fast or slow pulse, low Calcium and Potassium amounts, inability to smell, increase in acidity of body fluids

- If you have an adverse reaction to sunlight (phototoxicity) seek help immediately

General Advice and Precautions

- Grapefruit and grapefruit juice increase the effect of this medicine so it is best to avoid it for an hour before taking Amlodipine

- Stimulants like Guarana and Ma Huang (should be avoided anyway due to reports of dangerous side effects) should be avoided along with Ginseng, Peppermint Oil, Hawthorn,

Saw Palmetto, Eleuthero Root, Goldenseal and Licorice. St. John's Wort should be used only under the guidance of a doctor

- Depressants like alcohol may make blood pressure drop even lower, so use with caution

- Tobacco and Marijuana smoking should be avoided as they reduce effectiveness, and marijuana may also increase angina and change electrocardiogram results

- Only stop using drug slowly and watch for recurrence of angina

- Some herbs that will help lower blood pressure (as alternatives or as a complementary therapy only under the advice of your physician) include Garlic, Calcium, and Indian Snakeroot

Angiotensin II Receptor Antagonist Family (ARBs)

Includes: Candesartan, Eprosartan, Irbesartan, Losartan, Telmisartan, Valsartan
Brand Names: Candesartan: Atacand
Eprosartan: Teveten
Irbesartan: Avapro, Avalide [CD]
Losartan: Cozaar, Hyzaar [CD]
Telmisartan: Micardis
Valsartan: Diovan

 ## Used For

- High blood pressure control

- Preventing death from congestive heart failure

- Assisting kidney health of diabetics through the use of Losartan

- People who are allergic or have adverse cough from use of ACE Inhibitors

 ## Known Contraindications and/or Interactions

- These drugs should be avoided during pregnancy, if at all possible, and definitely during breast-feeding

- Caution should be exercised when dosing patients with liver problems with Losartan and Valsartan. Hyzaar should not be used at all

- Some kidney problems may require a lower dose of Valsartan

- Interaction may occur if ARBs are taken with ACE inhibitors, corticosteroids, Fluconazole, Lithium, Moxonidine, Rifampin, Ritonavir, Amiloride, Triamterene, Spironolactone, or Cytochrome P450 3A4 inhibitors like grapefruit juice, Erythromycin and antifungals (Ketoconazole)

 ## Common Side Effects

- Change in taste, or taste related disorders may appear

- Flushing or sweating with use of Candesartan

- Headache

- Excessively low blood pressure when first begin dosing

 ## Occasional/Long-Term Side Effects

- Rarely, some people experience allergy, impotence or decreased sexual desire with use of Losartan or Valsartan, dizziness, cough, diarrhea, swelling of face, migraines, anemia, loss of glandular white blood cells, gout, liver or kidney problems, Potassium increase, nightmares or vivid dreams, nose bleed (very unlikely)

 ## Toxicity/Adverse Reaction (Contact your doctor)

- Signs of overdose: Changes in speed of heart rate, decrease in blood pressure resulting in dizziness, or light-headedness

General Advice and Precautions

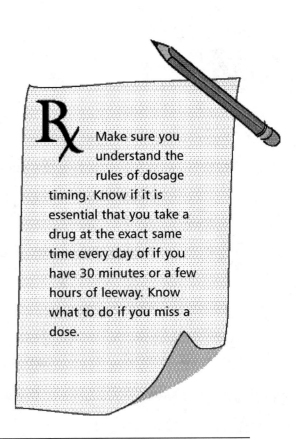

- Food can slow the absorption of Losartan and Valsartan

- Grapefruit and grapefruit juice may be especially problematic by making any type of ARB less effective

- People who are elderly or dehydrated may require lower doses of these drugs

- As with any other antihypertensive, avoid herbs that increase blood pressure (Ginseng, Ginko, Hawthorn, Saw Palmetto, Goldenseal, Yohimbe, Licorice, and Eleuthero Root)

Rx Make sure you understand the rules of dosage timing. Know if it is essential that you take a drug at the exact same time every day of if you have 30 minutes or a few hours of leeway. Know what to do if you miss a dose.

- Stimulants like caffeine, Guarana and Yerba Mate should be avoided (caffeine is less dangerous than the other two, but should not be consumed in excess)

- Marijuana and alcohol may intensify blood pressure drops, so should be used with caution and doctor knowledge

- Excessive heat or exercise resulting in profuse sweating may cause dehydration and extremely blood pressure

- Caution with sun exposure is advised. Do not take with St. John's Wort due to enhanced photosensitivity

Anti-Alzheimer's Drug Family

Brand Names: Donepezil, Aricept; Rivastigmine, Exelon; Tacrine, Cognex; Galantamine, Reminyl.

 ## Used For

- Treatment of symptoms of Alzheimer's disease

 ## Known Contraindications and/or Interactions

- Do not take a drug in this family if you have had an allergic reaction to it in the past.

- Do not take tacrine if you have bronchial asthma, hyperthyroidism, peptic ulcer, an intestinal or urinary tract obstruction, or have had tacrine liver toxicity, or galantamine if you have significant liver or kidney problems

- Consult your doctor before taking if you have a slow heartbeat, low blood pressure, an AVO conduction defect, glaucoma, asthma, if you are anemic, if you have a history of seizure disorder, peptic ulcer, liver disease, if you take muscle relaxants, or if you are scheduled for surgery

- Drug interactions may occur with Bethanechol, Theophylline, Succinylcholine, anticholinergic medications, Cimetidine, Carbamazepine, Dexamethasone, Erythromycin, Paroxetine, Ibuprofen, Ketoconazole, Quinidine, Ritonavir, NSAIDs, Riluzole

 ## Common Side Effects

- Stomach upset/indigestion, weight loss

Occasional/Long-Term Side Effects

- Tacrine, Galantamine and Donepezil may make bronchial asthma or peptic ulcer disease worse

 Toxicity/Adverse Reaction (Contact your doctor)

- Mild adverse reaction: Rash, itching, increased salivation, increased urination, dizziness, confusion, insomnia, low blood pressure, nausea, vomiting, diarrhea, loss of appetite, muscle aches

- Serious adverse reaction: Anaphylaxis, changes in liver function, aggravation of asthma, bronchospasm or pulmonary edema possible in susceptible people, anemia, slow heart rate or abnormal rhythm, seizures

- Call your doctor if there is a significant change in stool color

- Signs of overdose: Severe nausea and vomiting, reduced heartbeat and blood pressure, weakness, convulsions

 General Advice and Precautions

- Herbs and Minerals: Galantamine is derived from daffodils, so consult your doctor if you have an allergy. No definitive study on Ginkgo Biloba exists; talk to your doctor if you are considering supplementation

- Supplementing with B vitamins is recommended

- These drugs may cause confusion and/or dizziness. Driving and other activities (e.g., operating machinery) may not be possible

- Tacrine may cause increased sweating. As a precaution, drink extra fluids when exposed to heat

- These drugs should not be stopped suddenly. Discontinue gradually, under your doctor's supervision

Anti-Leukotriene Family – Montelukast, Zafirlukast , Zileuton

Brand names: Montelukast, Singulair; Zafirlukast, Accolate; Zileuton, Zyflo

 Used For

- Prevent asthma attacks. Montelukast is approved for allergic rhinitis

 Known Contraindications and/or Interactions

- Should not be used to treat an asthma attach in progress

- Do not use these anti-leukotrienes if you are allergic to them or if you have liver disease

- Drug interactions may occur with Aspirin, Astemizole (Hismanal – no longer sold in U.S.), Beta-Blockers, Terfenadine (Seldane)

- A doctor should be consulted before Zafirlukast is given to children under 12, people taking Warfarin, heavy drinkers or people with impaired kidney function

- Consult your doctor about these medications if you are pregnant or breast-feeding

 Common Side Effects

- These drugs are generally well tolerated

 Occasional/Long-Term Side Effects

- These medicines can affect the liver, promoting borderline conditions into full-scale disorders

 Toxicity/Adverse Reaction (Contact your doctor)

- Mild adverse reaction: Skin rash, headache, fatigue, weakness, digestive disorders, dizziness, muscle pain

- Serious adverse reaction: Allergic reactions, liver toxicity, Churg-Strauss Syndrome, drug-induced lupus erythematosus

 General Advice and Precautions

- Do not double doses

- Zafirlukast should be taken on an empty stomach

- Herbs and minerals: Do not take St. John's Wort with Zafirlukast or Montelukast. Asthmatics should avoid fir and pine needles

- May cause dizziness

Aspirin

Brand Names: Analgesic Pain Reliever, Aggrenox, Alka-Selzer, Anacin, Ancasal, APC, APO-ASA, Arthritis Pain Formula, A.S.A. Enseals, Asasantine, Acriptin, Aspergum, Asprimox, Astrin, Axotal, Azdone, Bayer, Bufferin, BC Powder, Buffaprin, Cama Arthritis Pain Reliever, Cardioprin, Carisoprodol Compound, Cope, Coricidin, Coryphen, C2 Buffered, Darvon Compound, Dristan, Easprin, Ecotrin, Empirin, Entrophen, Excedrin, Fiorinal, Genacote, Genprin, Goody's Headache Powder, Halprin, Hepto, Lortab ASA, Marnal, Measurin, Midol, Momentum, Norgesic, Novasen, Orphenadrine, PAP w/Codeine, Percodan, Phenaphen, Propoxyphene, Riphen-10, Robaxisal, Roxiprin, 692, SK-65 Compound, Soma Compound, Supasa, Synalgos, Talwin Compound, Talwin Compound-50, Tecnal, Triaphen-10, Vanquish, Verin, Wesprin, Zorprin

✔ Used For

- Pain relief

- Inflammation relief

- Fever reduction

- Blood clot, heart attack, stroke, colon cancer, coronary disease prevention

 ## Known Contraindications and/or Interactions

- Do not take this drug if you have had an allergic reaction to it in the past

- Do not take this drug if you have a bleeding disorder, peptic ulcers are pregnant or breast-feeding

- Consult your doctor before taking if you are taking anticoagulants, COX II inhibitors, oral antidiabetics, have surgery planned, have a history of peptic ulcers, gout, lupus, asthma, carditis, rhinitis, nasal polyps, liver or kidney problems, drink alcohol on a regular basis, are pregnant or nursing

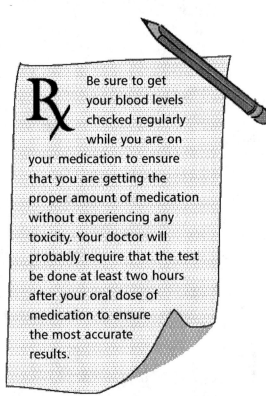

℞ Be sure to get your blood levels checked regularly while you are on your medication to ensure that you are getting the proper amount of medication without experiencing any toxicity. Your doctor will probably require that the test be done at least two hours after your oral dose of medication to ensure the most accurate results.

- Children with viral infections or who have been exposed to viral infections should never take Aspirin as this increases the risk of Reye's Syndrome

- Drug interactions may occur with adrenocortical steroids, Insulin, Heparin, Methotrexate, anticoagulants, antidiabetic drugs, Ticlodipine, Tiludronate, thrombolytics, ACE Inhibitors, beta-adrenergic blocking drugs Captopril, Enalapril, Furosemide, NSAIDs, Phenytoin, Probenecid, Spironolactone, Sulfinpyrazone, Tiludronate, Alendronate, Biphosphates, Capsaicin, Celecoxib, Cilostazol, Clopidogrel, Cortisone-like drugs, Diltiazem, Eptifibatide, high blood pressure, Ibuprofen, Intrauterine devices, Lithium, Heparins, Methotrexate, Niacin, Quinidine, Tirofiban, Valproic Acid, Varicella Vaccine, Verapamil, Zafirlukast, Acetazolamide, Cimetidine, Para-Aminobenzoic Acid, Antacids, Cholestyramine, urinary alkalinizers

 ## Common Side Effects

- Drowsiness

- Impaired wound healing

 ## Occasional/Long-Term Side Effects

- Psychological dependence

- Anemia

- Stomach ulcer

- Bleeding

- Kidney problems

- Asthma, nasal problems

 ## Toxicity/Adverse Reaction (Contact your doctor)

- Mild adverse reaction: Skin rash, allergy-like symptoms, irritated stomach, nausea, vomiting, constipation, tinnitus

- Serious adverse reaction: Anaphylactic reaction, bruising, anemia, Stevens-Johnson syndrome, stroke, bleeding, stomach bleeding, ulcers, bone marrow disorders, weakness, hepatits, hearing problems, kidney problems, worsened angina pain, bronchospasm

- Signs of overdose: Painful vomiting, nausea, dizziness, ringing in the ears, hearing difficulty, stupor, fever, rapid breathing, shock, hallucinations, convulsions

General Advice and Precautions

- Herbs and minerals: Avoid Evening Primrose Oil, Ginkgo, Garlic, Ginger, Ginseng, Guggul, Feverfew, St. John's Wort, White Willow Bark. Speak to your doctor before you take any herbal medicine or vitamin while taking Aspirin

- Avoid taking Vitamin C

- Do not drink alcohol while taking Aspirin

- May cause mild drowsiness. Avoid driving and/or operating machinery until you know how this drug affects you

- Especially when taken as a preventative measure for heart disease and other conditions, do not suddenly stop taking this drug. Discontinue gradually under your doctor's supervision

Atenolol

Brand Names: Apo-Atenolol, Novo-Atenolol, Nu-Atenolol, PMS-Atenolol, Tenoretic [CD], Ternormin

Used For

- Treatment of angina and high blood pressure

- Improves prognosis after heart attack

- Migraine headaches

Known Contraindications and/or Interactions

- Do not take this drug if you've had an allergic reaction to it before; advise your doctor if you've had adverse reactions to beta-blockers

- Do not take if you have an abnormally slow heart rate

- If possible drug should be avoided by pregnant and nursing women

- Drug should not be administered within 14 days of the patient taking any monoamine oxidase (MAO) type A inhibitor

- Do not administer drug to someone in cardiogenic shock

- Consult your physician if you have a history of respiratory problems (even including hay fever), hyperthyroidism, kidney or liver problems, diabetes

- Drug interactions may take place with other antihypertensive drugs, Reserpine, Amiodarone, Ampicillin/Bacampicillin, Calcium channel blockers, Clonidine, Digoxin, Dolasetron, Insulin, Quinidine, Ritodrine, Digitalis

- Antacids and Aspirin may reduce the effectiveness of atenolol

 ## Common Side Effects

- Lethargy, fatigue, cold hands and feet, reduced heart rate, light-headedness when upright

 ## Occasional/Long-Term Side Effects

- May decrease libido and/or potency

 ## Toxicity/Adverse Reaction (Contact your doctor)

- Mild adverse reaction: Skin rash, headache, dizziness, indigestion, fluid retention, joint and/or muscle discomfort

- Serious adverse reaction: Includes asthma attacks (in people with asthma), chest pain, shortness of breath

- Signs of overdose: Slow pulse, low blood pressure, fainting, clammy skin, heart failure, coma, convulsions

 ## General Advice and Precautions

- Herbs and minerals to avoid include Ginseng, Guarana, Hawthorn, Saw Palmetto, Goldenseal, Yohimbe, Ma Huang, and Licorice, which may raise blood pressure; Garlic and Calcium help lower blood pressure.

- Best taken on an empty stomach

- Do not double up doses

- Do not stop this drug suddenly; discontinuing drug should be under doctor's supervision

- Carry a card in your wallet that says you take this medication

- Consult your doctor before using a nasal spray while on beta-blocker medication

Atorvastatin

Brand Names: Lipitor

 Used For

- Reducing total cholesterol, LDL cholesterol, triglycerides

- Increasing HDL (good) cholesterol

- Prevention of repeated heart problems

- Occasionally used to prevent Alzheimer's, cancer and bone loss

 Known Contraindications and/or Interactions

- Do not use while pregnant or breast-feeding

- Drugs with known interactions include fibric acid derivatives (Clofibrate), Amprenavir, Ritonavir, Saquinavir, Antacids, azole antifungals, birth control pills, Clopidogrel, Cyclosporine, Digoxin, Erythromycin, Fluconazole, Itraconazole, Fosphenytoin, Gemfibrozil, Cytochrome P450 3A4 nhibitors, Nefazodone, Niacin, Quinupristin/Dalfopristin

- Discuss all your medications with your doctor first

! **Common Side Effects**

- Usually none with normal doses

- May cause drowsiness

 Occasional/Long-Term Side Effects

- Allergic reaction, headache, vision changes, flu symptoms, temporary hair loss, flatulence, impotence

- Muscle pain, lowered blood platelets, memory problems

- Abnormal liver function with long-term use

- Coenzyme Q10 decrease

- May develop a tolerance

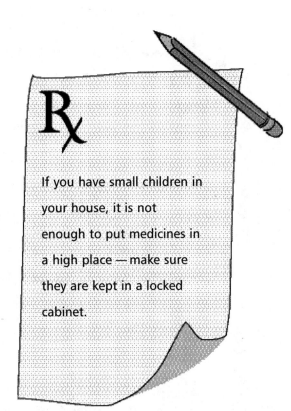

If you have small children in your house, it is not enough to put medicines in a high place — make sure they are kept in a locked cabinet.

Toxicity/Adverse Reaction (Contact your doctor)

- Report any muscle pain (usually with 20 mg dose) especially if fever and weakness occur simultaneously

- Signs of overdose: Gastrointestinal distress including indigestion, nausea, diarrhea

- The drug may need to be reduced or stopped if liver enzyme amounts climb too high

 ## General Advice and Precautions

- Eat a low-cholesterol diet. High quantities of vegetables, soy and fish are often recommended

- Only use Garlic or Cholestin under supervision of a doctor

- Eat more oat bran, but not less than two hours before taking medication or four to six hours after

- Do not take with grapefruit juice due to risk of elevated blood levels and muscle damage

- Avoid excessive alcohol consumption

- Don't stop this medication without consulting your doctor as blood cholesterol may suddenly increase, resulting in a tripled risk of heart attack or death

Beclomethasone

Brand Names: Apo-Beclomethasone-AQ, Beclodisk, Becloforte, Beclovent, Beclovent Rotacaps, Becolvent Rotahaler, Beconase AQ Nasal Spray, Beconase Nasal Inhaler, Med-Beclomethasone-AQ, Nu-Belomethasone, Propaderm, Propaderm-C, QVAR, Vancenase AQ Nasal Spray, Vancenase Nasal Inhaler, Vanceril

 ## Used For

- Treating severe asthma
- Prevention of nasal polyps
- Treatment of seasonal and allergic rhinitis
- Combination therapy for lung disease
- Sometimes used as treatment in juvenile rheumatoid arthritis

Known Contraindications and/or Interactions

- Do not take this drug if you have had an allergic reaction to it in the past

- Do not take this drug if you have severe acute asthma, if you take other antiasthma drugs, or if you are pregnant or nursing

- Children under six years of age should not take this medication

- Consult your doctor before taking if you have chronic bronchitis, tuberculosis, active infections, chicken pox, liver damage, or if you are prone to nosebleeds

- Drug interactions may occur with antiepileptic drugs, Flunisolide, Inhalant Bronchodilators, including Epinephrine, Isoetharine, Isoproterenol, and oral bronchodilators, including Aminophylline, Ephedrine, Terbutaline, Theophylline, Alendronate

 ## Common Side Effects

- Fungal infections (such as thrush)

- Headache

- Changes in sense of taste

 ## Occasional/Long-Term Side Effects

- Increased risk of cataracts

 ## Toxicity/Adverse Reaction (Contact your doctor)

- Mild adverse reaction: Skin rash, dry mouth, sore throat, nosebleed, stunted growth in children

- Serious adverse reaction: Lung inflammation, wheezing, shrunken nasal tissues, yeast infections, severe chicken pox, suppressed adrenal gland, pressure in head, osteoporosis

- Signs of overdose: Fluid retention, flushing, stomach irritation, nervousness

 ## General Advice and Precautions

- Herbs and minerals: Avoid Fir and Pine Needle Oil, Ephedra/Ma Huang

- Smoking makes this drug less effective, so consider quitting

- Do not suddenly stop taking this drug. Discontinue gradually under your doctor's supervision

- This drug will not help in acute asthma attacks

- Carry a card that says you are taking this drug

- Have a bone-mineral test conducted every two years when taking this drug

- Tell you doctor if you have any unexplained joint pain when taking this medication

Benztropine

Brand Names: Bensylate, Cogentin

 Used For

Parkinson's Disease

 Known Contraindications and/or Interactions

- Do not take this drug if you have had an allergic reaction to it in the past; you have untreated narrow-angle glaucoma or tardive dyskinesia. Do not give to a child under three years of age

- Consult your doctor before taking if you have had a negative reaction to atropine-like drugs in the past; if you have glaucoma, heart disease, high blood pressure, an enlarged prostate, a history of livery or kidney problems or bowel obstructions, if you have taken a MAO Type A Inhibitor within the last 14 days or if you will be exposed to extreme heat over an extended period.

- Drug interactions may occur with: phenothiazines, antihistamines, MAO Type A Inhibitors, tricyclic antidepressants, Amantadine, Belladonna, Clozapine, Procainamide.

- MAY INTERACT WITH OVER-THE-COUNTER MEDICATIONS—consult your doctor before taking, especially allergy, cough or cold preparations

 Common Side Effects

- Nervousness, blurred vision, dry mouth, constipation, heat intolerance

- May cause confusion, nightmares, increased eye pressure, and urination problems in people over 60

Occasional/Long-Term Side Effects

- Long-term use may bring about glaucoma

- May cause male impotence or infertility

 ## Toxicity/Adverse Reaction (Contact your doctor)

- Mild adverse reaction: Rash, headache, drowsiness, dizziness, muscle cramps, rapid heart rate, nausea, vomiting, memory problems

- Serious adverse reaction: behavior problems, bowel obstruction, hyperthermia, tardive dyskinesia

- Signs of overdose: Weakness, drowsiness, stupor, confusion, excitement, hallucinations, racing pulse, hot dry skin, rash, dilated pupils

 ## General Advice and Precautions

- Herbs and minerals: Avoid Calabar Bean, Betel Nut, and Octacosanol

- May cause drowsiness and dizziness. Avoid driving or operating machinery until you know how this drug affects you

- Alcohol may increase the sedative effect of this drug. Use of marijuana may cause heart rate to speed up to unsafe levels

- This medication affects your ability to sweat and make people more susceptible to heatstroke. Use caution with regard to exercise and/or saunas

- Do not suddenly stop taking this drug. Discontinue gradually under your doctor's supervision

Betaxolol

Brand Names: Betoptic, Betoptic-Pilo [CD], Betoptic-S, Kerlone, Novo-Betaxolol

 ## Used For

- Mild to moderate high blood pressure

- Chronic, open-angle glaucoma

Only keep one emergency medication at your bedside, like nitroglycerin, so you don't get confused when you are in a panicked state in the dark and take the wrong kind.

Known Contraindications and/or Interactions

- Avoid this drug if you are allergic to it, have an abnormally slow heart rate, or have taken an MAO inhibitor drug within the last 14 days

- Consult your physician if you have adverse reactions to beta-blockers, if you have serious heart disease, a respiratory condition (including hay fever), hyperthyroidism, low blood sugar, diabetes, kidney or liver problems

- Drug should be avoided by pregnant and breast-feeding women

- Drug interactions may occur with other antihypertensive drugs, Reserpine, Verapamil, Amiodarone, Calcium channel blockers, Clonidine, Digoxin, Fluoroquinolone, Fluvoxamine, Insulin, Methyldopa, oral antidiabetics, Phenothiasines, Rifabutin, Ritonavir, Venlafaxine, Zileuton, Indomethacin

 ## Common Side Effects

- Lethargy, fatigue, cold hands and feet, reduced heart rate, dizziness when upright

 ## Occasional/Long-Term Side Effects

- May cause decreased libido and/or sexual potency

- May disrupt menstrual cycle

 ## Toxicity/Adverse Reaction (Contact your doctor)

- Mild adverse reaction: Headache, dizziness, fatigue, disturbed sleep, nausea, diarrhea, joint pain, fluid retention

- Serious adverse reaction: Reduced heart rate, increased blood sugar, chest pain, shortnerss of breath, depression/anxiety

- Signs of overdose: Slow pulse, low blood pressure, fainting, clammy skin, heart failure, coma, convulsions

- (Note: Side effects from eye drops are rare)

 ## General Advice and Precautions

- Herbs and minerals: Ginseng, Guarana, Hawthorn, Saw Palmetto, Goldenseal, Yohimbe, Ma Huang, and Licorice may raise blood pressure; Garlic and Calcium help lower blood pressure. If you are using this medication for Glaucoma, also avoid Belladonna, Ephedra, Henbane, Scopolia root

■ Do not double up doses

■ Do not stop this drug suddenly; discontinuing drug should be under doctor's supervision

■ Carry a card in your wallet that says you take this medication

■ Consult your doctor before using a nasal spray while on beta-blocker medication

■ Consult your doctor before starting an exercise program

■ This drug may make you more susceptible to hot and cold; exercise caution.

Carteolol

Brand Names: Cartrol, Ocupress, Occupress

 Used For

■ Treatment of mild to moderate high blood pressure

■ Treatment of intraocular (eye) pressure

■ Other uses include prevention of angina, treatment of aggressive behavior, panic attacks

 Known Contraindications and/or Interactions

■ Do not take this drug if you are allergic to it or have asthma or pulmonary disease

■ This drug should not be administered to someone with congestive heart failure, or who has an abnormally slow heart rate

■ Consult your physician if you have adverse reactions to beta-blockers, if you have serious heart disease, a respiratory condition (including hay fever), hyperthyroidism, low blood sugar, diabetes, kidney or liver problems

■ Drug should be avoided by pregnant and breast-feeding women

■ Drug interactions may occur with other antihypertensive drugs, Reserpine, Theophyllines, Verapamil, Amiodarone, Clonidine, Digoxin, Diltiazem, Epinephrine, Fluoxetine, Fluvoxamine, Insulin, Nifedipine, oral antidiabetic drugs, Phenothiazines, Ritodrine, Sibutramine, Zileuton, Indomethacin

Common Side Effects

- Lethargy, fatigue, cold hands and feet, reduced heart rate, dizziness when upright

- Tearing and irritation with eye drops

 ## Occasional/Long-Term Side Effects

- May cause decreased libido and/or sexual potency

 ## Toxicity/Adverse Reaction (Contact your doctor)

- Mild adverse reaction: Headache, dizziness, fatigue, nausea, diarrhea, joint pain, fluid retention

- Serious adverse reactions: Irregular heartbeat, chest pain, shortnerss of breath, depression, asthma attacks (in people with asthma)

- Signs of overdose: Slow pulse, low blood pressure, fainting, clammy skin, heart failure, coma, convulsions

 ## General Advice and Precautions

- Herbs and minerals: Ginseng, Guarana, Hawthorn, Saw Palmetto, Goldenseal, Yohimbe, Ma Huang, and Licorice may raise blood pressure; Garlic and Calcium help lower blood pressure

- Do not double up doses

- Do not stop this drug suddenly; discontinuing the drug should be done under a doctor's supervision

- Carry a card in your wallet that says you take this medication

- Consult your doctor before using a nasal spray while on beta-blocker medication

- Consult your doctor before starting an exercise program

- This drug may make you more susceptible to hot and cold; exercise caution.

Carvedilol

Brand Names: Coreg, Dilatrend, Eucardic, Proreg

 ## Used For

- Treatment of mild to moderate high blood pressure, congestive heart failure

- Improves prognosis for heart attack patients

 ## Known Contraindications and/or Interactions

- Do not take this drug if you've been allergic to it before or if you have any respiratory disorders. Check with your doctor to ensure you do not have one of these conditions: sick sinus syndrome, decompensated heart failure, bracycardia, or a second or third degree heart block

- Consult your physician if you have adverse reactions to beta-blockers, if you have serious heart disease, a respiratory condition (including hay fever), hyperthyroidism, low blood sugar, diabetes, kidney or liver problems

- Drug should be avoided by pregnant and breast-feeding women

 ## Common Side Effects

- Lethargy, fatigue, cold hands and feet, reduced heart rate, dizziness when upright

 ## Occasional/Long-Term Side Effects

- Impotence (rare)

Toxicity/Adverse Reaction (Contact your doctor)

- Mild adverse reaction: Headache, dizziness, nervousness, fatigue, nausea, diarrhea, urination problems, cough, joint pain

- Serious adverse reaction: Slow heartbeat, chest pain, irregular heartbeat, shortness of breathfainting, asthma attack (in people with asthma)

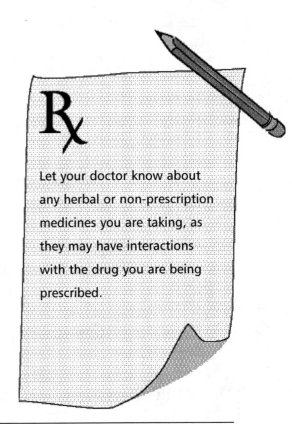

Let your doctor know about any herbal or non-prescription medicines you are taking, as they may have interactions with the drug you are being prescribed.

- Signs of overdose: Slow pulse, low blood pressure, fainting, clammy skin, heart failure, coma

 ## General Advice and Precautions

- Herbs and minerals: Ginseng, Guarana, Hawthorn, Saw Palmetto, Goldenseal, Yohimbe, Ma Huang and Licorice may raise blood pressure; Garlic and Calcium help lower blood pressure

- Do not skip doses

- Do not double up doses

- Do not stop this drug suddenly; discontinuing drug should be under doctor's supervision

- Carry a card in your wallet that says you take this medication

- Consult your doctor before using a nasal spray while on beta blocker medication

- Advise your doctor if you become depressed

- Avoid heavy exercise

- This drug may make you more susceptible to hot and cold; exercise caution

Cephalosporin Antibiotic Family

Includes: Cefaclor, Cefadroxil, Cefixime, Cefprozil, Ceftriaxone, Cefuroxime, Cephalexin, Loracarbef

Brand Names: Cefaclor: Ceclor

Cefadroxil: Duricef, Ultracef

Cefixime: Suprax

Cefprozil: Cefzil

Ceftriaxone: Rocephin

Cefuroxime: Ceftin, Kefurox, Zinacef

Cephalexin: Apo-Cephalex, Cefanex, Ceporex, Keflet, Keflex, Keftab, Novo-Lexin, Nu-Cephalex

Loracarbef: Lorabid

 ## Used For

- Ceftriaxone is used for home intravenous treatment of Lyme disease and severe bone infection

- Other forms used to treat skin, postoperative wound, upper and lower respiratory, ear, and throat infection

- Treats urinary tract infections and gonorrhea

 ## Known Contraindications and/or Interactions

- Doses should be lowered and blood levels checked specifically when giving Cefriaxone

- Depending on the drug, doses may be given as usual or need to be decreased, either slightly or significantly

- Doctor should be consulted about use if you are pregnant or breast-feeding

- Drugs may interact with aminoglycoside antibiotics, anticoagulants, birth control pills, Cholestyramine, Cyclosporine, Thyphoid vaccine (live), diuretics like Ethacrynic Acid, Nilvapidine, or Probenecid

 ## Common Side Effects

- Superinfections (infections resulting from antibiotic resistance)

- Vomiting, diarrhea, nausea

 ## Occasional/Long-Term Side Effects

- Occasionally, some people have been noted to experience allergic reaction, sore mouth, temporary decrease in white blood cell or platelet count, difficulty with blood clotting, joint pain, swelling and itching, liver enzyme increase with jaundice, gallbladder problems, increased urea nitrogen or serum creatinine

 ## Toxicity/Adverse Reaction (Contact your doctor)

- Signs of overdose: Typically include gastrointestinal problems like vomiting, diarrhea, abdominal cramps

 ## General Advice and Precautions

- Stopping these drugs without doctor knowledge may lead to severe superinfections and other bacterial resistance

- These drugs may cause a false-positive test result on blood sugar when taken with other drugs, so be sure to notify your physician

- It is best not to take the forms Cefaclor and Loracarbef with food, wait one hour before, two hours after eating

- Avoid herbal supplements of Marshmallow Root, Licorice, Oak Bark, and Mistletoe

- Alcohol may interact negatively with Ceftriaxone resulting in unpleasant nausea and vomiting

- Some forms may require refrigeration

Citalopram

Brand Names: Celexa. (Note: Escitalopram is a different isomer of Citalopram; studies indicate it may provide greater benefits with fewer side effects.)

 ## Used For

- Depression

- May be used to treat other conditions, including alcohol abuse

 ## Known Contraindications and/or Interactions

- Do not take this drug if you took a MAO Type A Inhibitor within the preceding 14 days

- Consult your physican before taking if you have a seizure disorder, liver or kidney problems, have attempted suicide in the past, or have had negative reactions to antidepressant drugs in the past

- Drug should be avoided by women who are pregnant or breast-feeding

- Drug interactions may occur with Dofetilide, Imipramine, Metoprolol, Sildenafil, Azole Antifungals, Buspirone, Carbamazepine, Cimetidine, Cisapride, Clarithromycin, Delavirdine, Dextromethorphan (the "DM" in some cough syrups), Diltiazem, Fenfluramine, Lithium, MAO Type A Inhibitors, Naratriptan, Selegiline, Sibutramine, Tryptophan, Tricyclic Antidepressants, Tramadol, Verapamil

 ## Common Side Effects

- Cough, sweating, weight loss, drop in blood pressure when standing

- Causes withdrawal symptoms if stopped suddenly

- May cause women's menstrual period to stop; may inhibit orgasm in both sexes

Occasional/Long-Term Side Effects

- No long-term effects reported

 ## Toxicity/Adverse Reaction (Contact your doctor)

- Mild adverse reaction: Rash, headache, dizziness, disrupted sleep patterns, tremor, change in sense of taste, increased appetite, nausea, indigestion, vomiting, increased heart rate, sweating, urination

- Serious adverse reaction: Mania, thoughts of suicide, low sodium levels, drug-induced seizures

- May activate epilepsy in susceptible people

- Signs of overdose: Agitation, tremor, vomiting, seizure, changes in heart rate

 ## General Advice and Precautions

- Herbs and minerals: Avoid St. John's Wort, Ginkgo, Ma Huang, Yohimbe, Indian Snakeroot and Kava Kava

- Drug may cause drowsiness, delayed reaction time, and/or impaired judgment. Avoid driving if these effects are present

- Do not stop this medication suddenly. Discontinue over two to four weeks under the supervision of a medical professional

- Caution: Notwithstanding treatment, some people suffering depression develop suicidal tendencies. If you (or someone you know) display signs of suicidal thinking, contact your doctor immediately

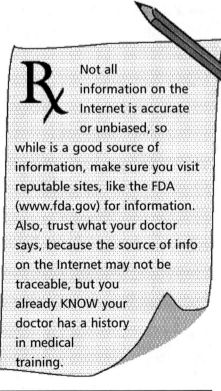

Rx Not all information on the Internet is accurate or unbiased, so while is a good source of information, make sure you visit reputable sites, like the FDA (www.fda.gov) for information. Also, trust what your doctor says, because the source of info on the Internet may not be traceable, but you already KNOW your doctor has a history in medical training.

Clonazepam

Brand Names: Apo-clonazepam, Klonopin, Med-clonazepam, Novo-clonazepam, Rhoxal-clonazepam, Rivotril

 Used For

- Treatment for panic attacks and some types of seizures

 Known Contraindications and/or Interactions

- Do not take this drug if you have had an allergic reaction to it in the past, if you have liver disease or if you have acute narrow-angle glaucoma

- Consult your doctor before taking it if you are allergic to any type of benzodiazepine drug, have a history of alcohol or drug abuse, are pregnant or planning pregnancy, have liver or kidney problems, have lung disease, or conditions including asthma, emphysema, or chronic bronchitis, or have a history of depression or mental disorder

- Should be avoided by women who are pregnant or breast-feeding

- Drug interactions may occur with some over-the-counter antihistamines, Amiodarone, Carbamazepine, Cimetidine, Desipramine, Disulfiram, Imipramine and other tricyclic antidepressants, MAO inhibitors, macrolide antibiotics, oral contraceptives, Phenytoin, Fosphenytoin, Primidone, Rifampin, Ritonavir, Theophylline, Valproic Acid

 Common Side Effects

- Drowsiness, salivation

 Occasional/Long-Term Side Effects

- Can affect mental function

- May increase sex drive

 Toxicity/Adverse Reaction (Contact your doctor)

- Mild adverse reaction: Rash, hives, muscle weakness, lack of coordination, weight gain, headache, dizziness, vision problems, memory problems, depression, nausea, vomiting, diarrhea, occasionally incontinence

- Serious adverse reaction: Psychological reactions of hyperactivity, agitation, anger, hallucinations, seizures, breathing problems

- Signs of overdose: Significant drowsiness, weakness, confusion, slurring, tremor, stupor, coma

 ## General Advice and Precautions

- Herbs and minerals: Avoid Hawthorn, Valerian, Kava Kava, Kola nut, siberian Ginseng, mate, Ephedra, Ma Huang, evening primrose oil, Ginkgo (when contaminated with other compounds), St. John's Wort

- Try to avoid alcohol completely while on this medication

- This drug may interfere with alertness, coordination and reaction time. Avoid driving or operating heavy machinery until you know how it affects you

- Can cause dependency

- About one-third of users develop a tolerance after approximately three months, requiring an adjustment in dosage

- Do not stop suddenly, particularly if the drug is being used to treat seizures. Discontinue gradually, under a doctor's supervision

Clonidine

Brand Names: Apo-Clonidine, Catapres, Combipres [CD], Dixarit, Duraclon, Novo-Clonidine, Nu-Clonidine

 ## Used For

- Treatment of High Blood Pressure

- Pain relief for cancer patients when used in conjunction with opioids or narcotics

- May be useful in treating narcotic or nicotine withdrawl, or with some women suffering hot flashes due to menopause

 ## Known Contraindications and/or Interactions

- Dose should be decreased in liver compromised patients and increased in people with decreased kidney function

- Only take this medication when pregnant or breast-feeding under explicit instructions of your physician

- Adverse effects may result from taking Clonidine with Levodopa, beta-blockers, Cyclosporine, Mirtazapine, Naloxone, Niacin (may actually be beneficial to avoid face flushing with use of Niacin), NSAIDs, Verapamil, or tricyclic antidepressants

 ## Common Side Effects

- Feelings of drowsiness

- Lack of moisture in nose and mouth

- Constipation

- Slowed heart rate

- Lowered blood pressure when moving from a sitting or lying position to standing straight up quickly

- Arrhythmias upon sudden stop of medication

- Some skin itching or rash can occur with use of a patch version of this drug

 ## Occasional/Long-Term Side Effects

- Sometimes people will experience headache, pain in the mouth (salvitory gland), urination at night, allergic reaction, nightmares or vivid dreams, anxiety, sleepiness, eyes that feel hot and dry – a burning sensation

- Long-term use may result in the development of a tolerance to the drug excess water and salt retention resulting in apparent weight gain or temporary sexual impotence

 ## Toxicity/Adverse Reaction (Contact your doctor)

- Extreme drowsiness, slow pulse, very low blood pressure, vomiting, feeling of weakness, inability to move, dry mouth, coma

General Advice and Precautions

- Alcohol may increase effects of this drug, leading to possible health risks

- Excess salt will be retained by your body, so it's best to eat a reduced salt diet

- Talk to your doctor about taking Garlic, Calcium, or Indian Snakeroot to lower your dose of clonidine

- Avoid herbs that may raise blood pressure like Ginseng, Hawthorn, Guarana, Saw Palmetto, Goldenseal, Yohimbe, Licorice, and definitely Eleuthero Root

- Extreme heat may increase the chance of sudden blood pressure drops on standing up

- Cold weather/water may also cause adverse reactions like pain in the hands and feet

- This drug can cause severe withdrawl symptoms if suddenly stopped, so gradual reduction over a few days is usually the best course

Codeine

Brand Names: Too numerous to list. Any time you are given a prescription-strength cough medication or painkiller, ask your doctor if it contains codeine

 ## Used For

- Treatment of moderate pain, cough

 ## Known Contraindications and/or Interactions

- Do not take this drug if you are having an asthma attack or shallow breathing, or if you have had an allergic reaction to it in the past. This drug may not be appropriate for people with asthma, emphysema or bronchitis

- Talk to your doctor before taking it if you have lung, liver or kidney problems, gallbladder disease, a seizure disorder; if you are hypothyroid, or on sedatives; if you have a history of drug abuse or porphyria; if you are due for a procedure where you will be under general anesthesia

- Avoid this drug if you are pregnant or breast-feeding

- Drug interactions may occur with atropinelike drugs, MAO inhibitors, Naltrexone, Quinidine, Rifabutin, Ritonavir, Sedatives, Tramadol

 ## Common Side Effects

- Drowsiness, dry mouth, fluid retention, constipation

 ## Occasional/Long-Term Side Effects

- Drug dependence, chronic constipation

- Opiates can variously dull or sharpen sexual response

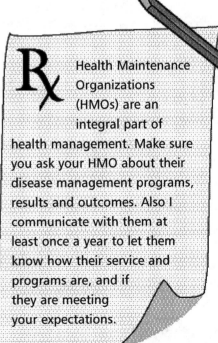

R Health Maintenance Organizations (HMOs) are an integral part of health management. Make sure you ask your HMO about their disease management programs, results and outcomes. Also I communicate with them at least once a year to let them know how their service and programs are, and if they are meeting your expectations.

Toxicity/Adverse Reaction (Contact your doctor)

- Mild adverse reaction: Rash, hives, "drunk" feeling, inability to concentrate, confusion, depression, vision problems, nausea, vomiting

- Serious adverse reaction: Anaphylaxis, hallucinations, delerium, porphyria, pancreatitis, liver or kidney toxicity

- Signs of overdose: Drowsiness or agitation, dizziness, weakness, nausea, vomiting, stupor, seizures, coma

 ## General Advice and Precautions

- Herbs and minerals: Avoid Valerian, Kava Kava and St. John's Wort

- Do not drink alcohol while on this medication

- Do not take this drug if you suspect head injury

- Remember that many codeine products contain Acetaminophen. Include these amounts when calculating your daily intake of Acetaminophen: you should not exceed 4,000 mg/day

- Should be used short-term only; if taken long-term, taper off the drug when discontinuing to avoid withdrawal problems

Colesevelam

Brand Names: Welchol

 ## Used For

- Lowering total cholesterol and LDL cholesterol

 ## Known Contraindications and/or Interactions

- Do not take this drug if you have had an allergic reaction to it in the past

- Do not take this drug if your bowels are obstructed

- Consult your doctor before taking it if pregnant or nursing, if you have hypothyroidism, stomach/intestinal disorders, or if you have a fat-soluble vitamin deficiency

- Drug interactions may occur with Alendronate, Fosamax, fibrates, Tricor, Verapamil, Calan, vitamin B_{12}, Atorvastatin, Lipitor, Lovastatin, Mevacor, Simvastatin, Zocor

 ## Common Side Effects

- Constipation

- Changes in fat/vitamin absorption

 ## Occasional/Long-Term Side Effects

- Deficiencies of vitamins A, D, E, K, folic acid

- Binding of vitamin B_{12}

 ## Toxicity/Adverse Reaction (Contact your doctor)

- Mild adverse reaction: Joint pain, constipation, indigestion, heartburn, gas, nausea, vomiting

- Serious adverse reaction: Vitamin deficiency, serious constipation

- Signs of overdose: Serious constipation

 ## General Advice and Precautions

- Herbs and minerals: Avoid Garlic

- Avoid eating cheese, soy products

- Speak to your doctor about vitamin supplementation when taking this medication

- Do not suddenly stop taking this drug. Discontinue gradually under your doctor's supervision

- Ensure you are drinking enough liquids when taking this medication

- Take this medication right before or with meals

COX II Inhibitor Family

Brand Names: Celecoxib, Celebrex; Rofecoxib, Valdecoxib, Bextra.

NOTE: The medication "Celexa" – while having a name similar to Celebrex – is an antidepressant, not a COX II inhibitor. Always check your prescription carefully to ensure no mistakes have been made

 ## Used For

- Treatment of non-arthritic pain and inflammation, osteoarthritis, rheumatoid arthritis, dysmenorrhea

 ## Known Contraindications and/or Interactions

- Do not take these drugs if you have had an allergic reaction to a COX II inhibitor or NSAID medication in the past, or if you have developed urticaria or bronchospasm when taking Aspirin or another NSAID in the past

- Do not take if you have a peptic ulcer, are in your third trimester of pregnancy, or have liver disease

- Rofecoxib should be used with caution in people who have ischemic heart disease

- This drug should be avoided by women who are breast-feeding

- Consult your physician before taking a COX II inhibitor if you have a history of heart disease, high blood pressure, peptic ulcers, kidney or liver disorders, or if you currently have a bleeding disorder, ulcerative colitis, ischemic heart disease, asthma; if you are or are planning to get pregnant; if you smoke or if you drink more than three alcoholic drinks a day

- Drug interactions may occur with ACE inhibitors, adrenocortical steroids, Alendronate, Carbamazepine, cortisone-like drugs, Diltiazem, Fluconazole, Fluoxetine, high blood pressure medication, Lithium, Methotrexate, oral anticoagulants, other NSAIDs, Propafenone, Ritonavir, Sertraline; certain drugs that affect liver activity

 ## Common Side Effects

- Acid indigestion, upset stomach (mild), dizziness

 ## Occasional/Long-Term Side Effects

- Erosion of stomach lining (long-term effect of Rofecoxib and Celecoxib, as evidenced by anemia)

Toxicity/Adverse Reaction (Contact your doctor)

- Mild adverse reaction: rash, dizziness, heartburn, diarrhea, fluid retention

- Serious adverse reaction: anaphylaxis, gastrointestinal bleeding, erosion of stomach lining, kidney or liver problems, bronchospasm (in patients with nasal polyps or asthma). May worsen angina. Rofecoxib and Celecoxib may be associated with clot-related cardiovascular problems

- Signs of overdose: No overdose data available. Note, however, drinking more than three alcoholic drinks a day increases risk of stomach bleeding

 ## General Advice and Precautions

- Herbs and minerals: Avoid Alfalfa, Cinchona Bark, Clove Oil, Feverfew, Ginkgo, Ginseng, White Willow Bark

- May cause dizziness. Avoid driving and/or operating heavy machinery until you know how this medication affects you

Cyclosporine

Brand Names: Neoral, Sandimmune, SangCya, Sangstat

 ## Used For

- Treatment of severe rheumatoid arthritis

- Treatment of other severe cases of inflammatory autoimmune disorders

- Prevention of organ rejection in transplant patients

 ## Known Contraindications and/or Interactions

- Do not take this drug if you have had an allergic reaction to it in the past

- Do not take this drug if you are involved in radiation or PUVA treatment, have high blood pressure, lymphoma or an active infection

  Consult your doctor before taking it if you take other

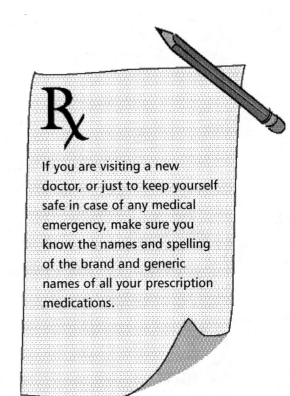

If you are visiting a new doctor, or just to keep yourself safe in case of any medical emergency, make sure you know the names and spelling of the brand and generic names of all your prescription medications.

immunosuppresants, are pregnant or nursing, have kidney or liver problems, hypertension, gout, gastrointestinal problems, take Potassium supplements, suffer from seizures, blood cell problems

- Drug interactions may occur with ACE inhibitors, Acyclovir, Aminoglycoside, Amphotericin B, Amprenavir, Aspirin, NSAIDs, Atorvastatin, Fluvastatin, Lovastatin, Simvastatin, Azathioprine, C channel blockers, Clonidine, Ciprofloxacin, Fluoroquinolones, Cotrimoxazole, Cyclophosphamide, Digoxin, Furosemide, Ganciclovir, Antihistamines, I, Milastatin, Methyprednisolone, Metronidazole, Nifedipine, Propafenone, Pravastatin, Sauinavir, Sirolimus, Spironolactone, Sulfamethoxxazole, Trimethoprim, Tacrolimus, thiazide diuretics, Triamterine, vaccines, Valproic acid, Verapamil, Warfarin, Acetazolamide, Allopurinol, Amiodarone, Ceftriaxone, Cimetidine, Cisapride, Clarithromycin, Clotrimazole, Colchicine, Dalfopristin, Danazol, anabolic steroids, Diltiazem, Econazole, Erythromycin, Fluconazole, Fluvoxamine, Glipizide, Glyburide, Grepafloxacin, Imatinib, Itraconazole, Ketoconazole, Methotrexate, Methyltestosterone, Metoclopramide, Miconazole, birth control pills, Ritonavir, Tamoxifen, Terconazole, Ticarcillin, Carbamazepine, Carvedilol, Clinamycin, Isoniazid, Nafcillin, Octreotide, Orlistat, Omeprazole, Phenobarbitol, Phenytoin, Fosphenytoin, Quinine, Rifampin, Sulfadimidine, Ticlopidine, Warfarin

 ## Common Side Effects

- Susceptability to infection

- Fever

 ## Occasional/Long-Term Side Effects

- Irreversable kidney damage

- Hypertension

- Growth of gums

- Enlargement of breasts in men

- Changes to facial features

 ## Toxicity/Adverse Reaction (Contact your doctor)

- Mild adverse reaction: Skin rash, hair growth, confusion, anxiety, headache, tremors, nausea, vomiting

- Serious adverse reaction: Anaphylactic reaction, hypertension, total cholesterol increases,

HDL cholesterol decreases, seizures, blindness, hearing loss, hallucinations, dementia, nerve damage, liver injury, pancreas injury, low white blood cell count, low blood platelets, abnormal blood clots, high blood sugar, high Potassium, lymphoma, lupus, increased risk of some cancers

- Signs of overdose: Headache, pain, bleeding gums, high blood pressure, atrial fibrillation, respiratory problems, seizures, coma, hallucinations, nerve disorders, liver disorders

 ## General Advice and Precautions

- Herbs and minerals: Avoid Echinacea, Mistletoe, Oak Bark, Marshmallow Rroot, St. John's Wort

- Speak to your doctor about vitamin supplementation while taking this drug

- May cause confusion, hallucinations, and seizures. Avoid driving and/or operating machinery until you know how this drug affects you

- Do not suddenly stop taking this drug. Discontinue gradually under your doctor's supervision

- Do not drink grapefruit juice, milk or alcohol while taking this drug

Dexamethasone

Brand Names: Aeroseb-Dex, Ak-Dex, Ak-Trol, Baldex, Dalalone, Dalalone DP, Dalalone LA, Decaderm, Decadron, Decadron Nasal Spray, Decadron-LA, Decadron Phosphate Ophthalmic, Decadron Phosphate Respinaler, Decadron Phosphate Turbinaire, Decadron w/Xylocaine, Decadron dose pack, Decaject, Decaject LA, Decaspray, Deenar, Deone-LA, Deronil, Dex-4, Dexacen-4, Dexacen LA-8, Dexacidin, Dexacort, Dexameth, Dexasone, Dexasone-LA, Dexo-LA, Dexon, Dexone-E, Dexone-4, Dexone-LA, Dexsone, Dexsone-E, Dexsone-LA, Dezone, Duedezone, Gammacorten, Hexadrol, Maxidex, Mymethasone, Neodecadron Eye-Ear, Neodexair, Neomycin-Dex, Ocu-Trol, Oradexon, PMS-Dexamethasone, SK-Dexamethasone, Sofracort, Solurex, Solurex-LA, Spersadex, Tobradex, Turbinaire

 ## Used For

- Symptom relief in asthma, rhinitis, lymphoma, brain edema, lupus, bursitis, tendonitis, arthritis, rheumatoid arthritis

- Symptom relief for ulcerative disease of the colon

- Used topically as treatment for eczema, psoriasis, dermatitis

- Also used to help treat vomiting caused by chemotherapy, refractory depression, brain cancer, multiple myeloma, pneumonia

- Can be used to suppress male hormones in women with acne, hair loss or excessive hair growth

 ## Known Contraindications and/or Interactions

- Do not take this drug if you have had an allergic reaction to it in the past

- Do not take this drug if pregnant/nursing, if you have peptic ulcers, active herpes simplex, fungal infections, psychoneurosis, psychosis, tuberculosis

- Consult your doctor before taking it if you have a family history of tuberculosis, if you have diabetes, glaucoma, high blood pressure, thyroid conditions, osteoporosis, if you have recently had a heart attack, or if you plan to have surgery

- Drug interactions may occur with Amprenavir, Indinavir, Caspofungin, Donepezil, Insulin, Isonaizid, Quetiapine, salicylates (including Aspirin), vaccines, NSAIDs, birth control pills, Carbamazepine, Irinotecan, loop diuretics, oral anticoagulants, oral antidiabetic drugs, neuromuscular blocking agents, ritodrine, ritonavir, protease inhibitors, Thalidomide, thiazide diuretics, antacids, barbiturates, Fosphenytoin, Phenytoin, Primidone, Rifabutin, Rifampin

 ## Common Side Effects

- Increased appetite, weight gain, salt and water retention

- Increase in head pressure

- Potassium loss

- Increased likelihood of infection

- Increased facial hair

- Increased white blood cell count

 ## Occasional/Long-Term Side Effects

- Increased blood sugar (diabetes)

- Increased fat deposits

- Thinning of skin

- Weakening bones

- Osteoporosis

- Cataracts/glaucoma

- Body hair

- Stunted growth in children

 Toxicity/Adverse Reaction (Contact your doctor)

- Mild adverse reaction: Skin rash, headache, dizziness, insomnia, depression/euphoria, high blood pressure, indigestion, distension, muscle cramping and weakness, stunted growth in children and infants, easy bruising, vaginal itching

- Serious adverse reaction: Anaphylaxis, mental and emotional disturbances, reactivation of tuberculosis, pneumonia, peptic ulcer, pancreatitis, thrombophlebitis, increase in cholesterol, abnormal heart beat, Cushing's syndrome, diabetes, low Potassium, fluid in the lungs, bone death, osteoporosis, altered menstruation

- Signs of overdose: Fatigue, muscle weakness, stomach irritation, indigestion, sweating, flushing, swelling, increased blood pressure

 General Advice and Precautions

- Herbs and minerals: Avoid Hawthorn, Ginger, Garlic, Ma Huang/Ephedra, Ginseng, Nettle, Licorice, Fir or Pine Needle Oil, Echinacea

- Talk to your doctor about supplementing with vitamin D and Calcium when taking this medication

- May cause dizziness. Avoid driving and/or operating machinery until you know how this drug affects you

- Do not drink alcohol when taking this medication

- Do not smoke cigarettes or Marijuana when taking this medication

- Eating high-Potassium foods may be advisable

- Carry a card that indicates you are taking this medication

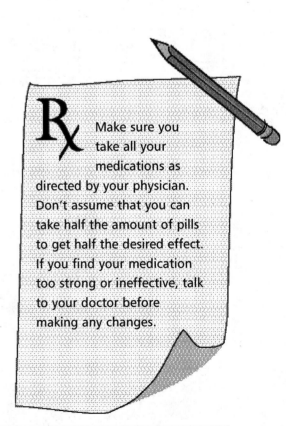

R͟x Make sure you take all your medications as directed by your physician. Don't assume that you can take half the amount of pills to get half the desired effect. If you find your medication too strong or ineffective, talk to your doctor before making any changes.

- If you are to get a vaccination, discontinue use of this drug 72 hours before vaccination, and resume taking your medication 14 days after your vaccination. Discuss this with your doctor

- Talk to your doctor if you experience unexplained joint pain while taking this drug

- Children may be especially sensitive to a topical version of this medication

- Do not suddenly stop taking this drug. Discontinue gradually under your doctor's supervision

Diazepam

Brand Names: Apo-Diazepam, Diastat, Diazemuls, Dizac, E-Pam, Meval, Novo-Dipam, Q-pam, Rival, T-Quil, Valcaps, Valium, Valrelease, Vazepam, Vivol, Zetran

 Used For

- Treatment of anxiety, nervous tension, muscle spasm, alcohol withdrawal, certain types of seizures

 Known Contraindications and/or Interactions

- Do not take this drug if you have had an allergic reaction to it in the past or have acute narrow-angle glaucoma. Consult your doctor before taking it if you are allergic to any types of benzodiazepine drug, have a history of alcohol or drug abuse, are pregnant or planning pregnancy, have liver or kidney problems, have lung disease or conditions including asthma, emphysema or chronic bronchitis, or have a history of depression or mental disorder

- Should be avoided by women who are pregnant or breast-feeding

- Drug interactions may occur with some over-the-counter antihistamines, Digoxin, Phenytoin, Fosphenytoin, Levodopa, Fluoxetine, Fluvoxamine, macrolide antibiotics, MAO inhibitors, Mirtazapine, narcotics, Olanzapine, Propoxyphene, Quinupristin/Dalfopristin, Ampernavir, oral contraceptives, Cimetidine, Cisapride, Disulfiram, Isoniazid, Itraconazole, Ketoconazole, Omeprazole, Ritonavir, Sertraline, Valproic Acid, Ranitidine, Rifampin, Theophylline.

Common Side Effects

■ Drowsiness, lethargy, feeling like you have a "hangover"

 ## Occasional/Long-Term Side Effects

■ Can cause drug dependence

■ May affect menstrual cycle

■ May interfere with potency in men, inhibit orgasm in women

 ## Toxicity/Adverse Reaction (Contact your doctor)

■ Mild adverse reaction: Rash, hives, dizziness, fainting, vision problems, slurred speech, sweating, nausea, loss of coordination

■ Serious adverse reaction: Anaphylaxis, drop in blood pressure and heart rate, leading to cardiac arrest, amnesia, obsessive-compulsive disorder, emotional reactions of agitation and anger. Intravenous form may result in blood clots, heart arrhythmias

■ Signs of overdose: Significant drowsiness, weakness, "drunk" feeling, tremor, stupor, coma

 ## General Advice and Precautions

■ Herbs and minerals: Avoid Hawthorn, Valerian, Kava Kava, Skull Cap, Kola Nut, Siberian Ginseng, Guarana, Mate, Ephedra, Ma Huang, evening Primrose Oil, Ginkgo (when contaminated with other compounds), St. John's Wort

■ Cut back on caffeine (coffee, tea, cola); avoid grapefruit juice

■ Try to avoid alcohol completely while on this medication

■ This drug may interfere with alertness, coordination, reaction time. Avoid driving or operating heavy machinery until you know how it affects you

■ Do not stop suddenly, particularly if the drug is being used to treat seizures. Discontinue gradually, under a doctor's supervision.

Digoxin

Brand Names: Digitaline, Nativelle, Digitek, Lanoxicaps, Lanoxin, NovoDigoxin, SK-Digoxin

 Used For

- Regulating heart rhythm

- Stimulant in cases of heart failure

 Known Contraindications and/or Interactions

- Do not take this drug if you have had an allergic reaction to it in the past

- Do not take this drug if you have a life-threatening heart rhythm

- Consult your doctor before taking if pregnant or nursing, have recently taken this drug, have lung disease, take diuretics, have heart damage, have an inflamed heart, low blood Potassium, low blood Magnesium, liver or kidney problems, thyroid conditions

- Drug interactions may occur with Acarbose, Calcium, Digoxin Immune Fab, Diuretics, Dofetilide, Metformin, Pancuronium, Vecuronium, Propranolol, beta-blockers, Quinidine, Succinylcholine, Alprazolam, Amiloride, Amiodarone, Amphotericin, Atorvastatin, Benzodiazepines, Captopril, Carvedilol, Cotrimoxazole, Cyclosporine, Diltiazem, Disopyramide, Erythromycin, Clarithromycin, Azithromycin, Ethacrynic Acid, Esomeprazole, Omeprazole, Flecainide, Fluoxetine, Fluvoxamine, Gatifloxacin, Hydroxychloroquine, Ibuprofen, Indomethacin, Itraconazole, Methimazole, Mibefradil, Nefazodone, Nifedipine, Omeprazole, Phenytoin, Propafenone, Propylthiouracil, Quinine, Quinupristin, Dalfopristin, Ritonavir, Spironolactone, Telmisartan, Tetracyclines, Tolbutamide, Tramadol, Trazodone, Trimethoprim, Verapamil, Activated Charcoal, Aluminum, Magnesium, Antacids, Bleomycin, Carmustine, Cholestyramine, Colestipol, Cyclophosphamide, Cytarabine, Doxorubicin, Laolin/Pectin, Methotrexate, Metoclopramide, Miglitol, Neomycin, Penicillamine, Procarbazine, Rifampin, Rifabutin, Sucralfate, sulfa antibiotics, Slufasalazine, Thryroid medications, Vincristine

 Common Side Effects

- Slow heart rate

- Black feces

- Breast enlargement in men

Occasional/Long-Term Side Effects

- Decreased libido

- Cornification of the vagina

- Mental changes

 ## Toxicity/Adverse Reaction (Contact your doctor)

- Mild adverse reaction: Skin rash, headache, drowsiness, confusion, vision changes, nightmares, appetite loss, vomiting, diarrhea

- Serious adverse reaction: Hallucinations, facial neuralgia, nerve damage, blindness, low blood platelets, psychosis, seizures, disorientation, serious rashes, heart rhythm problems

- Signs of overdose: Drooling, vomiting, diarrhea, major changes in heart rate, intestinal bleeding, drowsiness, confusion, hallucinations, convulsions

 ## General Advice and Precautions

- Herbs and minerals: Avoid St. John's Wort, Aluminum, Magnesium, Calcium, Hawthorn, Coenzyme Q_{10}, Couch Grass, Nettle, Aloe, Lily of the Valley, Pheasant's Eye, Squill, Ginseng

- May cause drowsiness and vision changes. Avoid driving and/or operating machinery until you know how this drug affects you

- Do not smoke tobacco or Marijuana while taking this medication

- Avoid caffeine while taking this medication

- Do not suddenly stop taking this drug. Discontinue gradually under your doctor's supervision

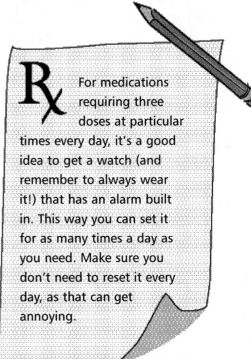

Rx For medications requiring three doses at particular times every day, it's a good idea to get a watch (and remember to always wear it!) that has an alarm built in. This way you can set it for as many times a day as you need. Make sure you don't need to reset it every day, as that can get annoying.

Estrogens

Also known as: Chlorotrianisene, conjugated estrogens, esterified estrogens, Estradiol, Estriol, Estrone, Estropipate, Quinestrol

Brand Names: Activella, Alora, C.E.S., Climacteron, Climara, Climestrone, Congest, Delestrogen, Depo-Estradiol, DV, Esclim, Estinyl, Femogen, Femogex, Femhrt, Gynetone, Gynodiol, Gynogen LA, Menest, Menotab, Menotab-M, Menrium, Milprem, Minestrin, PMS-Estradiol, Premarin, Premphase, Prempro, Progynon Pellet, TACE, Valergen-10, Vivelle, Vivelle-Dot, White Premarin

 ## Used For

- Relief of vasomotor symptoms like night sweats and hot flashes in menopausal women

- Relief of deteriorating vaginitis, vaginal dryness or deterioration of body tissues (skin thinning)

- Prevention of osteoporosis in post-menopausal women

- Reducing clotting and inflammation (when used with simvastatin)

 ## Known Contraindications and/or Interactions

- Estrogen/progestin combination is not effective for preventing recurring heart attack, Alzheimer's, dementia

- Estrogens are not easily wasted from the body and thus, may cause problems with people who have mild liver disease, or compromised livers. Lower doses should be sought be people with sever kidney problems

- Can predisposition female children to certain cancers if taken during pregnancy, but estrogen does not seem to harm a baby during breast feeding

- May adversely affect/be affected by Amprenavir, Atorvastatin, Fluconazole, Lamotrigene, Naratriptan, antidiabetics, progestins, Tacrine, thyroid hormones, trycyclic antidepressants, Warfarin, Carbamazepine, Primidone, penicillin or other antibiotics, Belladonna and other phenobarbitals, Fosphenytoin, Phenytoin, Rifampin, or constant high doses of vitamin C

- Inform your doctor if you have estrogen or horse allergy, or if you have (or your family has) any history of the diseases that may be caused or activated by estrogen. (See: Occasional/Long-Term Side Effects.)

Common Side Effects

- Fluid retention, spotting in mid-menstrual cycle ("breakthrough" bleeding), menstrual flow resumes after postmenopausal bleeding, yeast infections, weight gain

 ## Occasional/Long-Term Side Effects

- Some studies have shown that combination therapies may increase the chance of breast cancer, coronary problems, blood clots or stroke

- Use of estrogen may activate diabetes, hypertension, porphyria or liver problems that were previously unnoticed

- Allergy, erythema, high blood pressure, gallbladder disease, jaundice, pancreatitis, leg swelling and pain, stroke in women who have a uterus, blood clot moved to lung, benign liver tumors, come cancers, hypocalcaemia are rare, but may occur

- May cause sensitivity to sunlight

 ## Toxicity/Adverse Reaction (Contact your doctor)

- Signs of overdose: Headache, drowsiness, vaginal bleeding that is irregular or unusual and excessive, stomach discomfort including nausea and vomiting, discomfort or enlargement of the breasts

 ## General Advice and Precautions

- Because there are so many adverse effects, it is now recommended that estrogens be taken in the smallest dose to be effective for as short an amount of time as possible

- Hot flashes from withdrawal may occur if medication is stopped too quickly

- Smoking increases the risk of heart attack with use of estrogen

- It's a good idea to consume less caffeine and DHEA

- Consuming a lot of salt can adversely affect fluid retention

- The use of Ginko Biloba, Echinacea, and St. John's Wort increased infertility while using it with estrogen, St. John's Wort was also indicated as making people more prone to photosensitivity

- People seeking alternative to estrogens may seek Black Cohosh, Clonidine, Fluoxetine (Prozac), Venlafaxine (Effexor), or Gabapentin (Neurontin) — depending on the symptoms

they are seeking to treat

Extended Release Niacin/Lovastatin

Brand Names: Advicor

 Used For

- Lowering total cholesterol

- Lowering LDL cholesterol

- Lowering triglycerides

- Prevention of heart disease

- Slowing atherosclerosis

- Reducing risk of stroke

- Reducing risk of some cancers

 Known Contraindications and/or Interactions

- Do not take this drug if you have had an allergic reaction to it in the past

- Do not take this drug if pregnant or nursing, planning pregnancy, you have peptic ulcers, liver disorders, or if you are bleeding from an artery

- Consult your doctor before taking it if you have low blood pressure, you regularly drink alcohol, you have vision disorders, an irregular heart beat, peptic ulcers or bowel disease, gout, a muscular disorder or diabetes

- Drug interactions may occur with medications for hypertension, antidiabetics, Aspirin, Probenecid, Sulfinpyrazone, Isoniazid, Cholestyramine, Colestipol, Lovastatin, nicotine atches, Amprenavir, Clofibrate, Colesevelam, Cyclosporine, Diltiazem, Erythromycin, Fluconazole, Intraconazole, Ketoconazol, Voriconazole, Gemfibrozil, Levothyroxine, Nefazodone, Quinupristin, Dalfopristin, Ritonavir, Indinavir, protease inhibitors, Warfarin

 Common Side Effects

- Flushing, tingling, unexplained warmth, itching

- Hypotension

Occasional/Long-Term Side Effects

- Myopathy

- Hyperglycemia, diabetes

- High levels of uric acid, gout

 ## Toxicity/Adverse Reaction (Contact your doctor)

- Mild adverse reaction: Headache, dizziness, fainting, vision changes, nausea, changes in senses of taste and smell, vomiting, diarrhea, dry skin

- Serious adverse reaction: Hepatitis, jaundice, anaphylaxis, arthritis, angioedema, fever, skin death, diabetes, gout, impaired wound heeling, changes in heart beat, muscle pain, ulcers

- Signs of overdose: Nausea, painful vomiting, low blood pressure

 ## General Advice and Precautions

- Herbs and minerals: Avoid Cholestin, multivitamins with high Niacin content, and Garlic

- Do not drink grapefruit juice while taking this medication

- Do not drink alcohol or smoke cigarettes while taking this drug

- May cause dizziness and vision problems. Avoid driving and/or operating machinery until you know how this drug affects you

- Do not suddenly stop taking this drug. Discontinue gradually under your doctor's supervision

- Speak to your doctor about vitamin supplementation while taking this medication

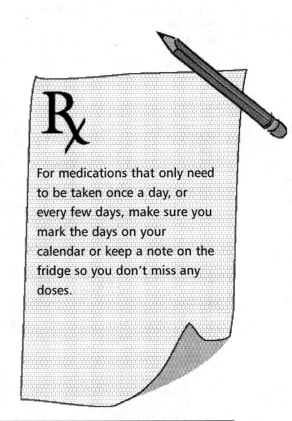

For medications that only need to be taken once a day, or every few days, make sure you mark the days on your calendar or keep a note on the fridge so you don't miss any doses.

Fentanyl

Brand Names: Actiq, Duragesic, Innovar, Oralet, Sublimaze

 Used For

- Pain relief

 Known Contraindications and/or Interactions

- Do not take this medication if you have had an allergic reaction to it in the past

- Do not take for mild pain. Do not use Fentanyl Oralet at home – it is for hospital use only

- Consult your physician before taking if you have chronic lung disease, a kidney or liver disorder, an abnormally slow heartbeat or heart disease, a brain tumor or seizure disorder, have a history of alcoholism or drug abuse, take a benzodiazepine drug (e.g., Diazepam, Valium)

- Avoid using this drug if you are pregnant or breast-feeding

- Drug interactions may occur with Amiodarone, Benzodiazepines, central nervous system depressants (barbituates, opiates, tranquilizers, tricyclic antidepressants), Clonidine, MAO inhibitors, Rifabutin, Ketoconazole, Voriconazole, Erythromycin, Phenytoin-Dilantin, Fosphenytoin-Cerebyx, Ritonavir and other protease inhibitors, Sibutramine, Sildenafil

 Common Side Effects

- Drowsiness or euphoria, dry mouth, constipation. Many older patients are given medication for constipation as soon as this drug is started

 Occasional/Long-Term Side Effects

- May develop a tolerance or even dependence on the drug

- May cause impotence in men. May dull orgasm sensation in both men and women

Toxicity/Adverse Reaction (Contact your doctor)

- Mild adverse reaction: Skin rash, vision problems, tremor, nausea, vomiting

- Serious adverse reaction: Anaphylaxis, erratic behavior, speech problems, raised or lowered blood pressure, hallucinations, seizures, shallow breathing

- Signs of overdose: Shallow breathing, apnea, dizziness, amnesia, stupor

General Advice and Precautions

- Herbs and minerals: Avoid Valerian, Kava Kava and St. John's Wort

- Should NOT be combined with other opioids, benzodiazepines, alcohol or narcotic drugs

- Be extremely careful to keep this medication from children as doses may look tempting but are potentially fatal

- Do not stop taking this drug suddenly; discontinue gradually under a doctor's supervision

Fluoroquinolone Antibiotic Family

Includes: Ciprofloxacin, Gatifloxacin, Levofloxacin, Lomefloxacin, Moxifloxacin, Norfloxacin, Ofloxacin, Sparfloxacin, Trovafloxacin
Brand Names: Ciprofloxacin: Ciloxan, Cipro
Gatifloxacin: Tequin
Levofloxacin: Levaquin, Quixin, Maxaquin
Moxifloxacin: Avelox
Norfloxacin: Chibroxin, Noroxin
Ofloxacin: Apo-Oflox, Floxin, Ocuflox, Ofloxacine
Sparfloxacin: Zagam
Trovafloxin: Trovan, Trovan/Zithromax Compliance Pak

 ## Used For

- Ciprofloxacin and Ofloxacin are used to treat lower respiratory tract infections

- Treatment of urinary tract, bones, joint, skin

- Treatment of bacterial eye infections

- Treatment for diarrhea

- Treatment of some prostate infections

- Effective treatment of streptococcus by sparfloxacin

- Treatment of outer ear infections by ciprofloxacin

- Cystic fibrosis patients, in higher doses than normal

Known Contraindications and/or Interactions

- Interacts with Probenecid, Amiodarone, Zzlocillin, Caffeine, Corticosteroids, Cyclosporine, Dofetilde, Foscarnet, Ibutilide, Lithium, Typhoid Vaccine (live), Olanzapine, Phenytoin, Riluzole, Theophylline, Warfarin, antacids, Calcium supplements, iron salts, Didanosine, Morphine, Magnesium, Nitrofurantoin, Sucralfate, and Zinc salts

- Sparfloxacin is especially prone to cause arrhythmias (abnormal heart beats) when taken with Amiodarone, Astemizole, Bepridil, beta-blockers, Chlorpromazine, Cisapride, Disopyramide, Macrolide Antibiotics, Phenothiazines, Procainamide, Quinidine, Tricyclic antidepressants

- Moxifloxacin could cause changes in hearts that are unstable, or abnormal, if taken with antiarrhythmic drugs in class 1A or class III

- In cases of liver problems you should not use Ciprofloxacin, Norfloxacin or Trovafloxin without extreme caution

- For kidney problems doses should be decreased for most types of these antibiotics

- Should not be used during pregnancy or while breast-feeding unless advised by your physician

 # Common Side Effects

- Infections as a result of antibiotic resistance (superinfections)

- Infants may experience a permanent tooth discoloration of a greenish tone

- Photosensitivity is a common side effects

 # Occasional/Long-Term Side Effects

- In some cases this drug has resulted in people experiencing tendon rupture, especially those on corticosteroids, over 60 years old, or with high cholesterol or triglycerides

- Mental confusion or disorientation may occur as a result of neurological compromise

- Occasional side effects include vaginitis, pain during menstruation, excessive menstrual bleeding, blood in urine, allergic reaction, skin rashes, muscle pain, burning in eye for eye treatments, vision problems, kidney disease, arrhythmias, changes in blood sugar levels, intracranial hypertension, bone marrow depletion and more severe myasthenia gravis

Toxicity/Adverse Reaction (Contact your doctor)

■ It is imperative you stop taking the medication and call your doctor immediately if you notice any changes in your thinking, such as unusual confusion, disorientation, trouble speaking or hallucinations or if you experienced tremors or a seizure

■ Signs of overdose: Headache, gastrointestinal distress, confusion, seizure, hallucinations and toxicity in liver or kidneys

 General Advice and Precautions

■ Sometimes the term "Norflox" is used to describe Norfloxacin by doctors prescribing the medication, but this is not a proper drug name and has occasionally been confused by pharmacists with a drug that is actually a muscle relaxant, so be wary of what you are prescribed

■ Caffeine amounts can be increased and stay in your system longer

■ Dairy products should be eaten two hours before, or six hours after a dose

■ Similarly, Calcium, Zinc, Iron supplements, or Fennel Seeds should not be taken before or after these times

Flunisolide

Brand Names: AeroBid, AeroBid-M, Bronalide, Nasalide, Nasarel, Nu-Flunisolide, Rhinalar

 Used For

■ Treatment of allergic rhinitis

■ Treatment of chronic bronchial asthma

■ Treatment of hayfever (perennial allergic rhinitis)

■ Treatment of nasal polyps

 Known Contraindications and/or Interactions

■ Do not take this drug if you have had an allergic

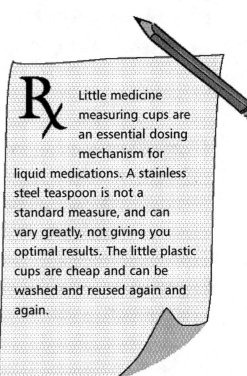
Little medicine measuring cups are an essential dosing mechanism for liquid medications. A stainless steel teaspoon is not a standard measure, and can vary greatly, not giving you optimal results. The little plastic cups are cheap and can be washed and reused again and again.

reaction to it in the past

- Do not take this drug if you are pregnant or nursing

- Do not take this drug if you have severe acute asthma or chronic bronchitis

- Do not take if you suffer nosebleeds

- Consult your doctor before taking if you take other cortisone-related medications, if you have had or have tuberculosis, herpes simplex, chicken pox, measles, nasal surgery, or you think you have a respiratory infection

- Drug interactions may occur with albuterol, bitolterol, epinephrine, aminophylline, ephedrine, terbutaline, theophylline, stanozolol, antiepileptic medications, isoetharine, isoproterenol

 ## Common Side Effects

- Yeast infections

- Adrenal gland suppression

- Changes in sense of taste

 ## Occasional/Long-Term Side Effects

- Acne

- Cataracts

- Changed menstrual cycle

- Osteoporosis

 ## Toxicity/Adverse Reaction (Contact your doctor)

- Mild adverse reaction: skin rash, hives, headache, dizziness, moodiness, insomnia, loss of sense of smell or taste, respiratory infection, heart palpitation, increased blood pressure, indigestion, nausea, vomiting, diarrhea

- Serious adverse reaction: lung inflammation, bronchospasm, wheezing, hypertension, tachycardia, osteoporosis, cataracts

- Signs of overdose: fluid retention, flushing, irritated stomach, nervousness

General Advice and Precautions

- Herbs and minerals: Avoid Fir and Pine Needle Oil, Ephedra, Echinacea, Ragweed, Chrysanthemum, Chamomile, Feverfew, St. John's Wort

- Do not suddenly stop taking this drug. Discontinue gradually under your doctor's supervision

- Consider avoiding alcohol and quitting smoking

Fluoxetine

Brand Names: Alti-Fluoxetine, Apo-Fluoxetine, Gen-Fluoxetine, Med-Fluoxetine, Prozac, Sarafem

 Used For

- Depression, PMS, bulimia, obsessive-compulsive disorder

- May be used to treat other conditions, including kleptomania, obesity, tinnitus

 Known Contraindications and/or Interactions

- Do not take this drug if you took a MAO Type A Inhibitor within the preceding 14 days

- Consult your physican before taking if you have a Parkinson's or a seizure disorder, liver or kidney problems, have a history of psychosis or have had negative reactions to antidepressant drugs in the past

- Drug should be avoided by women who are pregnant or breast-feeding

- Drug interactions may occur with beta-blockers, Diazepam, Digitalis (Digitoxin, Digoxin), Diltiazem, Dofetilide, ergot derivatives, Flecainide, Phenytoin, Propafenone, Propranolol, Quinidine, Sildenafil, Valproic Acid, Warfarin, antidiabetic drugs, Aspirin (rare), some antihistamines, Buspirone, Carbamazepine, Cimetidine, Clarithromycin, Clozapine, Cotrimoxazole, Delavirdine, Dextromethorphan (the "DM" in some cough medications), Fenfluramine, Haloperidol, Ketorolac, Lithium, Loratadine, medicines that reduce liver function, MAO Type A Inhibitors, Morphine, Naratriptan, Olanzapine, Ondansetron, Selegiline, Sibutramine, Sulfamethoxazole, Thioridazine, Tramadol, any tricyclic antidepressant, Trimethoprim, Tryptophan, Ziprasidone, Zolpidem

Common Side Effects

- Decreased appetite, weight loss

- May impair erection in men and orgasm in both sexes

- May cause breast milk production in women

 ## Occasional/Long-Term Side Effects

- No long-term side effects reported

 ## Toxicity/Adverse Reaction (Contact your doctor)

- Mild adverse reaction: rash or hives (call your doctor immediately), headache, nervousness, dizziness, disrupted sleep patterns, change in sense of taste, nausea, diarrhea, vomiting, nosebleeds, hair loss, increased heart rate, sweating

- Serious adverse reaction: allergic reaction that mimics flu, drug-induced seizures, mania, psychosis, hallucinations, obsession with suicide, liver toxicity, heart rhythm disorders

- May activate epilepsy in susceptible people

- Signs of overdose: Agitation, nausea, vomiting, seizures

 ## General Advice and Precautions

- Herbs and minerals: Avoid St. John's Wort, Ginkgo, Ma Huang, Yohimbe, Indian Snakeroot and Kava Kava. Calcium may be beneficial—talk to your doctor

- Does not cause weight gain; may cause weight loss

- If taking long term, drink two quarts of water daily

- Drug may cause drowsiness, delayed reaction time, and/or impaired judgment. Avoid driving if these effects are present

- Caution: Notwithstanding treatment, some people suffering depression develop suicidal tendencies. If you or someone you know display signs of suicidal thinking, contact your doctor immediately. Also, if you don't feel the medication is working, call your doctor. There are many antidepressants and another drug choice may be more appropriate for you

Fluticasone

Brand Names: Advair, Advair Diskus, Cutivate, Flonase, Flovent, Flovent Diskus, Flovent Rotadisc

 ## Used For

- Relief of seasonal allergic rhinitis

- Treatment of eczema

- Treatment of asthma

 ## Known Contraindications and/or Interactions

- Drugs with known interactions include, Nizoral (Ketoconazole), Norvir (Ritonavir), systemic steroids (Prednisone)

- Tell your doctor if you have diabetes, acne, warts, fungal infections, herpes simplex, tuberculosis, joint pain

- Tell your doctor if you have been exposed to measles or chicken pox

- Do not use for sudden onset asthma

- Children under four should not take this drug

- Ask your doctor about risk/reward profile if pregnant or nursing

 ## Common Side Effects

- Nosebleeds

- Yeast infections in mouth or throat

 ## Occasional/Long-Term Side Effects

- Yeast infections in the nose

- Increased risk of osteoporosis, glaucoma, cataracts, Cushing's syndrome

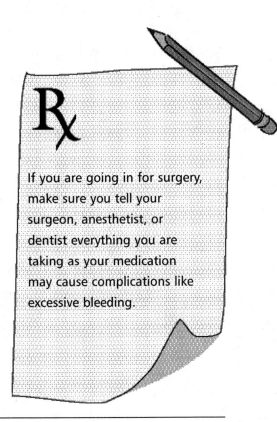

If you are going in for surgery, make sure you tell your surgeon, anesthetist, or dentist everything you are taking as your medication may cause complications like excessive bleeding.

Toxicity/Adverse Reaction (Contact your doctor)

- Headache, nausea, vomiting

- Increased heart rate

- Pressure in the head

- Inflammation of blood vessels

- Blood sugar problems

- Anaphylaxis

 General Advice and Precautions

- Herbs and minerals to avoid include Fir Needle, Pine Needle, Ephedra, Ragweed, Chrysanthemum, Daisy, Echinacea, Chamomile, Feverfew, St. John's Wort

- Supplementation of Calcium and vitamin D suggested

- May cause dizziness

- Use of this drug disqualifies you from piloting

- Do not stop taking this drug abruptly

Fluvastatin

Brand Names: Lescol, Lescol XL

 Used For

- Lowering total cholesterol levels

- Lowering triglyceride levels

- Slowing progression of atherosclerosis

- Could be used to decrease risk of osteoporosis, Alzheimer's, cancer

Known Contraindications and/or Interactions

- Do not take this drug if you have had an allergic reaction to it in the past

- Do not take this drug if you have liver disease, liver compromise, or if you are pregnant or nursing

- Consult your doctor before taking it if you are planning pregnancy, if you regularly consume alcohol, if you have cataracts or other vision impairment, if you have muscle pain, or if you have major surgery scheduled

- Drug interactions may occur with Digoxin, Warfarin, Amprenavir, Ritonavir, protease inhibitors, Clofibrate, Clopidogrel, Plavix, Cyclosporine, Erythromycin, Macrolide antibiotics, Fluconazole, Itraconazole, Ketoconazole, Gemfibrozil, Levothyroxine, Niacin, Omeprazole, Quinupristin, Dalfopristin, Ranitidine, Sildenafil/Viagra, Cholestyramine

 ## Common Side Effects

- Decreased levels of coenzyme Q_{10}

- Changes in liver function tests

 ## Occasional/Long-Term Side Effects

- Liver disorders, hepatitis

- Loss of the drugs effects

- Changes in vision

 ## Toxicity/Adverse Reaction (Contact your doctor)

- Mild adverse reaction: Rash, headache, insomnia, dizziness, indigestion, nausea, constipation, diarrhea, low blood pressure

- Serious adverse reaction: Abnormal liver function, muscle pain, kidney failure, skin rash, neuropathy, lupus-like symptoms

- Signs of overdose: Stomach distress, diarrhea

 ## General Advice and Precautions

- Herbs and minerals: Avoid Garlic

- Speak to your doctor about vitamin supplementation while taking this drug

- Consider substituting meat with soy products in your diet

- Do not drink alcohol when taking this medication

- Do not suddenly stop taking this drug. Discontinue gradually under your doctor's supervision

- Stop taking this drug under the supervision of a doctor if you become pregnant

Fluvoxamine

Brand Names: Fluvoxamine, Luvox

 ## Used For

- Depression

- Treatment of obsessive-compulsive disorder

- May be used to treat other conditions, including compulsive exhibitionism, panic disorders, binge eating

 ## Known Contraindications and/or Interactions

- **Warning: Do not take this medication with Seldane (Terfenadine) or Hismanal (Astemizole)**

- Do not take this drug if you are taking Cisapride

- Consult your physican before taking this drug if you have a seizure disorder, heart problems (currently or have in the past), or if you have taken a MAO Type A Inhibitor within the last 14 days

- Drug should be avoided by women who are pregnant or breast-feeding

- Drug interactions may occur with Amitriptyline, Astemizole, Benzodiazepines, beta-blockers, Carbamazepine, Cimetidine, Cisapride, Clomipramine, Clozapine, Cyclosporin, Dextromethorphan (the "DM" in some cough medications), Diltiazem, Dofetilide, ergot derivative, Imipramine, Lithium, MAO inhibitors, Maprotiline, Methadone, Olanzapine, oral antidiabetic drugs, Phenytoin, Fosphenytoin, Ritonavir, Sibutramine, Sumatriptan, Tacrine, Terfenadine, Theophylline, Tramadol, tricyclic antidepressants, triptans, Tryptophan, Warfarin

Common Side Effects

- Nausea, vomiting (usually stops after two to three days; call your doctor if it persists)

 ## Occasional/Long-Term Side Effects

- No long-term side-effects have been reported

- May inhibit orgasm in both sexes

 ## Toxicity/Adverse Reaction (Contact your doctor)

- Mild adverse reaction: Rash, hives, headache, nervousness, dizziness, disrupted sleep patterns; nausea, vomiting (that persists beyond two days), dry mouth, constipation nosebleeds, hair loss

- Serious adverse reaction: Anaphylaxis, rash, prolongued bleeding, seizures, tremors, Tourette's, liver toxicity

- Signs of overdose: Nausea, vomiting, seizures

 ## General Advice and Precautions

- Herbs and minerals: Avoid St. John's Wort, Ginkgo, Ma Huang, Yohimbe, Indian Snakeroot, Valerian, and Kava Kava

- Avoid caffeine while on this medication

- Drug may cause drowsiness. Do not drive or operate mechanical equipment if this symptom is present

- Because this drug interacts with so many other medications, tell all your doctors and healthcare providers that you take it

- Do not suddenly stop taking this medication. Discontinue gradually, under a doctor's supervision

- Caution: Notwithstanding treatment, some people suffering depression develop suicidal tendencies. If you or someone you know display signs of suicidal thinking, contact your doctor immediately

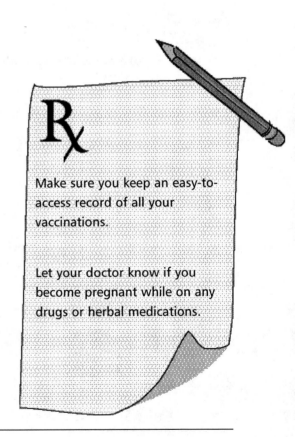

R͓x

Make sure you keep an easy-to-access record of all your vaccinations.

Let your doctor know if you become pregnant while on any drugs or herbal medications.

Furosemide

Brand Names: Albert Furosemide, Apo-Furosemide, Fumide MD, Furocot, Furomide MD, Furose, Furosemide-10, Furoside, Lasaject, Lasimide, Lasix, Lasix Special, Lo-Aqua, Luramide, Myrosemide, Novo-Semide, Ro-Semide, SK-Furosemide, Uritol

 Used For

- Removes excess water to help with congestive heart failure, liver, kidney, and lung diseases

- Acts to relieve mild or moderately high blood pressure

- Assists other anti-hypertensives in lowering blood pressure

 Known Contraindications and/or Interactions

- Furosemide increases the effects of other antihypertensives, Digoxin, and Lithium

- May interact with oral antidiabetic drugs, Charcoal, adrenocortical steroids, aminoglycides, Bepridil, cephalosporin antibiotics, Clofibrate, Cholestyramine, Cortisone and corticosteroids, Colestipol, Cyclosporin, Lomefloxacin, Metformin, NSAIDs, and drugs like Fosphenytoin or Phenytoin

- People with liver or kidney problems may need larger doses to see effects, while people suffering from cystic fibrosis will be advised to take smaller doses as they are more sensitive to the drug

- If you are pregnant it is best to avoid this drug for the baby's safety, most certainly for the first trimester

! **Common Side Effects**

- A feeling of light-headedness when getting up from sitting or lying down

- Loss of Potassium and Magnesium, resulting in muscle pain and cramping

- Increased blood sugar, affecting diabetics

- Increase or development of gout from excess uric acid

- Rise in cholesterol

 Occasional/Long-Term Side Effects

- May result in allergy, numbness, tingling, vision problems, stomach irritation, jaundice, liver problems, temporary ringing in ears or loss of hearing, arrhythmias, vitamin deficiency, kidney stones, increased risk of hip fracture, lungs gathering fluid, abdominal pain due to an inflamed pancreas or fatigue, weakness, bleeding and bruising from bone marrow being depleted

- Long-term use may induce hyperglycemia in some individuals, or may cause mineral imbalances between salt, Magnesium, Potassium, and water levels in blood, blood clots, or dehydration

 ## Toxicity/Adverse Reaction (Contact your doctor)

- Signs of overdose: feeling of dehydration characterized by thirst and dry mouth, feelings of weakness and fatigue, drowsiness, sluggishness, nausea, vomiting, muscle cramps. This may progress to a shocked or dazed state, or even coma

 ## General Advice and Precautions

- It's a good idea to take this drug in the morning to avoid frequent urges to urinate throughout the night

- Don't double-up on doses, if you forget one dose and it's very close to your next dosing time, just skip the previous dose and take the one coming up at the scheduled time

- It may be a good idea to eat more Potassium-rich foods, but it's always best to take Furosemide an hour before or two hours after eating

- Some herbs that increase blood pressure would be good to avoid for obvious reasons, these include: Guarana, Hawthorn, Ginseng, Eleuthero Root, Saw Palmetto, Goldenseal, and Licorice. Couch Grass may also negate the effects of Furosemide on congestive heart problems or other edema. Yohimbe should also be avoided. Herbs like Garlic, Calcium, and Indian Snakeroot may contribute to efforts to lower blood pressure. Don't start taking any herbal supplements before talking to your physician

- This drug may increase photosensitivity, especially if taken with St. John's Wort. It's best to avoid excessive heat or exercise, but speak to you doctor about your options

- Avoid drinking too much alcohol because it can affect your blood pressure

- Surgery may require discontinuation of this drug five or seven days in advance. Usually effects of patients taking Furosemide are successful and don't have major side effects if taken slowly, so there should not be any problems should discontinuation be necessary

Insulin

Brand Names: Humalog, Humalog Mix 75/25, Humulin, Iletin, Initard, Insulatard, Insulin aspart, NovoLog, Insulin Human, Insulin-Toronto, Lantus, Lente, Lente Iletin, Mixtard, Novolin, Novolin, Novolin-Lente, NovolinPen, Novolinset, Novolin-Toronto, Novolin-Ultralente, NPH, Protamine, Regular Insulin, Regular Purified Pork Insulin, Semilente, Ultralente, Velosulin

 ## Used For

- Controlling Type 1 diabetes

- Controlling Type 2 diabetes that has not responded to other treatments

- Controlling gestational (pregnancy) diabetes

 ## Known Contraindications and/or Interactions

- Effects of Insulin are decreased by birth control pills, thyroid treatments, thiazide diuretics, Furosemide, Phenytoin, corticosteroids and Chlorthalidone

- Insulin's effects may increase if taken with oral antidiabetics, MAO Inhibitors, Aspirin, Acarbose, non-selective beta-blockers, other beta-blockers, Clofibrate, Dispyramide, and Fenfluramine

- Insulin is often the chosen method of diabetic control for mothers with diabetes, however, women with diabetes are two to four times more likely to have a child with a birth defect, but it's not certain whether this is due to medication, the disease, or other factors

 ## Common Side Effects

- People taking Insulin have a high chance of developing drastic blood sugar drops (hypoglycemia), most commonly from taking inappropriate amounts of medication, other medications, or leading an inappropriate lifestyle

- Sometimes people will experience pain if the injection is made too deep (into the muscle layer), a lump if the injection is made too shallow, allergy, or infection from contamination of the needle or dirty injection site

- People may also gain weight while taking Insulin

Occasional/Long-Term Side Effects

- On rare occasions, loss of libido, allergy, problems with tasting, inflammation of ears, irregular heart hearts (arrhythmias), or anemia may occur

- With long-term use some people experience Insulin resistance or a tissue thinning at injection site.

 ## Toxicity/Adverse Reaction (Contact your doctor)

- Overdose usually results in hypoglycemia, which appears as impaired judgment or strange behavior that can seem like intoxication. It may also include shaking, sweating, weakness, fatigue, faintness, pale face, confusion, trouble seeing, coma, seizure, or death. This can be remedied — if caught at the first signs — by giving the person something with sugar, such as a soft drink (substitutes like diet soda won't work)

 ## General Advice and Precautions

- Diabetics have to follow a strict diet. Diets usually consist of portion control, sugar control, rice bran, starches, and vegetables, especially legumes like beans that are high in soluble fiber, which reduces the speed at which food flows through the intestines, promoting absorption of glucose. Diet can be very specific and will usually be outlined by your doctor, or a course may be offered to help you plan and follow your diet

- Extreme heat, like that in saunas or hot tubs can make Insulin absorb faster, causing hypoglycemia. Be prepared to take corrective action during these activities or during any heavy physical exertion

- Insulin should be kept cool, in a refrigerator, but not frozen. Strong light and heat can be damaging to the medication. Always use fresh Insulin that has not gone past its expiry date

- Some foods and herbs may complement diabetes treatment or may contribute to cases of hypoglycemia, so it's important to speak to your doctor before taking Alpha Lipoic Acid, Vitamin D, Magnesium, Chromium, or Vanadium. Also watch for supplements of Aloe, Bitter Melon, Ginger, Garlic,

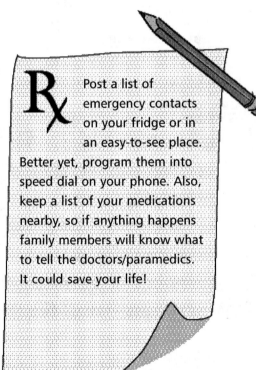
℞ Post a list of emergency contacts on your fridge or in an easy-to-see place. Better yet, program them into speed dial on your phone. Also, keep a list of your medications nearby, so if anything happens family members will know what to tell the doctors/paramedics. It could save your life!

Eucalyptus, Fenugreek, Ginseng, Glucomannan, Guar Gum, Nettle, Hawthorn, Licorice, Yohimbe, Prickly Pear Cactus, Red Sage. Do not take Echinacea, Pupurea, or Blonde Psyllium Seed if you have diabetes.

- Marijuana and Tobacco smoking may alter effectiveness of Insulin

- Alcohol is not advised for diabetics as it may induce hypoglycemia

- It's important to get regular checkups and to look for unnoticed cuts or sores that may not be painful due to nerve damage (diabetic neuropathy). Moisturize dry skin to avoid cracks and infection, wear well-fitting shoes, and check your body — especially your feet — for any damage on a daily basis. Drink lots of water to avoid dehydration, and wear cotton underwear to prevent infection and improve air flow

Isosorbide Dinitrate

Brand Names: Angipec, Apo-ISDN, Cedocard-SR, Coradur, Coronex, Dilatrate-SR, Iso-BID, Isochron, Isonate, Isordil, Isordil Tembids, Isordil Titradose, Isotrate Timecelles, Novo-Sorbide, Sorbitrate, Sorbitrate-SA

 Used For

- Prevention and treatment of pain associated with angina

- Treatment of congestive heart failure

- Treatment after a heart attack

- Treatment of achalasia

- Topical application for treatment of anal fissures

- Treatment of leg cramps

 Known Contraindications and/or Interactions

- Do not take this drug if you have had an allergic reaction to it in the past

- Do not take this drug if you are anemic, you have high intraocular (eye) pressure, you have recently had head trauma, you have hyperthyroidism, you have abnormal growth of the heart, you take Viagra or have recently taken Viagra, you have high blood pressure or tachycardia

- Consult your doctor before taking if you are pregnant or nursing, if you have been unable to tolerate other nitrates, you have low blood pressure, you have glaucoma, you have had a brain hemorrhage, you are planning pregnancy, you are allergic to Tartrazine, you have G6PD deficiency, you have a compromised liver, or if you have hyperthyroidism

- Drug interactions may occur with Viagra/sildenafil, propranolol, hydralazine, antihypertensive drugs, over-the-counter allergy/cough/cold medications

 ## Common Side Effects

- Flushing

- Headache

- Heart palpitations, rapid heart rate

 ## Occasional/Long-Term Side Effects

- Tolerance

- Abnormal hemoglobin

- Spells of low blood pressure, fainting

 ## Toxicity/Adverse Reaction (Contact your doctor)

- Mild adverse reaction: Skin rash, headache, dizziness, fainting, nausea, vomiting

- Serious adverse reaction: Dermatitis, transient ischemic attacks, impaired vision, impaired speech, anemia, changes in heart rate, low blood pressure, myocardia ischemia

- Signs of overdose: Headache, dizziness, flushing, difficulty breathing, coma, weakness

 ## General Advice and Precautions

- Herbs and minerals: Avoid Hawthorn, Coenzyme Q_{10}, Couch Grass, Nettle, and Soy products

- May cause dizziness and fainting. Avoid driving and/or operating machinery until you know how this drug affects you

- Avoid alcohol, tobacco, and Marijuana completely when taking this medication

- Do not suddenly stop taking this drug. Discontinue gradually under your doctor's supervision

- Take this medication on an empty stomach

- Talk to your doctor about taking rest periods from taking this drug to avoid tolerance issues

- Over-the-counter cold/cough/allergy medications can interact with this medication, speak to your doctor before you take any of these formulations

- Speak to your doctor about Omega-3 fatty acid and B-vitamin supplementation when taking this medication

- Avoid excessively hot and cold environments

- Speak to your doctor before exercising when taking this medication

Isosorbide Mononitrate

Brand Names: Elan, Elantan, Imdur, Ismo, Monoket

 Used For

- Prevention of recurrent angina

- May be used as treatment for congestive heart failure

- May be used as treatment for myocardial ischemia

- May be used as treatment for heart attacks

- Can help patients with stomach bleeding due to cirrhosis of the liver

 Known Contraindications and/or Interactions

- Do not take this drug if you have had an allergic reaction to it in the past

- Do not take this drug if you have severe anemia, you take Viagra, you have an overactive thyroid, if you have hypertrophic cardiomyopathy

- Consult your doctor before taking if you are pregnant or nursing, if you have low blood pressure or high blood pressure, if you have had a recent head trauma, if you have hyperthyroidism, if you are planning pregnancy, if you have had a brain hemorrhage, if you have had trouble with other nitrates, or if you have had a recent heart attack

Drug interactions may occur with antihypertensive drugs, Calcium channel blockers, Hydralazine, Propranolol, Viagra, over-the-counter cough/cold medication

 ## Common Side Effects

- Flushing

- Headache

- Heart palpitation, rapid heart beat

- Low blood pressure

 ## Occasional/Long-Term Side Effects

- Abnormal hemoglobin

- Increased eye pressure

- Impotence, decreased libido

 ## Toxicity/Adverse Reaction (Contact your doctor)

- Mild adverse reaction: Skin rash, itching, headache, dizziness, fainting, blurred vision, nausea, vomiting, discolored urine, increased liver enzymes

- Serious adverse reaction: Transient ischemia, bone marrow depression, abnormally low blood pressure, abnormal heartbeat, tolerance, worsening of symptoms

- Signs of overdose: Headache, dizziness, vomiting, weakness, difficulty breathing, coma

 ## General Advice and Precautions

- Herbs and minerals: Avoid Hawthorn, Coenzyme Q_{10}, soy products

- Never take with Viagra/Sildenafil

- Speak to your doctor about vitamins C and B, and Omega-3 fatty acid supplementation while taking this drug

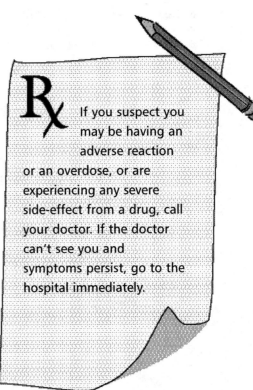

R If you suspect you may be having an adverse reaction or an overdose, or are experiencing any severe side-effect from a drug, call your doctor. If the doctor can't see you and symptoms persist, go to the hospital immediately.

- Avoid alcohol, tobacco, and Marijuana while taking this drug

- May cause dizziness or low blood pressure. Avoid driving and/or operating machinery until you know how this drug affects you

- Do not suddenly stop taking this drug. Discontinue gradually under your doctor's supervision

- Avoid excessively hot or cold environments

- Aspirin or Acetaminophen may relieve the headaches associated with this medication, speak to your doctor

- People over 60 may be more susceptible to side effects when taking this drug

- Speak to your doctor before exercising when taking this medication

Isotretinoin

Brand Names: Accutane, Amnesteem

 Used For

- Treatment of severe cystic acne

- Treatment of other serious skin conditions

- May treat hypertropic lupus erythematosus

- Treatment of refractory rosacea

 Known Contraindications and/or Interactions

- Do not use it if you are pregnant or planning pregnancy

- Do not use while breast-feeding

- Do not use if you have not received warnings (verbal and written) from your doctor about this prescription medication and birth defects/fetal damage

- Do not use if you have mild acne

- Do not use if you cannot use two forms of contraception

- Do not use if allergic to parabens

- Tell your doctor if you wear contact lenses

- Tell your doctor if you have a history of depression

- Tell your doctor if you have diabetes

- Tell your doctor if you have a cholesterol disorder

- Tell your doctor if you routinely give blood or are considering giving blood

- Do not use if you have taken two confirmed negative pregnancy tests

- Children and infants should not take this drug

- Drugs with known interactions include Tegretol, drugs that increase sensitivity to sun, drugs that increase your risk of osteoporosis (such as corticosteroids), tetracyclines, cinocycline, micro-dosed progesterone

! Common Side Effects

- Dry nose, mouth, nosebleeds, dry, peeling skin, decreased night vision, conjunctivitis

 ## Occasional/Long-Term Side Effects

- Back or joint pain

- Reduced red/white blood cell counts

- Increased triglcerides

!! Toxicity/Adverse Reaction (Contact your doctor)

- Skin rash, thinning hair

- Insomnia, lethargy

- Depression, psychosis, thoughts of suicide, hallucinations

- Cataracts

- Kidney toxicity, pancreatitis, gastrointestinal bleeding

- Low libido

- Ejaculatory problems

- Change in menstrual cycle

- Seizures

- Violent behavior

- Hearing loss

- Headache/visual disturbances

- Nausea, vomiting

 ## General Advice and Precautions

- FDA requires monthly pregnancy tests by women taking this drug

- Periodic Bone Mineral Density tests suggested

- Can cause photosensitivity – wear sunscreen

- Do not smoke cigarettes while taking this drug

- Use two forms of contraception

- Heavy alcohol intake is not advisable

- Do not give blood

- Do not share this medication

- Herbs and minerals to avoid include St. John's Wort, medicinal yeast

- Do not take with other forms of vitamin A

Levodopa

Brand Names: Apo-Levocarb, Bendopa, Biodopa, Dopar, Larodopa, Prolopa [CD], Sinemet [CD], Sinemet CR [CD]

 ## Used For

- Treatment of Parkinson's Disease

 ## Known Contraindications and/or Interactions

- Do not take this drug if you have had an allergic reaction to it in the past

- Do not take this drug if you have narrow-angle glaucoma, a history of melanoma, or have taken an MAO Type A Inhibitor drug in the last 14 days

- Consult your doctor before taking this drug if you have chronic lung disease, diabetes, heart disease, epilepsy, high blood pressure, liver or kidney problems, hematopoiesis, abnormal heart rhythm; if you have had a heart attack; if you have a history of wide-angle glaucoma, depression or mental illness, or peptic ulcer disease; or if you are scheduled for surgery

- Avoid this drug if you are pregnant or breast-feeding

- Drug interactions may occur with: benzodiazepines, Bromocriptine, Bupropion, Cisapride, Clonidine, Entacapone, Fentanyl/Droperidol, Indinavir, Isoniazid, Metoclopramide, MAO Type A Inhibitors, Phenothiazines, Reserpine, Risperidone, Tolcapone, Tricyclic antidepressants, Zotepine, Amoxapine, Chlordiazepoxide, Olanzapine, Papaverine, Phenytoin or Fosphenytoin, Pyridoxine, Risperidone

 ## Common Side Effects

- Drowsiness, lethargy, change in sense of taste, body odor, pink, red, or dark urine, gout

 ## Occasional/Long-Term Side Effects

- Involuntary head/face/hand/foot movements (often reversible)

 ## Toxicity/Adverse Reaction (Contact your doctor)

- Mild adverse reaction: Rash, headache, dizziness, insomnia, nightmares, vision problems, nausea, vomiting diarrhea, constipation, dry mouth, altered sense of taste, hair loss

- Serious adverse reaction: High blood pressure, confusion, hallucinations, paranoia, depression, seizures, congestive heart failure; involuntary movements of head, face, hands, or feet, arrhythmia, low blood pressure, peptic ulcer, gastrointestinal bleeding

- People over 60 should be on the alert for behavior changes, including depression, confusion, dementia, nightmares, hallucinations

- Signs of overdose: Twitching muscles, including eyelids, nausea, vomiting, diarrhea, weakness, fainting, confusion, hallucinations

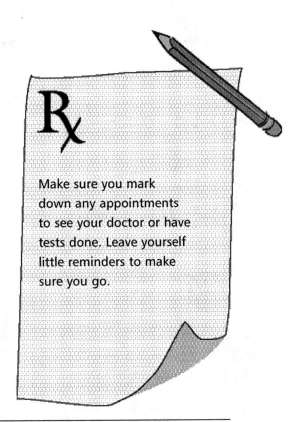

Make sure you mark down any appointments to see your doctor or have tests done. Leave yourself little reminders to make sure you go.

General Advice and Precautions

- Herbs and minerals: Avoid Calabar bean, Octacosanol

- Do not take medication with protein foods

- May cause dizziness and impair vision. Avoid driving and/or operating machinery until you know how this drug affects you

- Be careful about heat exposure: drug may make you more susceptible to heat exhaustion

- Do not suddenly stop taking this drug. Discontinue gradually under your doctor's supervision.

Levothyroxine

Brand Names: Alti-Thyroxine, Armour Thyroid, Eltroxin, Euthroid, Euthyrox, Levo-T, Levotabs, Levothroid, Levoxine, Levoxyl, L-Thyroxine, Proloid, Synthroid, Synthrox, Syroxine, Thyroid USP, Thyrolar, Unithroid, V-Throid

 ## Used For

- Hormone replacement therapy for people suffering from a deficiency (hypothyroidism)

- Treatment of chronic thyroiditis, thyroid gland cancer, and enlarged thyroid (simple goiter)

 ## Known Contraindications and/or Interactions

- Usually acceptable for use during pregnancy; consult doctor about use during breast-feeding

- Sometimes used in combination with Liothyronine, which is close to the natural hormone, to increase effectiveness

- Combination treatments of Levothyroxine and Triidothyronin requires a lowered dosage and the discontinuation of any use of thyroid extract

- May increase effects of Warfarin, may decrease Digoxin's effects, the effectiveness of Levothyroxine may be decreased by antibiotics, antacids, Calcium Carbonate, strogens, Cholestyramine, Colestipol, Iron salts, Lovastatin, Phenytoin, Rifampin, Ritonavir, Sucralfate and others. Discuss all your medications with your doctor

Common Side Effects

- Children receiving treatment may experience temporary hair loss in the first few months

- People with cardiovascular problems may experience an aggravation of their symptoms

- Altered menstruation during dose adjustments

 ## Occasional/Long-Term Side Effects

- Headache, mild allergy, seizures, osteoporosis, immune concentration of IgA decreased, increased angina or artery spasms are all very rare side effects.

- Osteoporosis of the spine and increase in abnormal heart growth on the left side may occur in long term use

 ## Toxicity/Adverse Reaction (Contact your doctor)

- Watch for headache, feeling of hotness, sweating, tremors, feelings of nervousness, arrhymia, diarrhea, muscle cramps, weight loss, insomnia, and heart attack as signs of an overdose

 ## General Advice and Precautions

- Use of drug for purposes other than thyroid problems (e.g. use on infertility, slow growth, nonspecific obesity or fatigue) is dangerous

- A discomfort in hot environments may occur

- Be cautious during heavy exercise if you have angina

- May be negatively affected by Horseradish Root, Cabbage, Iodine, Gamma Orizanol (from Rice Bran Oil), and Soy. Speak to your doctor before seeking alternative medicine therapies

- Take continually at regular times and do not discontinue medication without consulting your doctor

Lithium

Brand Names: Carbolith, Duralith, Eskalith, Liskonium, Lithane, Lithizine, Lithobid, Lithonate, Lithotabs

 Used For

- Mood stabilizer — Treatment of bipolar disorder, mania

 Known Contraindications and/or Interactions

- Do not take it if you've had an allergic reaction to it in the past, have uncontrolled diabetes or hypothyroidism, or have severe kidney or heart disorders

- Consult with your doctor first if you have brain disease, have a history of schizophrenia (or similar), grand mal epilepsy, diabetes, heart disease, hypothyroidism, kidney problems, are pregnant or planning pregnancy, or are due for anesthesia or ECT therapy

- Should not be used by women who are pregnant or breast-feeding

- Drugs known to interact with this medication include Acetazolamide, ACE Inhibitors, Aspirin, Bumetanide, Calcitonin, Calcium channel blockers, Carbamazepine, Celecoxib, Chlorpromazine, Cisplatin, Citalopram, Clozapine, Diazepam, diuretics, Ethacrynic acid, Filgrastim, Fludrocortisone, Fluoxetine, Fluvoxamine, Furosemide, Haloperidol, Ibuprofen, Levofloxacin, Losartan, Methyldopa, Metronidazole, MAO Type A Inhibitors, Nicotine, Piroxicam, Sibutramine, Sodium Bicarbonate, Theophylline, Thiazide Diuretics, Tricyclic Antidepressants, Vasartan, Verapamil

 Common Side Effects

- Increased thirst and urination, weight gain, fatigue and lethargy, increased white cell count, tremor, heart block, metallic taste in mouth

 Occasional/Long-Term Side Effects

- Hypothyroidism, goiter, reduced sugar tolerance, kidney damage. May promote Type II diabetes

- Decreased libido, erectile dysfunction

 Toxicity/Adverse Reaction (Contact your doctor)

- Drug should be stopped at the first sign of toxicity. Call your physican immediately, even for mild reactions

- Mild adverse reaction: Rash, headache, dizziness, weakness, blurred vision, nausea, vomiting, diarrhea, joint pain,

- Serious adverse reaction: Confusion, slurred speech, twitching muscles, abnormal changes in heart rate or rhythm, loss of bladder control, diabetes-like symptoms, high/low thyroid function, seizures

- Signs of overdose: Dizziness, drowsiness, uncoordinated, slurred speech, confusion, nausea, vomiting, diarrhea, muscle spasms, stupor, seizures, coma

 ## General Advice and Precautions

- Ongoing testing/monitoring is essential while on this drug

- Do not take Calcium supplements without your doctor's permission

- Avoid Guarana and Mate

- Drink eight to 12 cups of fluid daily

- Lithium may increase effects of alcohol. Alcohol consumption may lead to Lithium toxicity

- This drug may affect alertness, coordination, and reaction time. Restrict driving and/or the use of machinery until you know how the medication affects you

- Excessive sweating can cause reduced salt and water levels and lead to toxicity. Avoid saunas, drink fluids generously

- Lithium can be stopped suddenly (no need to taper off), but if discontinued before treatment is complete symptoms may recur

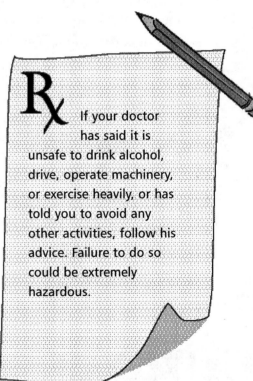

Rx If your doctor has said it is unsafe to drink alcohol, drive, operate machinery, or exercise heavily, or has told you to avoid any other activities, follow his advice. Failure to do so could be extremely hazardous.

Lorazepam

Brand Names: Alzapam, Apo-Lorazepam, Ativan, Dom-Lorazepam, Loraz, Novo-Lorazepam, Nu-Loraz, PMS-Loraz

 ## Used For

- Treatment of anxiety. Used intravenously as a sedative

Known Contraindications and/or Interactions

- Do not take this drug if you have had an allergic reaction to it in the past, have acute narrow-angle glaucoma, have extremely low blood pressure, depression, or psychosis

- Consult your doctor before taking it if you are allergic to any benzodiazepine drug, have a history of alcohol or drug abuse, are pregnant or planning pregnancy, have liver or kidney problems, have a history of asthma, emphysema, epilepsy

- Should be avoided by women who are pregnant or breast-feeding

- Drug interactions may occur with Clozapine, Heparin, Lithium, Oxycodone, Phenytoin, Fosphenytoin, Quetiapine, macrolide antibiotics, Probenecid, Valproic acid, oral contraceptives, caffeine, amphetamines, Theophylline

 ## Common Side Effects

- Drowsiness, "hungover" feeling

 ## Occasional/Long-Term Side Effects

- Can cause drug dependence

- Decreased male sex drive and/or impotence

 ## Toxicity/Adverse Reaction (Contact your doctor)

- Mild adverse reaction: Rash, hives, dizziness, amnesia, insomnia, fainting, vision problems, slurred speech, sweating, nausea

- Serious adverse reaction: Liver damage, swings in behavior between excitement and/or anger, seizures, twitching movements, shallow breathing

- Signs of overdose: Significant drowsiness, weakness, "drunk" feeling, shallow breathing, stupor, coma

 ## General Advice and Precautions

- Herbs and minerals: Avoid Hawthorn, Valerian, Kava Kava, Danshen, Skull Cap, Kola Nut, Siberian Ginseng, Guarana, Mate, Ephedra, Ma Huang, St. John's Wort, Dong Quai

- Cut back on caffeine (coffee, tea, cola), avoid grapefruit juice

- Avoid alcohol while on this medication

- This drug may interfere with alertness and coordination. Avoid driving or operating heavy machinery until you know how it affects you

- Do not stop suddenly, particularly if the drug has been used longer than four weeks. Discontinue gradually, under a doctor's supervision

Macrolide Antibiotic Family

Includes: Azithromycin, Clarithromycin, Erythromycin

Brand Names: Azithromycin, Zithromax, Clarithromycin, Biaxin, Prevpac [CD], AK-Mycin, Akne-Mycin, Apo-Erythro Base, Benzamycin [CD], C-Solve 2, E.E.S., Emgel, E-Mycin, Reamycin, Erybid, ERYC, Erycette, Eryderm, Erygel, Erymax, EryPed, Eryphar, Ery-tab, Erythrocin, Erythromid, E-Solve2, Ethril, ETS-2%, Ilosone, Ilotycin, Novo-Rythro, PCE, Pediamycin, Pediazole [CD], PMS-Erythromycin, Robimycin, Sans-Acne, SK-Erythromycin, Staticin, Stievamycin, T-Stat, Wyamycin

 ## Used For

- Treating acne and streptococcus of the skin

- Respiratory tract infections such as strep-throat

- Pneumonia

- Gonorrhea and syphilis

- Amebic dysentery

- Rheumatic fever prevention

- Otitis media

- Chlamydia

- Therapy of stomach ulcer due to Helicobacter plylori

- Legionnaire's disease

- Other bacteria infections

Known Contraindications and/or Interactions

- Liver and kidney problems may require changes in dose depending on the drug

- Some forms are dangerous during pregnancy (Clarithromycin and Erythromycin Estolate) or in breast-feeding; ask your doctor

- Increases effects of Amprenavir, Benzodiazepines Buspirone, Carbamazepine, Cilostazol, Cisapride, Clozapine, Digoxin, Entacapone, Ergotamine, Imatinib, antiarrhymic drugs, Methylprednisolone, Phenytoin, Quetiapine, Quinidine, Sibutramine, Sildenafil, Ithromycin, Theophylline, Tretinoin, Valporic Acid, Vinblastine, and Warfarin

- Decreases effects of Clindamycin, Lincomycin, Penicillins

- May cause additional adverse effects when taken with Atorvastatin (Lipitor), Pravastatin, Simvastatin, birth control pills, Cyclosporine, Disopyramide, Dofetilide, Fluoxetine, Grepafloxacin, Lansoprazole, Loratadine, and other allergy medicines and antihistamines, Midazolam, Nevirapine, Omeprazole, Esopraxole, proton-pump inhibitors, Prednisone, Corticosteroids, Rifabutin, Ritonavir, Sparfloxacin, Terfenadine, Triazolam, Valporic Acid, Zafirlukast, Zidovudine

- People with a history of liver disease or other liver problems should definitely not take Erythromycin Estolate

Common Side Effects

- Additional infections caused by antibiotic resistance causing itching at infection site (superinfection)

 ## Occasional/Long-Term Side Effects

- Superinfection may occur if used for long term or if complete dosage is not taken

- Occasionally adverse effects such as allergy, nausea, vomiting, diarrhea, and other stomach upset, hallucinations, liver problems, arrhythmia, hypothermia, pancreatitis, kidney problems, headache, cramps, loss of hearing, colon inflammation, extreme muscle weakness, fatigue, low blood platelet count, or lowered white blood cell count may occur, but these side-effects are rare

Toxicity/Adverse Reaction (Contact your doctor)

- Signs of overdose may include hallucinations (particularly with clarithromycin), diarrhea, abdominal pain, nausea, and vomiting

 ## General Advice and Precautions

- To prevent superinfections, avoid long-term use if possible, but do make sure you take the full dose prescribed by your physician, unless informed otherwise

- People over 60 may be especially prone to superinfections of yeast in the vaginal, genital and anal regions. This will cause an itchy feeling. Also watch for kidney, liver, or hearing problems

- High-fat meals, especially, but any type of food can decrease absorption of many forms of macrolides, especially Erythromycin. However, Biaxin XL should be taken with food

- Mistletoe, St. John's Wort, Marshmallow, and Licorice supplements should be avoided

- Fruit juices and carbonated drinks like cola should be avoided for an hour after taking the nonenteric-coated forms of Erythromycin

Alcohol should be avoided if you have liver problems or are taking Erythromycin Estolate

Metformin

Brand Names: Apo-Metformin, Avandamet, Dom-Metformin, Glucophage, Glucovance, Glycon, Metaglip, Novo-Metformin, PMS-Metformin, Riva-Metformin

 ## Used For

- Slowing progression of diabetes

- Prevention of complications in diabetes patients

- Prevention of diabetes in high-risk patients

- Used in combination therapy for blood sugar control

- Glucose control

Make sure you throw away drugs as soon as the expiry date passes. Do not use any drugs that are past their date. If it is an important drugs make sure you get a refill as soon as possible.

Known Contraindications and/or Interactions

- Do not take this drug if you have had an allergic reaction to it in the past

- Do not take this drug if you have kidney or liver problems, drink alcohol regularly, have alcoholism, heart or lung problems, need a radiology test, have acidosis or ketoacidosis, are breast-feeding

- Consult your doctor before taking if you have plans for surgery, an infection, megaloblastic anemia, or are pregnant

- Drug interactions may occur with ACE Inhibitors, Azole antifungals, beta-blockers, cationic drugs, media for x-rays, Cotrimoxazole, Digoxin, Dofetilide, Gatifloxacin, Levofloxacin, Itraconazole, Voriconazole, Procainamide, Quinidine, thyroid medications, cimetidine, MAO Inhibitors, Morphine, Nifedipine, antidiabetic drugs, Ranitidine, Trimethoprim

 ## Common Side Effects

- Hypoglycemia

- Problems absorbing vitamin B_{12}

 ## Occasional/Long-Term Side Effects

- B_{12} deficiency

- Folic acid and amino acid deficiencies

 ## Toxicity/Adverse Reaction (Contact your doctor)

- Mild adverse reaction: Rash, metallic taste, anorexia, nausea, vomiting, diarrhea, headache, nervousness, fatigue, dizziness

- Serious adverse reaction: Liver toxicity, lactic acidosis, anemia, red blood cell problems, porphyria, increased risk of cardiovascular death

- Signs of overdose: Vomiting, pulmonary edema, stomach hemorrhaging, lactic acidosis, seizures, low blood pressure, coma

General Advice and Precautions

- Herbs and minerals: Avoid Chromium, Vanadium, Aloe, Bitter Melon, Eucalyptus, Fenugreek, Ginger, Garlic, Ginseng, Glucomannan, Guar Gum, Hawthorn, Licorice, Nettle, Yohimbe, Prickly Pear Cactus, Red Sage, Psyllium Seed, Psyllium Husk, Echinacea

- Do not drink alcohol while taking this medication

- Do not smoke Marijuana while taking this medication

- This medication increases photosensitivity

- Speak to your doctor about the symptoms of lactic acidosis

- Speak to your doctor about an appropriate exercise regimen while taking this medication, heavy exertion not recommended

- May cause drowsiness and dizziness. Avoid driving and/or operating machinery until you know how this drug affects you

- Do not suddenly stop taking this drug. Discontinue gradually under your doctor's supervision.

Methylprednisolone

Brand Names: A-Methapred, Depmedalone-40, Depmedalone-80, Depo-Medrol, Enpak Refill, Mar-Pred 40, Medrol, Medrol Acne Lotion, Medrol Enpak, Medrol Veriderm Cream, Meprolone, Neo-Medrol Acne Lotion, Neo-Medrol Veriderm, Pre-Dep 40, Pre-Dep 80, Rep-Pred 80, Solu-Medrol

 Used For

- Treatment of allergies and inflammatory disorders

- Treatment of lupus, asthma, multiple sclerosis, ulcerative colitis, bursitis, tendonitis, rheumatoid arthritis

- Combination therapy in anaphylactic shock, acute lymphocytic leukemia, pneumonia in AIDS patients

- Treatment of chronic obstructive pulmonary disease, vomiting due to chemotherapy, bone cysts in children, croup, carpal tunnel

- Relief of cancer pain

Known Contraindications and/or Interactions

- Do not take this drug if you have had an allergic reaction to it in the past

- Do not take this drug if pregnant or breast-feeding

- Do not take this drug if you have peptic ulcer disease, if you have had bowel surgery, herpes simplex, tuberculosis, or systemic fungus infection

- Consult your doctor before taking it if you take any other cortisone-like drugs, if you have diabetes, glaucoma, high blood pressure, thyroid dysfunction, osteoporosis, kidney disease, fever, joint pain, plan to have surgery, or have been exposed to a viral illness

- Drug interactions may occur with Insulin, Isonaizid, Salicylates (including Aspirin), Vaccines, Amphotericin B, Carbamazepine, Cholestyramine, Clarithromycin, Cyclosporine, Clarithromycin, Ketoconazole, loop diuretics, neuromuscular blocking agents, NSAIDs, anticoagulants (including Warfarin/Coumadin, antidiabetic drugs, Primidone, Quinupristin, Rifampin, Ritonavir (and other protease inhibitors), Tacrolimus, Theophylline, Thiazide diuretics, antacids, barbiturates, Phenytoin, Fosphenytoin, Rifampin

Common Side Effects

- Increased appetite, weight gain, water or salt retention

- Potassium loss

- Adrenal gland suppression

- Increased eye pressure

- Easy bruising, susceptibility to infection, difficulty healing wounds

 # Occasional/Long-Term Side Effects

- Diabetes, high blood sugar

- Thinning of skin

- Bone weakening, osteoporosis

- Cataracts, glaucoma

- Decreases resilience to infection

- Stunted growth in children

- Change in menstrual cycle

Toxicity/Adverse Reaction (Contact your doctor)

- Mild adverse reaction: Skin rash, insomnia, headaches, dizziness, indigestion, distention, joint pain, facial hair

- Serious adverse reaction: Anaphylaxis, mental and emotional disturbances, seizures, ulcers, liver/kidney problems, cataracts, glaucoma, blindness, Cushing's syndrome, osteoporosis, hyperglycemia, muscle weakness, high blood pressure, arrhythmias, inflamed pancreas, thrombophlebitis, blood clot in lung

- Signs of overdose: Fatigue, weakness, irritated stomach, sweating, flushing, swelling, high blood pressure, bloating

 ## General Advice and Precautions

- Herbs and minerals: Avoid Hawthorn, Ginger, Garlic, Ma Huang, Ephedra, Ginseng, Guar Gum, Fenugreek, Nettle, Fir or Pine Needle Oil, Ragweed, Echinacea, Chamomile, Feverfew, St. John's Wort

- Avoid drinking alcohol and grapefruit juice

- Do not smoke cigarettes or Marijuana

- May cause dizziness. Avoid driving and/or operating machinery until you know how this drug affects you

- Do not suddenly stop taking this drug. Discontinue gradually under your doctor's supervision

- Carry a card that indicates you take this medication

- Avoid people with severe infections when taking this medication

- Children taking this medication should be monitored

- If you are scheduled for vaccination, stop taking this drug 72 hours before your vaccination. Do not resume taking this medication until 14 days after the vaccination

- Should be used sparingly in persons over 60 years of age

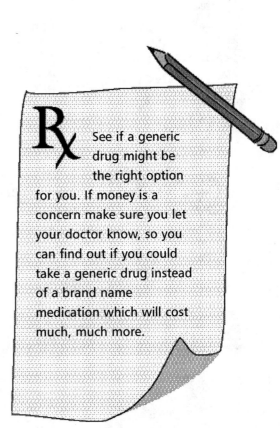

R̶x See if a generic drug might be the right option for you. If money is a concern make sure you let your doctor know, so you can find out if you could take a generic drug instead of a brand name medication which will cost much, much more.

Methysergide

Brand Names: Sansert

 Used For

- Migraine headaches and cluster neuralgia

 Known Contraindications and/or Interactions

- Do not take this drug if you have had an allergic reaction to it in the past or have one of the following: A severe infection, any kind of heart condition, cellulitis (lower legs), chronic lung disease, arteriosclerosis, high blood pressure, liver problems, peptic ulcer, phlebitis, Raynaud's disease or phenomenon

- Consult your doctor before taking if you have ever had a reaction to an ergot, or if you have a history of peptic ulcer or heart disease

- Do not take this drug if you are pregnant or breast-feeding

- Drug interactions may occur with beta-blocker drugs, macrolide antibiotics, Efavirenz, Sibutramine, Sildenafil, drugs in the triptan family

 Common Side Effects

- Fluid retention, weight gain, poor circulation in hands and feet

 Occasional/Long-Term Side Effects

- Fibrosis developing in chest and/or abdominal cavity and internal organs

 Toxicity/Adverse Reaction (Contact your doctor)

- Mild adverse reaction: Rash, hair loss, drowsiness, dizziness, irritability, vision problems, nausea, vomiting, diarrhea, muscle/joint pain

- Serious adverse reaction: Chest pain, leg spasms, narrowing of arteries, heart attacks, hallucinations, nightmares

- Signs of overdose: nausea, vomiting, diarrhea, dizziness, cold hands and feet

 General Advice and Precautions

- Herbs and minerals: Avoid St. John's Wort, Ma Huang. If you are allergic to plants in the aster family (such as ragweed), avoid Echinacea, Chamomile and Feverfew

- This drug may cause drowsiness and affect your vision. Avoid driving or operating heavy machinery until you know how it affects you

- Do not use this drug for headaches other than the kind it is prescribed for

- Should not be used on a continual basis for longer than six months

- Do not stop this drug suddenly; discontinue use over two to three weeks under your doctor's supervision

Metoprolol

Brand Names: Apo-Metoprolol, Betaloc, Co-Betaloc [CD], Logimax [CD], Lopressor, Novo-Metoprol, Nu-Metop, Toprol

 ## Used For

- Treatment of mild to moderate high blood pressure, angina

- Reduces risk of second heart attack

- Can be used to treat congestive heart failure

 ## Known Contraindications and/or Interactions

- Do not use this drug if you are allergic, have a heart rate slower than 45 beats per minute, are in cardiogenic shock, or have taken a MAO Type A drug within 14 days

- Consult your physician if you have adverse reactions to beta-blockers, if you have serious heart disease, a respiratory condition (including hay fever), hyperthyroidism, low blood sugar, diabetes, kidney, or liver problems

- Drug should be avoided by pregnant and breast-feeding women

- Drug interactions may occur with other antihypertensive drugs, Reserpine, Verapamil, Amiodarone, Clonidine, Digoxin, Fluoxetine, Fluvoxamine, Insulin, Lidocaine, Methyldopa, nifedipine, oral antidiabetic drugs, phenothiazines, Quinidine, Ritonavir, Tocainide, Venlafaxine, alpha one adrenergic blockers, Bupropion, Cimetidine, Ciprofloxacin, Calcium blockers, MAO Inhibitors, Methimazole, oral contraceptives, Propafenone, Propoxyphene, Propylthiouracil, Zafirlukast, Zileuton, barbituates, Indomethacin, Rifampin

 ## Common Side Effects

- Lethargy, fatigue, cold hands and feet, reduced heart rate, dizziness when upright

Occasional/Long-Term Side Effects

- Decreased sex drive in men, erectile dysfunction

 ## Toxicity/Adverse Reaction (Contact your doctor)

- Mild adverse reaction: Rash, headache, sleep disorders, dizziness, nervousness, fatigue, nausea, diarrhea, urination problems, cough, joint pain

- Serious adverse reaction: Depression, anxiety, hallucinations, chest pain, shortness of breath, asthma attack (in people with asthma), intermittant claudication

- Signs of overdose: Slow pulse, low blood pressure, fainting, clammy skin, heart failure, coma, convulsions

 ## General Advice and Precautions

- Herbs and minerals: Avoid Valerian, Kava Kava, Ginseng, St. John's Wort, Guarana, Hawthorn, Saw Palmetto, Ma Huang, Goldenseal, Yohimbe, Licorice. Calcium and Garlic may help lower blood pressure

- Do not skip or double doses

- Do not stop this drug suddenly; discontinuing drug should be under doctor's supervision

- Carry a card in your wallet that says you take this medication

- Consult your doctor before using a nasal spray while on beta-blocker medication

- Advise your doctor if you become depressed

- Avoid heavy exercise

- This drug may make you more susceptible to hot and cold; exercise caution.

Morphine

Brand Names: Alti-Morphine, Astramorph, Avinza, Duramorph, Epimorph, Infumorph, Kadian, M-Eslon, Morphitec, M.O.S., MS Contin, MS-IR, OMS Concentrate, Opium Tincture, Oramorph, Paregoric, RMS Uniserts, Roxanol, Statex

 ## Used For

- Moderate to severe pain

 ## Known Contraindications and/or Interactions

- Do not take this drug if you have had an allergic reaction to it in the past

- Do not take this drug if you are having an asthma attack or obstructed breathing, or are experiencing shallow breathing

- Do not take this drug if you suspect head injury

- Consult your physician before taking it if you took an MAO Type A Inhibitor in the last 14 days; are taking atropine-like drugs, antihypertensives, Metoclopramide or Zidovudine, sedatives; if you have an enlarged prostate, kidney or liver problems, constipation problems; if you have a history of asthma, emphysema, epilepsy, or seizure disorder, gallbladder disease, inflammatory bowel disease, sickle cell anemia, low blood surgery; if you are due for surgery under a general anesthetic

- Drug interactions may occur with antihypertensives, Metformin, sedatives, Metoclopramide, benzodiazepines, Cimetidine, Fluoxetine, Hydroxyzine, Metoclopramide, MAO Type Inhibitors, Naltrexone, phenothiazines, Rifampin, Ritonavir, Tramadol, Trovafloxacin, Zidovudine

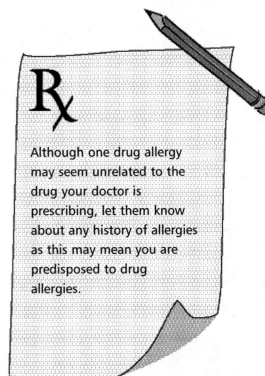

Although one drug allergy may seem unrelated to the drug your doctor is prescribing, let them know about any history of allergies as this may mean you are predisposed to drug allergies.

Common Side Effects

- Drowsiness, light-headedness, weakness, dry mouth, constipation, fluid retention

Occasional/Long-Term Side Effects

- Drug dependence, chronic constipation. Many doctors prescribe a constipation treatment alongside this medication

- Excessive use of this drug may cause breathing problems in people with asthma, emphysema, or chronic bronchitis

 Toxicity/Adverse Reaction (Contact your doctor)

- Mild adverse reaction: Rash, hives, headache, dizziness, inability to concentrate, "drunk" feeling, depression, vision problems, sweating, palpitations; nausea, vomiting, fluid retention, bile tract spasm

- Serious adverse reaction: Larynx spasm, swelling throat, hallucinations, drop in blood pressure (causing weakness, fainting), disorientation, tremor, problems walking, shallow breathing, seizures

- Signs of overdose: Significant drowsiness, confusion, restlessness, shallow breathing, tremos, convulsions, stupor, coma

 General Advice and Precautions

- Herbs and minerals: Avoid Valerian, Kava Kava, and St. John's Wort.

- Avoid alcohol while on this medication

Nadolol

Brand Names: Alti-Nadol, Apo-Nadol, Corgard, Corzide [CD], Novo-Nadolol, Radio-Nadol, Syn-Nadol

 Used For

- Treatment of mild to moderate high blood pressure and effort-induced angina

 Known Contraindications and/or Interactions

- You should not use this drug if you are allergic to it, have an abnormally slow heart rate, heart shock, obstructive lung disease, or bronchial asthma

- Consult your physician if you have adverse reactions to beta-blockers, if you have serious heart disease, a respiratory condition (including hay fever), hyperthyroidism, low blood sugar, diabetes, kidney or liver problems

- Drug should be avoided by pregnant and breast-feeding women

- Drug interactions may occur with other antihypertensive drugs, Reserpine, Verapamil, Ritodrine, Theophyllines, Amiodarone, antacids containing Aluminum, Clonidine, Digoxin, Calcium blockers, Epinephrine, Insulin, Lidocaine, oral antidiabetics, Indomethacin

 ## Common Side Effects

- Lethargy, fatigue, cold hands and feet, reduced heart rate, dizziness when upright

 ## Occasional/Long-Term Side Effects

- Reduced sex drive in men, erectile dysfunction

 ## Toxicity/Adverse Reaction (Contact your doctor)

- Mild adverse reaction: Rash and drug-induced fever, headache, dizziness, hallucinations/vivid dreams, slurred speech, hair loss, cough, nausea, diarrhea, abdominal pain

- Serious adverse reaction: Facial swelling, anaphylaxis, chest pain, shortness of breath, severe slowing of heartbeat, asthma attack (in people with asthma), bronchospasm, intermittant claudication

- Signs of overdose: Slow pulse, low blood pressure, fainting, clammy skin, heart failure, coma, convulsions

 ## General Advice and Precautions

- Herbs and minerals: Avoid Valerian, Kava Kava, Ginseng, St. John's Wort, Guarana, Hawthorn, Saw Palmetto, Ma Huang, Goldenseal, Yohimbe Licorice. Calcium and Garlic may help lower blood pressure

- Do not skip or double doses

- Do not stop this drug suddenly; discontinuing drug should be under doctor's supervision

- Carry a card in your wallet that says you take this medication

- Consult your doctor before using a nasal spray while on beta-blocker medication

- Avoid heavy exercise

- This drug may make you more susceptible to hot and cold; exercise caution

Nifedipine

Brand Names: Adalat, Apo-Nifed, Gen-Nifedipine, Novo-Nifedin, Nu-Nifed, Procardia

 ## Used For

- Treatment of angina, hypertension

 ## Known Contraindications and/or Interactions

- Do not take this drug if you have had an allergic reaction to it in the past; if you have liver disease; if you have low blood pressure, narrowing of the aorta, or have had a heart attack in the last month; if you are over 65 and have been prescribed immediate-release nifedipine capsules

- Consult your physician before taking it if you have had a negative reaction to any Calcium channel blocker; cardiomyopathy, aortic stenosis, liver or kidney problems (especially diabetes), circulation problems in your hands, if you take Digitalis, a beta-blocker, blood pressure medication; have a history of heart attack, stroke, or drug-induced liver damage

- Avoid this drug if you are pregnant or breast-feeding

- Drug interactions may occur with Amiodarone, beta-blocker drugs, Digitalis drugs, Cyclosporine, Digoxin, Diltiazem, Magnesium, oral blood thinners, oral antidiabetics, Phenytoin, Fosphenytoin, Quinupristin, Dalfopristin, Rifampin, Tacrolimus, Theophylline, Vincristine, Cimetidine, Quinidine, Ranitidine, Ritonavir, and some antifungals

 ## Common Side Effects

- Rapid heart rate, low blood pressure, swollen ankles, feeling hot, sweating

- People over 60 may experience weakness, dizziness, fainting. Contact your doctor if you have any of these symptoms

 ## Occasional/Long-Term Side Effects

- None identified

Toxicity/Adverse Reaction (Contact your doctor)

- Mild adverse reaction: Rash, hives, fever; headache, dizziness, agitation, depression, eye problems; pedal edema; altered sense of taste or smell, tinnitus, sleep disorders, heartburn, nausea, diarrhea, muscle tremors, or cramps

- Serious adverse reaction: Dermatitis, joint pain, increased angina, kidney toxicity, drop in blood pressure with fainting, or poor circulation to fingers

- Signs of overdose: Weakness, dizziness, fainting, racing pulse, drop in blood pressure

 ## General Advice and Precautions

- Herbs and minerals: Avoid Valerian, Kava Kava, Dong Quai, St. John's Wort, Ginseng, Guarana, Hawthorn, Saw Palmetto, Goldenseal, Ma Huang, Yohimbe, Eleuthero root, and Licorice. Calcium and Garlic may help lower blood pressure

- Because this drug may prevent you from experiencing chest pain when you do vigorous exercise, you will not get a "warning" in the event of a problem. Use caution

- Advise all healthcare providers that you take this medication

- Carry a wallet card identifying that you take this drug

- Do not stop this drug suddenly; discontinue gradually under your doctor's supervision

Nitroglycerin

Brand Names: Corobid, Deponit, Minitran Transdermal Delivery System, Nitrek, Nitro-Bid, Nitrocap TD, Nitrocine Timecaps, Nitrocine Transdermal Nitrodisc, Nitro-Dur, Nitro-Dur II, Nitrogard, Nitrogard-SR, Nitro-glyn, Nitrol, Nitrolin, Nitrolingual Spray, Nitrol TSAR Kit, Nitrong, Nitrong SR, Nitroquick, Nitrospan, Nitrostabilin, Nitrostat, Nitro Transdermal System, NTS Transdermal Patch, Transderm-Nitro, Trates S.R., Tridil

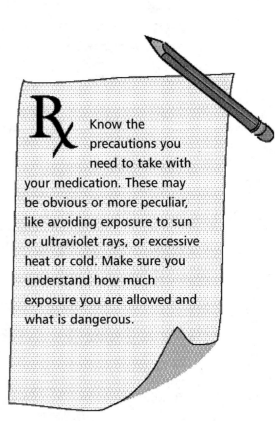

℞ Know the precautions you need to take with your medication. These may be obvious or more peculiar, like avoiding exposure to sun or ultraviolet rays, or excessive heat or cold. Make sure you understand how much exposure you are allowed and what is dangerous.

 ## Used For

- Relief for acute anginal attacks

- Prevention of angina

- Treatment for breathing difficulty caused by heart attack

- Treatment for symptomatic coronary artery disease

- Treatment for congestive heart failure

- Topical treatment for impotence

- Prevention of damage after heart attack

- Treatment of heart problems after cocaine use/addiction

- Used to delay contractions, relax uterus

- Treatment of diabetic neuropathy

 ## Known Contraindications and/or Interactions

- Do not take this drug if you have had an allergic reaction to it in the past

- Do not take this drug if you are anemic, if you have had head trauma, if you have high blood pressure, if you take Viagra, if you have hyperthyroidism, if you have high pressure in your eyes or glaucoma

- Use during pregnancy only if absolutely necessary

- Consult your doctor before taking it if you have not been able to tolerate other nitrates, have low blood pressure, abnormal growth of heart, a history of malabsorption, migraines, or if you are pregnant

- Drug interactions may occur with Acetylcysteine, Alteplase, Antihypertensive medications, Dihydroergotamine, Diltiazem, Heparin, Indomethacin, Isosorbide Dinitrate, Mononitrate, neuromuscular blocking agents, Viagra, Aspirin, NSAIDs, over-the-counter cough/cold medications

 ## Common Side Effects

- Flushing

- Headaches

- Low blood pressure

- Rapid heart rate, palpitations

Occasional/Long-Term Side Effects

- Tolerance, higher dose may be necessary

 ## Toxicity/Adverse Reaction (Contact your doctor)

- Mild adverse reaction: Skin rash, headaches, dizziness, nausea, vomiting, changes in sense of taste

- Serious adverse reaction: Allergic reactions, fainting, slow heartbeat, transient ischemic attacks, intracranial pressure, difficulty healing wounds, bleeding

- Signs of overdose: Severe headache, dizziness, vomiting, confusion, seizures, paralysis

 ## General Advice and Precautions

- Herbs and minerals: Avoid Hawthorn and Coenzyme Q_{10}

- May cause dizziness or fainting. Avoid driving and/or operating machinery until you know how this drug affects you

- Do not smoke cigarettes or Marijuana when taking this medication

- Do not drink alcohol when taking this medication

- Avoid excessively hot and cold environments

- Speak to your doctor before exercising when taking this drug

- No not put pills in a pillbox, leave in original container

- Do not suddenly stop taking this drug. Discontinue gradually under your doctor's supervision

- This drug can trigger migraine headaches

- Many over-the-counter cough cold medications interact with this drug, speak to your doctor before taking any over-the-counter drugs

Oxycodone

Brand Names: Endocet [CD], Endodan [CD], Oxycocet [CD], Oxycodan [CD], OxyContin, Percocet [CD], Percodan [CD], Roxicet, Roxicodone, Roxilox, Roxiprin [CD], SK-Oxycodone, Supeudol, Tylox [CD]

 ## Used For

- Pain relief

 ## Known Contraindications and/or Interactions

- Do not take this drug if you have had an allergic reaction to it in the past

- Do not take this drug if you have severe asthma, are having an attack, have respiratory depression. Do not take Percodan if you are allergic to Aspirin.

- Do not take this drug if you suspect head injury

- Consult your doctor before taking if you react badly to narcotic drugs, have had a head injury, have a lung disease that causes breathing problems, have kidney or liver problems, gallbladder disorder, epilepsy or seizure disorder, have hypothyroid problems, taking any sedatives, or are scheduled to have surgery under general anesthesia

- Avoid using while pregnant or breast-feeding

- Drug interactions may occur with atropinelike drugs, sedatives (including benzodi-azepines, tricyclic antidepressants, antihistamines, MAO inhibitors, Phenothiazines, and other opioid drugs), Naltrexone, Rifabutin, Ritonavir, Sertraline, Tramadol

 ## Common Side Effects

- Drowsiness, light-headedness, fluid retention, constipation. Many doctors prescribe a medication for constipation alongside this drug

 ## Occasional/Long-Term Side Effects

- Long term use may result in drug dependence, chronic constipation

- Excessive use of this drug may cause breathing problems in people with asthma, emphysema, or chronic bronchitis

- May dull sexual response

Toxicity/Adverse Reaction (Contact your doctor)

- Mild adverse reaction: Skin rash, hives, "drunk" feeling, dizziness, depression, vision problems, nausea, vomiting

- Serious adverse reaction: Breathing problems

- Signs of overdose: Drowsiness or agitation, dizziness, weakness, nausea, vomiting, seizures, stupor, coma

 General Advice and Precautions

- Herbs and minerals: use caution with any preparation that can contribute to drowsiness – Valerian, Kava Kava. St. John's Wort can alter the effectiveness of this drug

- Interacts with alcohol. Avoid drinking while on this medication

- A high fat meal can increase drug levels of OxyContin by up to 25% in people taking stronger doses

- Some brands – Percocet, for example – come in many strengths and formulations. Make sure you understand clearly the dosage amounts and times for your particular prescription

- This drug can affect alertness, judgment, coordinatoin, reaction time. Do not drive or operate machinery until you know how it affects you

- This drug is best used short-term. If used over a long term, discontinue gradually under a doctor's supervision to avoid withdrawal symptoms

Paroxetine

Brand Names: Paxil

 Used For

- Treatment of depression, obsessive-compulsive disorder, panic attacks

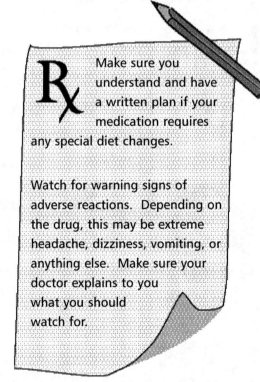

R Make sure you understand and have a written plan if your medication requires any special diet changes.

Watch for warning signs of adverse reactions. Depending on the drug, this may be extreme headache, dizziness, vomiting, or anything else. Make sure your doctor explains to you what you should watch for.

Known Contraindications and/or Interactions

- Do not take this drug if you have taken an MAO Type A Inhibitor in the last 14 days

- Consult your physician before taking if you have a history of seizures, many, liver or kidney problems, or if you generally don't drink a lot of water

- Drug should be avoided by women who are pregnant or breast-feeding

- Drug interactions may occur with benzodiazepines, Buspirone, Desipramine, Encainide, Flecainide, Galantamine, Haloperidol, Labetalol, activated Charcoal, Astemizole, Cimetidine, Dextromethorphan (the "DM" in some cough medications), Digoxin, Fenfluramine, Lithium, MAO Inhibitors, Phenytoin, Fosphenytoin, Propafenone, Quinidine, Risperidon, Ritonavir, Sibutramine, Sumatriptan, Tramadol, Tricyclic antidepressants, Tryptophan, Venlafaxine, Warfarin

 ## Common Side Effects

- Lowered blood pressure, possibly fainting; nausea

 ## Occasional/Long-Term Side Effects

- No long-term side effects reported

- May cause abnormal ejaculation, painful erection, or sexual dysfunction

 ## Toxicity/Adverse Reaction (Contact your doctor)

- Mild adverse reaction: Rash, headache, dizziness, nervousness, disrupted sleep patterns, loss of appetite, nausea, constipation, sweating, feeling of restlessness

- Serious adverse reaction: Excessive or prolonged bruising or bleeding, increased suicidal behavior in young patients, abnormal facial expressions

- Signs of overdose: Confusion, heart arrhythmia, seizure

General Advice and Precautions

- Herbs and minerals: Avoid St. John's Wort, Ginkgo, Ma Huang, Yohimbe, Indian Snakeroot, Valerian, and Kava Kava.

- Avoid alcohol while on this medication

- Drug may cause drowsiness. Do not drive or operate mechanical equipment if this symptom is present

- May cause excessive sweating. Increase fluid intake to compensate

- Do not suddenly stop taking this medication. Discontinue gradually, under a doctor's supervision

- Caution: Notwithstanding treatment, some people suffering depression develop suicidal tendencies. If you or someone you know display signs of suicidal thinking, contact your doctor immediately

Penicillin Antibiotic Family

Brand Names: Amoxicillin Apo-Amoxi, Clavulin, Larotid, Novamoxin, Nu-Amoxi, Polymox, Prevpac, Trimox, Wymox, Ampicillin, Ampilean, A-Cillin, Amoxicillin/Clavvlanate, Augmentin, Amcill, Ampicin, Ampilean, Apo-Ampi, D-Amp, Faspac Ampicillin: 500 Kit, Novo-Ampicillin, Nu-Ampi, Omnipen, Pardec Capsules, Penbritin, Polycillin-PRB, Pondocillin, Principen, SK-Ampicillin, Totacillin, Bacampicillin Penglobe, Spectrobid, Cloxacillin, Apo-Cloxi, Bactopen, Cloxapen, Novo-Cloxin, Nu-Cloxi, Orbenin, Tegopen, Penicillin VK, Apo-Pen VK, Beepen VK, Betapen-VK, Ledercillin VK, Nadopen-V, Novopen-VK, Nu-Pen-VK, Penapar VK, Pen-V, Pen-Vee, Pfizerpen VK, PVF, Robicillin VK, SK-Penicillin VK, Uticillin VK, V-Cillin K, VC-K 500, Veetids, Win-Cillin

 Used For

- Treatment of infections of the respiratory tract

- Treatment of genitourinary infections

- Treatment of pneumonia or acute sinusitis

- Treatment of other infections by microorganisms, but not viral infections

- Treatment of streptococcal infections

- Treatment of animal bites, Lyme disease

- Treatment of dental abscesses

- Treatment of resistant bacteria

- Prevents rheumatic fever in people with heart disease

Known Contraindications and/or Interactions

- Drugs with known interactions include Disulfiram, Antabuse, Entacapone, Comtan, live typhoid vaccine, Methotrexate, Mexate, Omeprazole, Prilosec, Probenecid, Allopurinol, Atenolol, Warfarin, Coumadin, birth control pills, antacids, histamine blockers, Chloramphenicol, Cholestyramine, Erythromycin, tetracyclines

- Do not take if allergic to Penicillin

- Speak to your doctor if pregnant or nursing

- Speak to your doctor if you have hay fever, asthma, hives, or are allergic to Cephalosporin antibiotics

- Dose adjustments may be necessary in patients with decreased kidney function

 ## Common Side Effects

- "Superinfections" – yeast infections

 ## Occasional/Long-Term Side Effects

- Drug-induced colitis

- Lowering of white blood cell count

- Compromised kidney function

- Possible decrease in sperm count

 ## Toxicity/Adverse Reaction (Contact your doctor)

- Skin rashes

- Black tongue

- Allergic reactions – anaphylactic, severe skin rashes, sore throat

- Abnormal bleeding or bruising

- Colitis

- Anemia

- Liver or kidney problems

- Nausea, vomiting, diarrhea

General Advice and Precautions

- Call your doctor if infection does not improve in 48 hours

- Take the full prescribed course of this medication, even if you are feeling better

- Some forms should be taken on an empty stomach

- Herbs and minerals to avoid include Echinacea, Mistletoe, Oak Bark, Marshmallow Root, Licorice, Guar Gum, St. John's Wort

- Some forms may cause photosensitivity

- Allergic reactions can be very serious – seek medical attention immediately if you feel you are having an allergic reaction to this medication

Pindolol

Brand Names: Alti-Pindol, Apo-Pindol, Dom-Pindolol, Novo-Pindol, Nu-Pindol, Syn-Pindolol, Viskazide [CD], Visken

 ## Used For

- Treatment of mild to moderate high blood pressure

- Prevention of angina

- May help prevent migraines, control aggressive behaviour

 ## Known Contraindications and/or Interactions

- You should not use this drug if you are allergic to it, have an abnormally slow heart rate, bronchial asthma or have taken an MAO Type A Inhibitor within the last 14 days

- Consult your physician if you have adverse reactions to beta-blockers, if you have serious heart disease, a respiratory condition (including hay fever), hyperthyroidism, low blood sugar, diabetes, kidney or liver problems

R If you are on a relatively new drug, understand that there may be unknown long-term side effects, and that should your doctor require tests on specific body tissues like your kidney or liver, you should comply fully to make sure you prevent any possible damages. Note: This may also be required with drugs that have been known to cause problems in long term use.

- Drug should be avoided by pregnant and breast-feeding women

- Drug interactions may occur with other antihypertensive drugs, Reserpine, Verapamil, Amiodarone, Clonidine, Digoxin, Epinephrine, Fentanyl, Fluoxetine, Fluvoxamine, Insulin, oral antidiabetics, Phenylpropanolamine, Ritodrine, Venlafaxine, Cimetidine, Methimazole, oral contraceptives, Propylthirouracil, Ritonavir, Zileuton, barbituates, Indomethacin, Rifampin, Theophylline

 ## Common Side Effects

- Lethargy, fatigue, cold hands and feet, reduced heart rate, dizziness when upright

 ## Occasional/Long-Term Side Effects

- Reduced sex drive in men, erectile dysfunction

 ## Toxicity/Adverse Reaction (Contact your doctor)

- Mild adverse reaction: Rash, headache, dizziness, unusually vivid dreams, fainting, indigestion, nausea, diarrhea, abdominal pain, joint/muscle pain, fluid retention

- Serious adverse reaction: Facial swelling, anaphylaxis, chest pain, shortness of breath, severe slowing of heartbeat, asthma attack (in people with asthma), intermittant claudication

- Signs of overdose: Slow pulse, low blood pressure, fainting, clammy skin, heart failure, coma, convulsions

 ## General Advice and Precautions

- Herbs and minerals: Avoid Ginseng, Guarana, Hawthorn, Saw Palmetto, Ma Huang, Goldenseal, Yohimbe, Licorice. Calcium and Garlic may help lower blood pressure

- Do not skip or double doses

- Do not stop this drug suddenly; discontinuing drug should be done under a doctor's supervision

- Carry a card in your wallet that says you take this medication

- Consult your doctor before using a nasal spray while on beta-blocker medication

- Avoid heavy exercise

- This drug may make you more susceptible to hot and cold; exercise caution

Prednisolone

Brand Names: A&D w/Prednisolone, Ak-Cide, Ak-Pred, Ak-Tate, Blephamide, Cortalone, Delta-Cortef, Duapred, Econopred Ophthalmic, Fernisolone-P, Hydelta-TBA, Inflamase, Inflamase Forte, Isopto Cetapred, Key-Pred, Meticortelone, Meti-Derm, Metimyd, Metreton, Minims Prednisolone, Mydrapred, Niscort, Nor-Pred, Nova-Pred, Novoprednisolone, Ophtho-Tate, Optimyd, Otobione, Pediaject, Pediapred, Polypred, Predcor, Pred Forte, Pred-G, Pred Mild, Prelone, PSP-IV, Savacort, Sterane, TBA Pred, Vasocidin

 Used For

- Treatment for serious skin conditions

- Treatment for asthma

- Treatment for inflammatory disorders

- Treatment for allergic conditions

- Treatment of arthritis, rheumatoid arthritis, bursitis, tendonitis

- Combination therapy in lymphoma, breast cancer, leukemia, liver tumors

- Treatment for anaphylactic shock

- Treatment of ulcerative colitis

 Known Contraindications and/or Interactions

- See Prednisone

 Common Side Effects

- See Prednisone

 Occasional/Long-Term Side Effects

- See Prednisone

 Toxicity/Adverse Reaction (Contact your doctor)

- Mild adverse reaction: See Prednisone

- Serious adverse reaction: See Prednisone

- Signs of overdose: See Prednisone

 General Advice and Precautions

- See Prednisone

Prednisone

Brand Names: Apo-Prednisone, Aspred-C, Deltasone, Liquid Pred, Meticorten, Metreton, Novoprednisone, Orasone, Panasol-S, Paracort, Prednicen-M, Prednisone Intensol, SK-Prednisone, Sterapred, Sterapred-DS, Winpred

 Used For

- Symptom relief of rheumatoid arthritis

- Symptom relief of lupus

- Symptom relief of a variety of allergic and inflammatory conditions

- Symptom relief in multiple sclerosis

- Symptom relief in Crohn's disease

- Treatment of serious skin disorders

- Combination therapy of leukemia, kidney transplant, breast cancer, liver tumors

 Known Contraindications and/or Interactions

- Do not take this drug if you have had an allergic reaction to it in the past

- Do not take this drug if pregnant, have peptic ulcers, active herpes simplex, tuberculosis, or severe fungal infection

- Consult your doctor before taking it if breast-feeding, over the age of 60, have diabetes, kidney failure, glaucoma, high blood pressure, thyroid disorders, osteoporosis, joint pain, measles, depression, diverticulitis, or plan to have surgery

- Drug interactions may occur with Insulin, Isoniazid, Salicylates, Aspirin, vaccines, Amphotericin B, Asparaginase, birth control pills, Clarithromycin, Cyclosporine, Foscarnet, Ketoconazole, Levofloxacin, loop diuretics, Macrolide antibiotics, Montelukast, neuromuscular blocking agents, NSAIDs, anticoagulants, oral antidiabetic drugs, Ritonavir, Theophylline, tiazide diuretics, antacids, barbiturates, Carbamazepine, Primidone, Riampin

⚠ Common Side Effects

- Increased appetite, weight gain, water, and salt retention

- High blood pressure

- Potassium loss

- Increased/decreased white blood cell count

- Depression, euphoria

- Easy bruising, impaired healing

Occasional/Long-Term Side Effects

- Increased blood sugar

- Increased fat deposits

- Thinning skin

- Weakening of bones

  Cataracts/glaucoma

- Stunted growth in children

⚠⚠ Toxicity/Adverse Reaction (Contact your doctor)

- Mild adverse reaction: Allergic reaction, skin rash, headache, dizziness, insomnia, indigestion, blue toes, muscle cramping, weakness, facial hair, acne

- Serious adverse reaction: Mental or emotional disturbances, reactivation of tuberculosis, peptic ulcer, inflammation of the pancreas, thrombophlebitis, Cushing's syndrome, bone weakness, osteoporosis, superinfections, muscle loss, seizures, blood clots

- Signs of overdose: Fatigue, weakness, stomach irritation, sweating/flushing, fluid retention/swelling, increased blood pressure

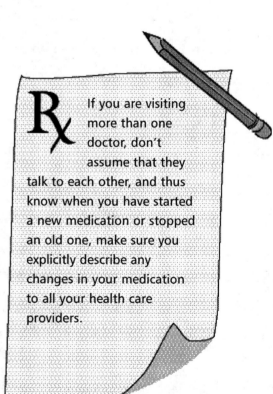

℞ If you are visiting more than one doctor, don't assume that they talk to each other, and thus know when you have started a new medication or stopped an old one, make sure you explicitly describe any changes in your medication to all your health care providers.

General Advice and Precautions

- Herbs and minerals: Avoid Hawthorn, Ginger, Garlic, Ma Huang, Ephedra, Ginseng, Guar Gum, Fenugreek, Nettle, Fir or Pine Needle Oil

- Avoid alfalfa

- Avoid alcohol, tobacco, and Marijuana

- May cause dizziness in rare instances. Avoid driving and/or operating machinery until you know how this drug affects you

- This drug may reduce your resistance to infection

- Carry a card that indicates you are taking this medication

- If you are to get a vaccination, discontinue use of this drug 72 hours before vaccination and resume taking your medication 14 days after your vaccination. Discuss this with your doctor

- Talk to your doctor if you experience unexplained joint pain while taking this drug

- Do not suddenly stop taking this drug. Discontinue gradually under your doctor's supervision

Propionic Acid

Brand Names: Fenoprofen: Nalfon, Flurbidprofen: Ansaid, Apo-Flurbiprofen, Froben, Ocufen, Ibuprofen: Aches-N-Pain, Actiprofen, Advil, Amersol, Apo-Ibuprofen, Arthritis Foundation Pain Reliever, Bayer Select, Motrin, Coadvil, Dimetapp, Dologesic, Dristan Sinus, Excedrin IB, Genpril, Guildprofen, Haltran, Ibu, Medipren, Medi-Profen, Midol IB, Novo-Profen, Nuprin, PediaProfen, Rufen, Superior Pain Medication, Supreme Pain Medication, Tab-Profen, Ketoprofen: Actron, Orudis, Oruvail, Rhodis, Naproxen: Aleve, Naprelan, Naprosyn, Naxen, Neo-Pro, Novo-Naprox, Nu-Naprox, Synflex, Oxaprozin, Daypro

Other Names: NSAIDs, or Nonsteroidal Anti-Inflammatory Drugs

 Used For

- Pain relief

- Inflammation relief

- Treatment of migraines and arthritis

- Fever reduction

 ## Known Contraindications and/or Interactions

- Do not take this drug if you have had an allergic reaction to it in the past

- Do not take this drug if you have asthma, nasal polyps, bleeding problems, herpes simplex, keratitis, kidney problems

- Consult your doctor before taking if you are pregnant, nursing, have ulcers, bleeding problems, liver or kidney problems, meningitis, high blood pressure, a history of heart failure, take Acetaminophen or Aspirin

- Drug interactions may occur with anticoagulants, Cyclosporine, Fosphenytoin, Lithium, Methotrexate, hypoglycemic edications, beta-blockers, diuretics, Aspirin, Dipyridamole, Eptifibatide, Indomethacin, Ketorolac, Heparins, Sulfinpyrazone, Valproic Acid, Warfarin, ACE Inhibitors, Alendronate, histamine blockers, Ofloxacin, Fluoroquinolones, Ritonavir, Tacrine, Tacrolimus

 ## Common Side Effects

- Fluid retention

- Tinnitus

- Discolored urine

 ## Occasional/Long-Term Side Effects

- Fluid retention

- Anemia

- Naproxen can affect ejaculation

- Ketoprofen can affect libido

- Ibuprofen, Naproxen, and Ketoprofen can affect your menstrual cycle

 ## Toxicity/Adverse Reaction (Contact your doctor)

- Mild adverse reaction: Skin rash, headache, dizziness, sleep disturbances, nausea, vomiting, constipation, diarrhea, palpitations

- Serious adverse reaction: Anaphylactic reaction, terrible skin rash, lung inflammation, aseptic meningitis, peptic ulcer, colon inflammation, porphyria, pancreatitis, lupus, Parkinson-like symptoms, esophagal inflammation, liver damage, kidney damage, bone marrow problems

- Signs of overdose: Drowsiness, dizziness, confusion, stupor, coma, diarrhea, vomiting

 ## General Advice and Precautions

- Herbs and minerals: Avoid Ginseng, Ginkgo, Alfalfa, Clove, Feverfew, Cinchona Bark, White Willow Bark, Garlic, Eucalyptus, Kava, Valerian, St. John's Wort, Hay Flower, Mistletoe, White Mustard Seed

- Avoid drinking alcohol while taking this drug

- Can be taken with food to avoid stomach irritation

- Remain upright for at least 30 minutes after taking this medication

- May cause drowsiness and dizziness. Avoid driving and/or operating machinery until you know how this drug affects you

- These drugs can cause photosensitivity in some individuals

- Do not suddenly stop taking this drug. Discontinue gradually under your doctor's supervision

Propranolol

Brand Names: Apo-Propranolol, Betachron, Detensol, Inderal, Inderide LA[CD], Innopran XL, Ipran, Novo-Pranol, PMS Propranolol

 ## Used For

- Treatment of effort-induced angina, heart rhythm disorders, high blood pressure

 ## Known Contraindications and/or Interactions

- You should not use this drug if you are allergic to it, have bronchial asthma, overt heart failure, coronary artery spasm, Raynaud's phenomenon, abnormally slow heart rate, or have taken an MAO Type A Inhibitor within the last 14 days

- Consult your physician if you have adverse reactions to beta-blockers, if you have serious heart disease, a respiratory condition (including hay fever), hyperthyroidism, low blood sugar, diabetes, kidney or liver problems, or are allergic to bee stings

- Drug should be avoided by pregnant and breast-feeding women

- Drug interactions may occur with other antihypertensive drugs, Lidocaine, Reserpine, Quinidine, Rizatriptan, Verapamil, Warfarin, Albuterol, Theophyllines, Amiodarone, Clonidine, Cocaine, Colestipol, Digoxin, Epinephrine, Fluoxetine, Fluvoxamine, Insulin, Nefazodone, oral antidiabetics, Sertraline, Venlafaxine, Zolmitriptan, Zotepine, Chlorpromazine, Cimetidine, Ciprofoxacin, Diltiasem, Disopyramide, Furosemide, Methimazole, Metoclopramide, Nicardipine, Propafenone, Propoxyphene, Propylthiouracil, Ritonavir, Zileuton, Antacids, Barbituates, Indomethacin, Rifampin, Sertraline, Simvastatin

 ## Common Side Effects

- Lethargy, fatigue, cold hands and feet, reduced heart rate, dizziness when upright

 ## Occasional/Long-Term Side Effects

- Reduced sex drive in men, erectile dysfunction

- May promote heart failure in patients with advanced heart disease

 ## Toxicity/Adverse Reaction (Contact your doctor)

- Mild adverse reaction: Rash, drug-induced fever, hair loss, headache, dizziness, disrupted sleep, indigestion, nausea, diarrhea, joint/muscle pain, dry eyes, weight gain

- Serious adverse reaction: Anaphylaxis, depression/anxiety, dramatic behavior changes, chest pain, shortness of breath, asthma attack (in people with asthma), intermittant claudication

- Signs of overdose: Slow pulse, low blood pressure, fainting, clammy skin, heart failure, coma, convulsions

General Advice and Precautions

- Herbs and minerals: Avoid Ginseng, Guarana, Hawthorn, Saw Palmetto, Ma Huang, Goldenseal, Yohimbe Licorice. Calcium and Garlic may help lower blood pressure. Cut back on salt while on this medication

- Do not skip or double doses

- Do not stop this drug suddenly; discontinuation of

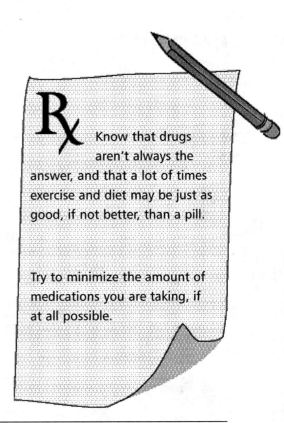

Rx Know that drugs aren't always the answer, and that a lot of times exercise and diet may be just as good, if not better, than a pill.

Try to minimize the amount of medications you are taking, if at all possible.

this drug should take place under doctor's supervision

- Carry a card in your wallet that says you take this medication

- Consult your doctor before using a nasal spray while on beta-blocker medication

- Avoid heavy exercise

- This drug may make you more susceptible to hot and cold; exercise caution

Protease Inhibitor Family

Brand Names: Atazanavir: Reyataz, Lopinavir, Ritonavir, Kaletra, Amprenavir: Agenerase, Indinavir, Crixivan, Nelfinavir: Viracept, Ritonavir, Kaletra, Norvir, Saquinavir, Fortovase, Invirase, Tenofovir: Viread

 Used For

- Treatment of HIV infection

- Used in combination therapy for HIV infection

- Decreasing secondary infections in HIV patients

- Lowering HIV levels

 Known Contraindications and/or Interactions

- Serious drug interactions known. Drugs with known interactions include Amiodarone, Cordarone, Ritonavir, Indinavir, antacids, Astemizole, Hismanal, azole antifungals, Bepridil, Vascor, birth control pills, Bupropion, Wellbutrin, Carbamazepine, Tegretol, Cimetidine, Tagamet, Cisapride, Propulsid, Cyclosporine, Sandimmune, Delavirdine, Rescriptor, Diazepam, Valium, Didanosine, Digoxin, Diltiazem, Dofetilide, Dronabinol, Efavirex, ergot derivatives, Felodipine, Flecainide, Fluticasone, Flonase, Fluvastatin, Lescol, Fluvoxamine, Luvox, Gemfibrozil, Glimepiride, Glipizide, Glyburide, oral hypo-glycemic drugs, Ibuprofen, Motrin, NSAIDs, Isradipine, Itraconazole, Ketoconazole, Macrolide Antibiotics, Methylenedioxymethamphetamine (MDMA or Ecstasy), Midazolam, Narcotics, Morphine, MS Contin, Methadone, Dolophine, Nevirapine, Viramune, oral hpyoglycemics, antiretrovirols, Paclitaxel, Taxol, Phenytoin, Dilantin, Fosphenytoin, Cerebyx, Propafenone, Quinidine, Quinupristin, Dalfopristin, Rifabutin, Riampin, Risperidone, Saquinavir, Sirolimus, Sildenafil, Viagra, Tramadol, Ultram, Triazolam, Halcion, Benzodiazepines, Tricyclic Antidepressants, Venlafaxine, Effexor, Warfarin, Coumadin, Zolpidem, Ambien

- Speak to your doctor if pregnant or breast-feeding

- This drug should not be taken in people under 18 years of age or over 65 years of age

- Tell your doctor if you have diabetes

- Tell your doctor if you are allergic to Sulfonamide

- Tell your doctor if you have had kidney stones or decreased kidney/liver functioning

- Tell your doctor if you have high cholesterol

! Common Side Effects

- Kidney stones

- Increased cholesterol levels

Occasional/Long-Term Side Effects

- Resistance to this drug can occur

- Blood sugar imbalances can occur

- PMS

- Ingrown toenails

!! Toxicity/Adverse Reaction (Contact your doctor)

- Rash, headache, chills, fever

- Nausea, vomiting

- Heart palpitations

- Joint pain

- Tingling feelings

- Anemia

- Blood clots

- Bleeding

- Serious increase in cholesterol level

- High blood sugar

- Kidney failure/kidney stones

General Advice and Precautions

- Follow your doctor's instructions exactly when taking this drug

- Be aware of the serious drug interactions that can occur

- Do not take with a high-fat meal

- Best taken on an empty stomach

- Do not smoke Marijuana or take Ecstasy while taking this drug

- Quitting smoking is advised

- Multivitamins recommended

- Herbs and minerals to avoid include Echinacea, Garlic, St. John's Wort

- Do not take vitamin E supplements while taking this drug

- Do not miss a dose of this medication

- Do not take double doses of this medication

- There is no known antidote for an overdose of this medication

- HIV can still be spread to other people while a patient takes this medication

- This drug is not a cure for HIV

- Learn the symptoms of high blood sugar

- This medication should not be refrigerated

- Shake this medication well before taking it

Quinidine

Brand Names: Apo-Quinidine, Binquin Durules, Cardioquin, Cin-Quin, Duraquin, Natisedine, Novo-Quinidin, Quinaglute Dura-Tabs, Quinate, Quinatime, Quinidex Extentabs, Quinobarb, Quinora, Quin-Release, SK-Quinidine Sulfate

 ## Used For

- Regulation of heart rhythm

Known Contraindications and/or Interactions

- Do not take this drug if you have had an allergic reaction to it in the past

- Do not take this drug if you are suffering from an infection, Digoxin toxicity, have kidney disease, AV block, or if you are nursing

- Consult your doctor before taking if you have an artery disease, sick sinus syndrome, thyroid conditions, blood platelet deficiency, imbalanced blood chemistry, take digitalis preparations, are planning for surgery under anesthesia, a history of fainting, rheumatic fever, or are pregnant

- Drug interactions may occur with Aspirin, beta-blocers, Cisapride, Clomipramine, Codeine, Dextromethorphan, Dofetilide, Fluoxetine, Gatifloxacin, Grepafloxacin, Moxifloxacin, Sparfloxacin, Antacids, Magnesium, Antiarrhythmics, Metformin, neuromuscular blocking agents, Nisoldipine, Tramadol, tricyclic antidepressants, Venlafaxine, anticoagulants, Digitoxin, Digoxin, Disopyramide, Propafenone, Warfarin, Amiodarone, Amprenavir, Cimetidine, Delavirdine, Diclofenac, Diltiazem, Erythromycin, Itraconazole, Ketoconazole, Voriconazole, Quiupristin, Dalfopristin, Ritonavir, protease inhibitors, Sertraline, Verapamil, arbiturates, Phenytoin, Fosphenytoin, Rifabuin, Rifampin, Sucralfate

! Common Side Effects

- Low blood pressure
- Fever

Occasional/Long-Term Side Effects

- None indicated

!! Toxicity/Adverse Reaction (Contact your doctor)

- Mild adverse reaction: Skin rash, stomach or esophagal irritation, nausea, vomiting, diarrhea

- Serious adverse reaction: Anaphylactic reaction, joint or muscle pain, hepatitis, fast heart rate, delirium, blurred vision, hearing loss, coma, heart attack, paranoia, depression, memory problems, lupus, carpal

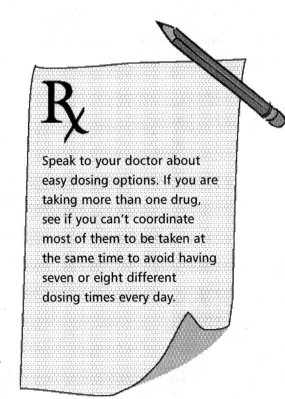

R

Speak to your doctor about easy dosing options. If you are taking more than one drug, see if you can't coordinate most of them to be taken at the same time to avoid having seven or eight different dosing times every day.

tunnel syndrome, swollen lymph glands, kidney toxicity, low white blood cell count, low platelet count

- Signs of overdose: Vomiting, tinnitus, headache, double vision, uncontrollable eye movements, confusion, seizures, coma

General Advice and Precautions

- Herbs and minerals: Avoid Kola, St. John's Wort, Ma Huang, Ephedra, Guarana, Yohimbe, Belladonna, Henbane, Scopolia, Pheasant's Eye, Lily of the Valley, Squill

- Do not drink alcohol or smoke cigarettes while taking this medication

- Avoid all forms of nicotine while taking this medication

- This medication can cause photosensitivity

- Avoid grapefruit juice and grapefruits while taking this medication

- Limit your caffeine intake while taking this drug

- May cause vision changes and dizziness. Avoid driving and/or operating machinery until you know how this drug affects you

- Do not suddenly stop taking this drug. Discontinue gradually under your doctor's supervision

Sertraline

Brand Names: Zoloft

Used For

- Depression, obsessive-compulsive disorder, panic disorder, post-traumatic stress disorder

Known Contraindications and/or Interactions

- Do not take this drug if you have taken an MAO Type A Inhibitor in the last 14 days, or if you take disulfiram oral solution

- Consult your physican before taking it if you take diuretics, have Parkinson's, have recently had a heart attack, a history of seizures, liver or kidney problems, adverse reactions to antidepressant drugs

- Drug should be avoided by women who are pregnant or breast-feeding

- Drug interactions may occur with antidiabetic drugs, Astemizole, Benzodiazepines, Bupropion, Carbamazepine, Cimetidine, Clozapine, Dextromethorphan (the "DM" in some cough medications), Erythromycin, Diazepam, Diltiazem, Dofetilide, Flecainide, Lamotrigine, Lithium, Metoclopramide, MAO Type A Inhibitors, Phenytoin, Fosphenytoin, Propafenone, Quinidine, Ritonavir, Sibutramine, Terfenadine, Theophylline, Tolbutamide, Tramadol, Warfarin, Zolpidem

 ## Common Side Effects

- Reduced appetite and weight loss

 ## Occasional/Long-Term Side Effects

- No long-term side-effects reported

- May cause sexual dysfunction in both sexes (but may also help some sexual disorders)

 ## Toxicity/Adverse Reaction (Contact your doctor)

- Mild adverse reaction: Rash, headache, fatigue, dizziness, nervousness, sleepwalking, sweating, muscle pain, dry mouth, nausea, vomiting, diarrhea

- Serious adverse reaction: Hallucinations, bronchospasm, drug-induced seizures, dermatitis, palpitations

- Signs of overdose: Agitation, nausea, vomiting, seizures

 ## General Advice and Precautions

- Herbs and minerals: Avoid St. John's Wort, Ginkgo, Ma Huang, Yohimbe, Indian Snakeroot, Valerian and Kava Kava.

- Do not drink grapefruit juice while on this medication

- Avoid driving, operating machinery and drinking alcohol until you know how this drug affects you

- May cause excessive sweating. Increase fluid intake to compensate

- May cause photosensitivity

- Do not suddenly stop taking this medication. Discontinue gradually, under a doctor's supervision

- Caution: Notwithstanding treatment, some people suffering depression develop suicidal tendencies. If you or someone you know display signs of suicidal thinking, contact your doctor immediately

Sildenafil Citrate

Brand Names: Viagra

 Used For

- Erectile dysfunction

 Known Contraindications and/or Interactions

- Do not take this drug without a prescription from a doctor who knows your medical history

- Do not take this drug if you have had an allergic reaction to it in the past

- Do not take this drug if you have low blood pressure, take nitrates, have a serious cardio-vascular illness

- Consult your doctor before taking if you have liver or kidney problems, heart disease, leukemia, multiple myeloma, vision problems, damage to the structure of your penis, heartburn

- If you are over the age of 65, do not take more than 50 mg of this drug

- Drug interactions may occur with nitrates (such as Nitroglycerin), Cimetidine, Delavirdine, Diliazem, Erythromycin, protease inhibitors, anti-fungals, Metronidazole, Nitroprusside, Saquinavir, Sertraline, Amprenavir, hypoglycemic drugs, Carbamazepine, Phenytoin, Rifabutin, Rifampin

- This drug is not approved for women, children, or infants

! **Common Side Effects**

- Dry eyes, vision changes

- Congestion

Occasional/Long-Term Side Effects

- Not available

 ## Toxicity/Adverse Reaction (Contact your doctor)

- Mild adverse reaction: Rash, flusing, headache, indigestion, blue/green color blindness

- Serious adverse reaction: Serious drug intereactions causing death, blindness, stroke, myocardial ischemia, heart attack, arrhythmia, fibrillation, sustained erection, priapism, ejaculation problems

- Signs of overdose: Not available, monitor dosage carefully

 ## General Advice and Precautions

- Herbs and minerals: Avoid St. John's Wort, Ma Huang, Ephedra, Kola, Yohimbe

- Do not drink grapefruit juice while taking this drug – serious interaction can occur

- Do not drink alcohol while taking this drug

- Carry a card in your wallet that indicates you are taking this drug

- Viagra is a serious drug; do not take it without a prescription from a doctor who knows your medical history; heed your doctor's advice while taking this medication

Spironolactone

Brand Names: Alatone, Aldactazide, Aldactone, Apo-Spirozide, Novo-Spiroton, Novo-Spirozine, Sincomen, Spironazide

 ## Used For

- Management of congestive heart failure

- Management of liver and kidney disorders

- Treatment of low blood Potassium levels (hypokalemia)

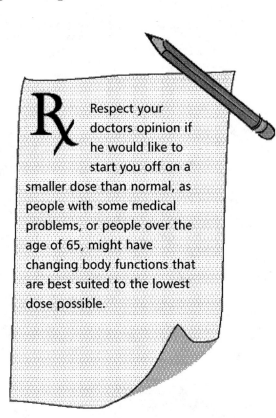

Respect your doctors opinion if he would like to start you off on a smaller dose than normal, as people with some medical problems, or people over the age of 65, might have changing body functions that are best suited to the lowest dose possible.

- Reduces risk of death and hospitalization in severe heart failure patients

- Can treat lung disorders

 ## Known Contraindications and/or Interactions

- Drugs with known interactions include Digoxin, Lanoxin, anticoagulants, Coumadin, Arginine, Captopril, Capoten, ACE Inhibitors, cortisone-like drugs, Digitoxin, Cyclosporine, Lithium, Norepinephrine, Potassium, Tacrolimus, Valsartan, Diovan, Warfarin, Aspirin, NSAIDs

- Do not use this drug if you have severely decreased liver or kidney function

- Do not use if you have high levels of Potassium in your blood

- Do not use this drug while pregnant or breast-feeding

- Tell your doctor if you have diabetes, liver disease, or kidney disease

- Tell your doctor if you are planning for surgery under general anesthesia

 ## Common Side Effects

- High blood Potassium levels

- Low blood sodium levels

- Dehydration

 ## Occasional/Long-Term Side Effects

- Male breast enlargement

- Excessive hair growth/deepening of voice in women

- Liver damage

 ## Toxicity/Adverse Reaction (Contact your doctor)

- Thirst, nausea, vomiting

- Irregular heart beat, low blood pressure

- Drowsiness, fatigue

- Skin rash/itching

- Taste disturbances

- Stomach ulcers

- Liver or kidney toxicity

- Low white blood cell count

- Decreased libido or impotence

- Weakness, dizziness

 General Advice and Precautions

- Avoid foods that are high in Potassium, including bananas, melons, prunes, avocados, potatoes, nuts, skim milk

- Do not restrict your salt intake

- Herbs and minerals to avoid include Hawthorn, Coenzyme Q_{10}, Soy products, Couch Grass, Nettle, Ginseng, Guarana, Eleuthero Root, Saw Palmetto, Ma Huang, Ephedra, Goldenseal, Licorice, Indian Snakeroot, Calcium, Garlic, Potassium

- Avoid drinking alcoholic beverages

- Withdraw using this drug under medical supervision

- Do not stop taking this drug without medical supervision

Sulfonamide Antibiotic Family

Contains: Sulfamethoxazole and Sulfisoxazole

Also known as Sulfa Drugs

Brand Names: Sulfamethoxazole: Apo-Sulfamethoxazole, Sulfatrim, Apo-Sulfatrim [CD], Azo Gantanol [CD], Bactrim [CD], Bethaprim [CD], Comoxol [CD], Cotrim [CD], Gantanol, Novo-Trimel [CD], Nu-Cotrimox, Protrin [CD], Roubac [CD], Septra [CD], Uro Gantanol [CD], Uroplus, Vagitrol, Sulfisoxazole, Azo Gantrisin, Novosoxazole, Pediazole [CD], SK-Soxazole, Sulfalar, Vagila

 Used For

- This is classified as an antibiotic

- Used to prevent and treat AIDS-related pneumonia

- Treats urinary tract infections, chancroid, cystitis, toxoplasmosis, otitis media (ear infection – mostly in children), cloroquine-resistant malaria, and can be used to treat chlamydia

 ## Known Contraindications and/or Interactions

- Sulfa drugs shouldn't be taken with Trizivir, Amantadine, anticoagulants, Sulfonylureas, Metformin, Methotrexate, Zidovudine, Metronidazole, Ritonavir, Warfarin, Antiarrythmics, Clarithromycin, Cotrimoxazole, Ondansetron, Ziprazidone, or Zolmitriptan unless advised by a doctor

- The following drugs may become less effective if taken with sulfas: birth control pills, Cyclosporine (transplant patients), live thyroid vaccines, and even penicillins

- This class of drugs shouldn't be used near the time of the baby's birth (within three months of due date) and it is probably best not to use them altogether

- People with liver or kidney problems should be monitored closely when using this drug, as the dosage of the drugs depends very strongly on the state of their health

 ## Common Side Effects

- Allergic reactions can occur and be either mild or severe

- Urine may be brownish, but this is of no danger

- The emergence of other infections

 ## Occasional/Long-Term Side Effects

- Headache, trouble balancing, dizziness, myopia, gastrointestinal distress, very severe allergy of the heart, skin, liver or lungs, symptoms from bone marrow depletion, fatigue, fever, weakness, bleeding, and bruising abnormally, hypoglycemia, hallucination, or seizures, pancreatitis, blood clotting problems, methemoglobinemia

- Long term use may result in liver or kidney damage, excessive excretion of vitamin C or the development of a goiter

 ## Toxicity/Adverse Reaction (Contact your doctor)

- Signs of overdose: Dizziness, headache, stomach upset, stomach cramps, toxic fever leading to jaundice, coma, or kidney failure

General Advice and Precautions

- Cannot be used to treat streptococcal infections of group A type

- Never stop taking an antibiotic just because you feel better. The doctor will describe to you the whole course of antibiotic treatment. You must continue the medication in the specified amount for the specified time to kill all the bacteria

- It is not recommended to take Echinacea, Mistletoe herb, Marshmallow Root, Licorice, Oak Bark or St. John's Wort

- Cranberry juice is recommended for its ability to prevent urinary infections. General increased fluid intake is also recommended

- Alcohol may cause undesired reactions with this drug, even when consumed in small doses

- Be cautious of overexposure to sunlight when taking sulfa drugs

Sumatriptan

Brand Names: Imitrex

 ## Used For

- Migraines, cluster headaches

 ## Known Contraindications and/or Interactions

- Do not take this drug if you have had an allergic reaction to it in the past, you have ischemic heart disease, peripheral vascular disease, a seizure disorder, uncontrolled hypertension; or if you have taken a ergot-based medication in the last 24 hours or MAO inhibitor within the last two weeks

- Not for basilar of hemiplegic migraine

- Do not use this drug if you are pregnant or breast-feeding

- Consult your physician before taking if you have high blood pressure or high cholesterol, chest pain,

R̞ Let your doctor know if you have difficulty swallowing large or even small pills. A liquid form may be a better choice for you, if it is available.

Always shake up your liquid medication to make sure the components are equally mixed, in case any separation may have occurred that could affect the amount of medication you're getting.

heart disease, irregular heartbeats, if you smoke, if you are over 40, if you have liver/kidney disease, or Raynaud's phenomenon

- Discuss any other migraine medications you've tried with your doctor.

- You must understand clearly how to perform a subcutaneous injection. Intravenous use is dangerous, so you must be able to master this procedure

- Drug interactions may occur with Citalopram, preparations containing Ergotamine, Mmethysergide, Fluoxetine, Flivoxamine, MAO Inhibitors, other "triptan" drugs, Paroxetine, Sertraline, Sibutramine, Venlafaxine

 ## Common Side Effects

- Thirst, with increased urination, altered sense of taste, vision changes, temporary blood pressure changes

 ## Occasional/Long-Term Side Effects

- No long-term side effects reported

 ## Toxicity/Adverse Reaction (Contact your doctor)

- Mild adverse reaction: Rash, itching, dizziness, confusion, tight feeling in chest, diarrhea, joint pain

- Serious adverse reaction: Anaphylaxis, dysphasia, fainting, seizure, changes in heart rate, rhythm, heart attack, difficulty breathing, kidney stones

- Signs of overdose: No human data available; effects seen in animal testing include tremers, convulsions, shallow breathing, cyanosis, ataxia, paralysis

 ## General Advice and Precautions

- Herbs and minerals: Avoid St. John's Wort, Ma Huang, Guarana, Kola, Ginseng. If you are allergic to plants in the aster family (e.g., Ragweed), you may be allergic to Echinacea, Chamomile, and Feverfew

- Note that missing meals, or eating food containing MSG or chocolate may trigger migraines

- This drug may cause drowsiness. Avoid driving or operating machinery until you know how it affects you

- Store this drug at room temperature, but not over 86 degrees F.

- Do not use if past expiry date

Tetracycline Antibiotic Family

Other Form: Doxycycline, Tetracycline

Brand Names: Doxycycline: Adoxia, Apo-Doxy, Atridox, Doryx, Doxy Caps, Doxychel, Doxycin, Doxy-Lemmon, Novo-Doxylin, Periostat, Vibramycin, Vibra-Tabs, Monodox, Achromycin, Acrocidin, Actisite, Apo-Tetra, Aureomycin, Bristacycline, Contimycin, Cyclinex, Cyclopar, Lemtrex, Medicycline, Mysteclin-F [CD], Neo-Tetrine, Nor-Tet, Novo-Tetra, Nu-Tetra, Panmycin, Retet, Robitet, SK-Tetracycline: Sumycin, Teline, Tetra-C, Tetracap, Tetra-Con, Tetracyn, Tetralan, Tetram, Tetrex-F, Tropicycline

 ## Used For

- Treatment of some acne forms over long-term use

- Treats gum disease (Actisite) in tetracycline form and in doxycycline form (Periostat)

- Gonorrhea and Syphilis treatment

- Tetracycline is the prime choice for treating cholera

- Assists in the prevention of malaria

- Doxycycline treats anthrax, plague, Brucellosis, cholera

 ## Known Contraindications and/or Interactions

- May cause problems or toxicity in people with compromised or diseased livers or kidneys

- Not to be taken while pregnant or breast-feeding

- Malnutrition may require a dose increase

- May increase effects of Cyclosporine, Lithium, Digoxin, Anticoagulants like Warfarin, and may decrease effects of birth control pills, and penicillins. Additional adverse effects may be noticed if taken with Furosemide, Methoxyflurane, Anesthesia, Theophylline, Antacids, Pepto-Bismol, Calcium supplements, cholesterol-lowering drugs, Carbamazepine, Colestipol, Phenobarbital, Phenytoin, Fosphenytoin, Quinapril, Rifampin, Sucralfate, Iron, Zinc, and Magnesium

⚠ Common Side Effects

- Additional infections caused by antibiotic resistance causing itching at infection site

- Metallic taste in mouth

- Children under eight may experience tooth discoloration

Occasional/Long-Term Side Effects

- Mild to severe allergic reactions, loss of appetite, irritation of mouth, cramping in stomach, skin problems, jaundice from hepatitis, pancreatitis, colitis, black tongue, inability for blood to clot, low Potassium, intracranial pressure (headache), blood cell disorders, and decreased male fertility are all possible to rare in occurrence

- Long-term use may lead to superinfections (infections from antibiotic resistance), liver and kidney problems, or bone marrow depression or impairment

 ## Toxicity/Adverse Reaction (Contact your doctor)

- Stomach distress resulting in nausea, vomiting, diarrhea, and heart burn

 ## General Advice and Precautions

- It is important to refrain from consuming dairy products like cheese, yogurt, milk, ice cream, iron-enriched or supplemented foods or products, and meat for two hours before and after taking the medication

- Alcohol can be affected by some forms of Tetracycline and Doxycycline

- Calcium, Zinc, and iron can make this medication less effective

- There is no data on how Echinacea or Mistletoe interact with tetracyclines

- Photosensitivity can occur, especially with use of St. John's Wort

- Drugs should be stopped before surgery requiring major anesthesia. Speak to your doctor before discontinuing use of any antibiotic

Thiazide Diuretics Family

Includes: Bendroflumethiazide, Chlorothiazide, Chlorthalidone, Hydrochlorothiazide, Hydroflumethiazide, Metolazone, Trichlormethiazide

Brand Names: Bendroflumethiazide: Naturetin

Chlorothiazide: Aldochlor [CD], Diachlor, Diupres [CD], Diurigen, Diuril, SK-Chlorothiazide, Supres [CD]

Chlorthalidone: Apo-Chlorthalidone, Combipres [CD], Demi-Regroton [CD], Hygroton, Hylidone, Novothalidone, Regroton [CD], Tenoretic [CD], Thalitone, Uridon

Hydrochlorothiazide: Atacand HCT [CD], Aldactazide [CD], Aldoril, Apo-Amilzide, Apo-Hydro, Apo-Methazide [CD], Apo-Triazide [CD], Apresazide [CD], Apresoline-Esidrix [CD], Avalide

[CD], Capozide [CD], Co-Betaloc [CD], Diaqua, Diuchlor H, Diazide [CD], Esidrex, Ezide, H.H.R., H-H-R, HydroDiuril, Hydromal, Hydro-Par, Hydropres, Hydroserpine [CD] , Hydro-T, Hydro-Z-50, Hyzaar [CD], Inderide [CD], Ismelin-Esidrex [CD], Lopressor HCT, Maxzide [CD], M Dopazide [CD], Microzide, Mictrin, Moduret [CD], Moduretic [CD], Natrimax, Neo-Codema, Normozide [CD], Novo-Doparil [CD], Novo-Hydrazide, Novo-Spirozine [CD], Novo-Triamzide [CD], Oretic, Oreticyl [CD], PMS Dopazide [CD], Prinzide [CD], Ser-Ap-Es [CD], Serpasil-Esidrex [CD], SK-Hydrochlorothiazide, Thiuretic, Timolide [CD], Trandate HCT [CD], Unipres [CD], Uniretic [CD], Urozide, Vaseretic [CD], Viskazide [CD] , Zestoretic [CD], Ziac [CD], Zide
Hydroflumethiazide: Diucardin, Saluron
Methyclothiazide: Aquatensen, Duretic, Enduron
Metolazone: Diulo, Microx, Mykrox, Zaroxolyn
Trichlormethiazide: Diurese, Marazide II, Metahydrin, Naqua, Naquival [CD]

 ## Used For

- This class of diuretics are primarily used to boost the effectiveness of other antihypertensives

- Lowering mild blood pressure

- These are often the first choice for treatment of hypertension in elderly people, as opposed to beta-blockers and may be even more effective in reducing left ventricular size than ACE inhibitors

 ## Known Contraindications and/or Interactions

- People with liver or kidney problems should be cautious with use of these drugs

- These drugs may negatively interact with Lithium, oral anticoagulants like Warfarin, antibiotic drugs taken orally like Sulfonylureas, Allopurinol, Amphotericin, Calcium, Carbamazepine, Cortisone, Cyclophosphamides, Digoxin, Digitoxin, Methotrexate, NSAIDs, Probenecid, Cholestyramine, Colestipol

- These drugs should not be used during pregnancy (unless under emergency circumstances) or breast-feeding

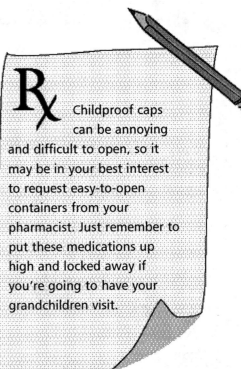

R̨ Childproof caps can be annoying and difficult to open, so it may be in your best interest to request easy-to-open containers from your pharmacist. Just remember to put these medications up high and locked away if you're going to have your grandchildren visit.

Common Side Effects

- Feeling lightheaded upon standing up from a drop in blood pressure, blood sugar or uric acid increases, low of Potassium, Zinc or Magnesium

 ## Occasional/Long-Term Side Effects

- Some forms have been found to cause impotence or loss of libido, allergic reactions, gout, fever, sore throat, unusual bleeding patterns, headache, dizziness, gastrointestinal distress, or inflammation of the pancreas

- If taking these drugs has resulted in a simultaneous loss of Magnesium and Potassium in blood over a long period of time, this could contribute to the risk of sudden death from cardiac complications

 ## Toxicity/Adverse Reaction (Contact your doctor)

- Signs of overdose: Dry mouth, muscle cramping, feeling thirsty, neausea, vomiting, feeling too tired to move, drowsiness, which may lead to coma

 ## General Advice and Precautions

- When taking thiazide diuretics, you may need to eat Potassium-rich foods and avoid alcohol

- The dose of other antihypertensives may need to be decreased if you also use these drugs

- Herbs that increase blood pressure, like Ginseng and Ginko, Hawthorn, Saw Palmetto, Mate Guarana, Eleuthero Root, and Licorice should be avoided

- Talk to your doctor before taking Garlic or Calcium supplements, which may cause hypotension

- Magnesium, Zinc, Potassium may need to be supplements if levels become low

- St. John's Wort is also ill advised since it will increase the already present effects of photosensitivity

- Excessive heat and/or exercise may also be dangerous due to an increased loss of water and salt from sweating

- Do not stop drugs suddenly as withdrawl symptoms may occur resulting in drastic fluid retention

Thiazolidinedione Family

Brand Names: Actos, Avandamet, Avandia, Rosiglitazone, Pioglitazone

 Used For

- Antidiabetic

- Controlling blood sugar

- Decreased risk of long-term complications of diabetes

 Known Contraindications and/or Interactions

- Drugs with known interactions include beta-blockers, Cholestyramine, corticosteroids, thiazide diuretics, birth control pills, protease inhibitors, azole antifungals, Carbamazepine, Sulfonylureas

- Children and infants should not take this drug

- Should be used with caution if over 65 years of age

- Do not take if you have Type I diabetes

- Do not use if you have liver disease

- Inform your doctor if you are pregnant or trying to conceive or breast-feeding

- Do not take if you have kidney damage

- Do not use if you have anemia

 Common Side Effects

- Abnormally low blood sugar (hypoglycemia)

- Fluid retention

 Occasional/Long-Term Side Effects

- Increased or enabling of fertility

- Edema (fluid retention)

- Effect of cholesterol

Toxicity/Adverse Reaction (Contact your doctor)

- Headache, weight gain, edema, diarrhea, allergic reaction

- Congestive heart failure, swelling in legs or ankles, shortness of breath

- Muscle aches

 General Advice and Precautions

- Herbs and minerals to avoid include St. John's Wort, Aloe, Fenugreek, Bitter Melon, Ginger, Garlic, Ginseng, Licorice, Nettle, Yohimbe, Echinacea, Psyllium seed or husk, Red Sage, Prickly Pear, Guar Gum

- Large doses of alcohol not recommended

- Follow diet prescribed by your doctor

- Regulate your dose to prevent hypoglycemia/learn how to treat hypoglycemia

- Talk to your doctor before changing dosing schedule or stopping medication

Timolol

Brand Names: Apo-Timolol, Apo-Timop, Betimol, Blocadren, Cosopt [CD], Dom-Timolol, Novo-Timolol, Timolide [CD], Timoptic, Xalacom

 Used For

- Treatment of effort-induced angina, high blood pressure and some heart rhythm problems

- Treatment of chronic open-angle glaucoma, detached retinas

- Prevention of repeat heart attack events

- Migraines

 Known Contraindications and/or Interactions

- You should not use this drug if you are allergic to this medication or Latanoprost or Dorzolamide; if you have asthma, bradycardia, overt heart failure, second or third degree AV block, or are in cardiogenic shock

- Consult your physician if you have congestive heart failure, diabetes, hypothyroidism, contact lenses or macular edema (re-vision treatments), are allergic to Sulfonamide, or have a history of diabetes or hypothyroidism

- Drug should be avoided by pregnant and breast-feeding women

- Drug interactions may occur with other antihypertensive drugs, Amiodarone, Lidocaine, Reserpine, Verapamil, Theophyllines, Clonidine, Epinephrine, Insulin, Methyldopa, oral hypoglycemic medications, Quinidine, Venlafaxine, Pilocarpine, Thimerosal, Chlorpromazine, Fluoxetine, Fluvoxamine, Methimazole, Propylthiouracil, Ritonavir, Ileuton, antacids, barbiturates, Indomethacin, Rifabutin, Rifampin

 ## Common Side Effects

- Lethargy, fatigue, cold hands and feet, reduced heart rate, dizziness when upright

 ## Occasional/Long-Term Side Effects

- Reduced sex drive in men, erectile dysfunction

- May promote heart failure in patients with advanced heart disease

 ## Toxicity/Adverse Reaction (Contact your doctor)

- Mild adverse reaction: Rash, hair loss, headache, dizziness, hallucinations, vivid dreams, nausea, diarrhea, vomiting, joint/muscle pain, tingling

- Serious adverse reaction: Laryngospasm, behavior changes, hallucinations, depression, chest pain, shortness of breath, asthma attack (in people with asthma), intermittant claudication

- Signs of overdose: Slow pulse, low blood pressure, fainting, clammy skin, heart failure, coma, convulsions

 ## General Advice and Precautions

- Herbs and minerals: Avoid Ginseng, Guarana, Hawthorn, Saw Palmetto, Ma Huang, Goldenseal, Yohimbe, Licorice. Calcium and Garlic may help lower blood pressure. Cut back on salt while on this medication

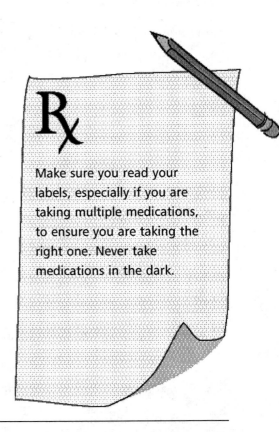

Make sure you read your labels, especially if you are taking multiple medications, to ensure you are taking the right one. Never take medications in the dark.

- Do not skip or double doses

- Do not stop this drug suddenly; discontinuing drug should take place under doctor's supervision

- Carry a card in your wallet that says you take this medication

- Consult your doctor before using a nasal spray while on beta blocker medication

- Avoid heavy exercise

- This drug may make you more susceptible to hot and cold; exercise caution

Valproic Acid

Brand Names: Alti-Valproic, Apo-Divalproex, Apo-Valproic, Atemperator, Depa, Depakene, Depakote (divalproex sodium), Deproic, Dom-Divalproex, Epival, Myproic, Novo-Divalproex, Novo-valproic, Nu-Valproic, Rhoproic, Valproic

 Used For

- Treatment of seizures, migraines, mania

 Known Contraindications and/or Interactions

- Do not take this drug if you have had an allergic reaction to it in the past, have liver disease, have a bleeding disorder.

- Do not take if you are pregnant or breast-feeding

- Consult your doctor before taking this drug if you have a history of liver disease, pancreatitis, bleeding disorder, or are taking anticoagulants, other anticonvulsants, antidepressants – both tricyclic and MAO Type A Inhibitors

- Drug interactions may occur with anticoagulants, antidepressants, benzodiazepines, Nimodipine, Phenobarbital, Phenytoin, Forphenytoin, Zidovudine, Acyclovir, Antacids, antiplatelet drugs, Aspirin, Carbamazepine, Cholestyramine, Clonazepam, Cyclosporine, Erythromycin, Felbamate, Fluoxetine, Isoniazid, Rifampin, Ritonavir

 Common Side Effects

- Fatigue, lethargy, drop in blood pressure upon standing

Occasional/Long-Term Side Effects

- Bone marrow depression

- May suppress sex drive

- May reduce effectiveness of oral contraceptives

 ## Toxicity/Adverse Reaction (Contact your doctor)

- Mild adverse reaction: Rash, headache, dizziness, confusion, tremor, slurred speech, nausea, indigestion, stomach pain, diarrhea, weight gain, bedwetting at night, temporary hair loss

- Serious adverse reaction: Psychosis, hallucinations, drug-induced hepatitis, increased blood-glucose levels, drug-induced pancreatitis, porphyria, hypothyroidism, pressure in the head, coordination problems

- Signs of overdose: Increased weakness, sleepiness, confusion – progressing to coma

 ## General Advice and Precautions

- Herbs and minerals: Avoid Kola, Guarana, Ma Huang, Valerian, Kava Kava, Eucalyptus, St. John's Wort. Note that Evening Primrose Oil and a contaminant that turns up in some Ginkgo preparations can increase seizure risk.

- Talk to your doctor about supplementing with Carnitine, Selenium, and Zinc

- Take capsules whole to prevent irritation. Do not put the syrup in carbonated drinks

- Avoid alcohol and Aspirin while on this medication

- This medication can make you drowsy. Avoid driving and operating machinery until you're aware of what effect the drug has on you

- Learn the symptoms of pancreatitis, so that you'll recognize them if they start

- Antihistamine medications will increase drowsiness effects

- Drug may cause photosensitivity

- Do not stop this drug suddenly – could result in rolling seizures. Discontinue gradually, under your doctor's supervision

Venlafaxine

Brand Names: Effexor

 ## Known Contraindications and/or Interactions

- Do not take this drug if you have taken an MAO Type A Inhibitor in the last 14 days, or if you take disulfiram oral solution

- Consult your physican before taking if you have a history of heart attack, high blood pressure, hyperlipidemia, seizures, suicidal tendencies, sleep disorders, mania

- Drug should be avoided by women who are pregnant or breast-feeding

- Drug interactions may occur with beta-blockers, Calcium channel blockers, Clarithromycin, Cimetidine, Cotrimoxazole, Dextromethorphan (the "DM" in some cough medications), Dofetilide, MAO Type A Inhibitors, Ondansetron, Quinidine, Ritonavir, Paroxetine, Sibutramine, Tramadol, Tricyclic antidepressants, triptans, Warfarin, Ziprazidone, Zolpidem

 ## Common Side Effects

- Headache, fatigue, dry mouth, constipation, weight loss

 ## Occasional/Long-Term Side Effects

- No long-term side-effects reported

- Rare cases of sexual dysfunction

 ## Toxicity/Adverse Reaction (Contact your doctor)

- Mild adverse reaction: Allergic reaction, anxiety, dizziness, disrupted sleep, blurred vision, palpitations, weight loss, nausea, vomiting

- Serious adverse reaction: Increased blood pressure, mania, allergic reaction, seizure

- Signs of overdose: Nausea, vomiting, seizure

 ## General Advice and Precautions

- Herbs and minerals: Avoid St. John's Wort, Ginkgo, Ma Huang, Yohimbe, Indian Snakeroot, Valerian, and Kava Kava.

- Restrict intake of grapefruit juice

- May cause drowsiness. Avoid driving, operating machinery, and drinking alcohol until you know how this drug affects you

- Do not suddenly stop taking this medication. Discontinue gradually, under a doctor's supervision

- Caution: Notwithstanding treatment, some people suffering depression develop suicidal tendencies. If you or someone you know display signs of suicidal thinking, contact your doctor immediately

Verapamil

Brand Names: Alti-verapamil, Apo-Verap, Calan, Chronovera, Covera-HS, Isoptin, Novo-Veramil, Nu-Verap, Tarka [CD], Verelan

 ## Used For

- Treatment of angina, rapid heart rate, tachycardia, hypertension

 ## Known Contraindications and/or Interactions

- Do not use this drug if you have had an allergic reaction to it in the past; if you have low blood pressure, liver disease, sick sinus syndrome, ventricular tachycardia, atrial fibrillation, or if you have a second or third-degree heart block

- Consult your doctor about any other prescription medicine you use; if you have had an adverse reaction to a Calcium channel blocker in the past; if you have recently had a heart attack or stroke; if you have aortic stenosis, poor circulation, liver or kidney problems, if the left side of your heart is weak, or if you have a history of heart rhythm disorders, angina, or congestive heart failure

- Avoid this drug if you are pregnant or breast-feeding

- Drug interactions may occur with Buspirone, Carbamazepine, Digitoxin, Digoxin, Lovastatin, Simvastatin, neuromuscular blocking agents, Sirolimus, Tacrolimus, Tretinoin, tricyclic antidepressants, Vincristine, Amiodarone, Aspirin, beta-blockers, Calcium supplements, Cilostazol, Colesevelam, Cyclosporine, Dantrolene, Dofetilide, Disopyramide, Flecainide, Lithium; Class I, IA, or III antiarrhythmics; Midazolam, NSAIDs, oral hypoglycemics, Phenytoin, Fosphenytoin,

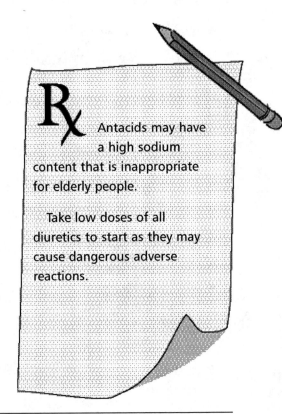
Antacids may have a high sodium content that is inappropriate for elderly people.

Take low doses of all diuretics to start as they may cause dangerous adverse reactions.

Prazosin, Quinidine, Ritampin, Ritonavir, Sulfinpyrazone, Terazosin, Theophylline, Warfarin, Cimetidine, Clarithromycin, Quinupristin/Dalfopristin

 ## Common Side Effects

- Low blood pressure, fluid retention (may cause swollen feet or ankles)

- Impotence

 ## Occasional/Long-Term Side Effects

- No long-term side effects reported

 ## Toxicity/Adverse Reaction (Contact your doctor)

- Mild adverse reaction: Rash, hives, flushing, headache, dizziness, fatigues; nausea, stomach problems, gum growth, cold hands and feet, cough, joint pain

- Serious adverse reaction: Severe rash; changes to heart rate or rhythm, heart attack; drug-induced liver damage; lung problems, low blood pressure, low blood sugar

- Signs of overdose: Feeling hot, sweating, light-headed, irritable, racing pulse, low blood pressure, loss of consciousness

 ## General Advice and Precautions

- Herbs and minerals: Avoid Ginseng, Guarana, Hawthorn, Saw Palmetto, Ma Huang, Goldenseal, Yohimbe, Licorice, St. John's Wort, Eleuthero Root, Ephedra, Indian Snakeroot. Calcium can reduce blood pressure, but may interact with this drug; consult your doctor. Garlic can lower blood pressure

- Do not take this drug with grapefruit juice

- Advise all your healthcare providers that you are taking this drug. Carry a card in your wallet saying you are on this drug.

- This drug may cause dizziness. Avoid driving or operating machinery until you know how it affects you

- This drug may cause photosensitivity. Guard against excessive exposure to sunlight

- The effects of this drug may increase in a hot environment. Watch for feelings of light-headedness or weakness

- Do not stop this drug suddenly. Discontinue gradually under your doctor's supervision

Warfarin

Brand Names: Athrombin-K, Carfin, Coumadin, Sofarin, Warnerin

 Used For

- Blood clots, including for prevention of stroke or recurrence of heart attack

 Known Contraindications and/or Interactions

- Do not take this drug if you have had an allergic reaction to it in the past; if you have a peptic ulcer, ulcerative colitis, arterial aneurysm, malignant hypertension, low blood platelets, infective pericarditis or endocarditis, liver disease, esophageal varices, if you have recently had a stroke; if you've had a spinal tap

- Consult your doctor before taking regarding any other medications you take; if you have congestive heart failure, high blood pressure, diabetes, liver or kidney problems, if you have an internal catheter, if you have a history of a bleeding disorder, if you are due or general or dental surgery

- Do not take this drug if you are pregnant or breast-feeding

- IMPORTANT NOTE: Warfarin, a blood thinner, can interact with hundreds of medications – both prescription and over-the-counter. Before your doctor puts you on Warfarin, make sure you disclose all the medications you take, even if they seem trivial, so that he can ensure this medication is safe for you

 Common Side Effects

- Epidsodes of bleeding

 Occasional/Long-Term Side Effects

- Long-term effect: "Blue toe" syndrome

- It is possible to develop a resistance to Warfarin

!! **Toxicity/Adverse Reaction (Contact your doctor)**

- Mild adverse reaction: Rash, hives, hair loss, nausea, vomiting, diarrhea, cramps

- Serious adverse reaction: Drug fever, bleeding into skin/tissues, nosebleeds, bleeding in gastrointestinal tract, lungs, urinary tract or other

- Signs of overdose: External or internal bleeding

General Advice and Precautions

- Herbs and minerals: Do not take any herbal preparations in combination with Warfarin. Garlic may be problematic as well. Talk to your doctor

- Advise all healthcare providers that you take this drug. Carry a card in your wallet identifying that you take this medication

- Stay with the brand you're given

- Keep all appointments for regular testing

- Limit alcohol intake to a maximum of one drink daily

- It is safe to stop this drug suddenly if abnormal bleeding occurs, but consult a doctor first if possible. Otherwise, discontinue this medication gradually, under your doctor's supervision

Avoid the

Harmful Side Effects

of Today's Commonly Prescribed Drugs

WHAT YOU NEED TO KNOW ABOUT COMMON HERBAL SUPPLEMENTS AND VITAMINS

NOTES

Herbs

Aloe Vera

Overview

Aloe vera has been in continuous use since the days of ancient Egypt. It's mentioned in the Bible. It was carried by explorers on their ships. Aloe is one of the most common herbal cures of our time and is also used in shampoos and lotions. Many people grow aloe as an attractive houseplant and cut off a leaf when they need to use it.

Benefits

Aloe juice, taken orally, treats constipation. Powdered gel extract is taken orally to treat intestinal problems, including ulcers, diverticulitis, and inflammatory bowel disease.

The gel from the succulent aloe leaf is used to treat cuts, scrapes, and skin irritations, again, reducing pain and promoting healing. Research indicates aloe vera has antifungal, antibacterial, and antiviral properties.

Aloe is an effective treatment for psoriasis. One of the most recent studies found that over 80% of those who applied aloe to affected areas experienced substantial improvement (versus six percent improvement in the control group).

Topically, aloe is used to treat first degree burns (typically sunburns) and minor second degree burns. It reduces pain and inflammation and promotes healing. In one study, people who used aloe vera healed in an average of 12 days, whereas those who treated the affected areas by covering them in gauze required six days longer.

Considerations

Aloe vera has not been shown effective for treating deep wounds or promoting healing after surgery.

Do not take aloe vera juice if you are pregnant or breast feeding. Aloe should not be used as a long-term laxative. Don't take it in conjunction with other laxatives. Use caution with other supplements or drugs that might lower blood sugar levels.

Side Effects

While there are rare cases of people allergic to aloe vera (evidenced by skin reactions – itching, rash, swelling), topical aloe vera is considered very safe. Taken orally as aloe vera juice, the only problems reported are due to a poorly processed product. If you experience cramps, stop taking the juice immediately. After your stomach returns to normal, buy a fresh supply of juice.

Dosage

Topically, apply about three to four times a day. Orally, take half a cup of liquid gel extract or two pills after a meal.

Black Cohosh

Overview

Also known as black snakeroot, black cohosh is a shrub-like plant native to North America. An attractive garden plant, the medicinal value comes from its roots and rhizomes.

Benefits

Antispasmodic for nerves and muscles. Historically used for "female problems" – menopausal concerns in particular – black cohosh may reduce pain and swelling associated with rheumatoid arthritis, sciatica, osteoarthritis, or inflammation resulting from joint and muscle injuries. It needs more research, but it may also help with sore throat and persistent cough associated with bronchitis and asthma.

Considerations

It should not be used by pregnant or breast-feeding women. It should also not be considered a substitute for hormone replacement therapy. Don't use it if you have a hormone-sensitive condition such as breast cancer or endometriosis. It has no known drug interactions, but don't use it with other drugs or supplements that might lower blood pressure. To be safe, don't use it with any herbs that might have estrogen-like effects.

Side Effects

May cause occasional stomach upset, headache, lowered heart rate and blood pressure. In a few studies, it has led to constipation, lack of bone mass, low blood pressure, nausea, vomiting, intestinal discomfort and even irregular heartbeat.

Dosage

Available in dried root, powdered extract, tablet, capsule, and tincture form. Its recommended dosage is 20 to 40 mg, twice a day, for up to six months.

Cayenne (Capsaicin)

Overview

Cayenne plants originated as perennials in Mexico and Central America, but today they are grown as annuals the world over. They grow to three feet in height, have white or yellow flowers, and bear fruit in the form of peppers, which are used as both food and medicine. Capsaicin is what makes hot peppers hot. When you eat them your brain receives a "pain message" and responds by releasing endorphins, your body's natural painkiller. This also results in a hot pepper "high."

Benefits

The capsaicin/endorphin interplay results in a product that can be used topically to treat arthritis pain, psoriasis, shingles, and other nerve pain syndromes. These actions are well-documented. It's also used orally as a digestive aid.

Considerations

Some people are sensitive to capsaicin and will react with skin irritations. Test on a small area before general use. Wash your hands thoroughly after applying, and take extra precautions to ensure the cream never comes in contact with the eyes, nose, or mouth. Do not take in conjunction with the asthma drug therophylline. Cayenne might reduce the effectiveness of some drugs: ACE Inhibitors, antacids, anticoagulants, and H2-blockers.

Side Effects

A burning sensation on the skin when you apply capsaicin is normal. Continue using regularly and it should stop within one week. Avoid contact with the eyes. It is possibly unsafe to use it for a long-term basis as an oral supplement. Taken orally, it can cause upset stomach and sweating.

Dosage

Capsaicin creams are sold over-the-counter; follow package directions. Orally, unless you enjoy the taste of hot peppers, you can take one or two capsules up to three times daily.

Chamomile

Overview

The medicinal Chamomile is the German or Hungarian variety, different from the typical Roman or English Chamomile. The dried flower is the part that gets used. Chamomile also has a long history of cosmetic use: for example, a strong brew of Chamomile tea allowed to cool and poured over your hair after washing (don't rinse out) will lighten hair color when it's allowed to dry in the sun.

Benefits

This anti-inflammatory speeds healing of minor injuries and rashes. It also soothes indigestion, reduces stress, and helps you relax. It is sometimes used as a treatment for ulcers, insomnia, colds, and bronchitis. The active ingredients are flavonoids and essential oils.

Considerations

Chamomile is so safe it's accepted for use by children and pregnant or breast-feeding women. You should avoid contact with your eyes. However, it's recommended you not take it in conjunction with Warfarin, heparin, or Trental because Chamomile might increase their blood-thinning effects. It also may increase the drowsiness caused by some drugs.

Side Effects

None indicated among non-allergic people at recommended doses. Some people who have allergies to the daisy family may experience adverse reactions. Eating large quantities of flowers may result in vomiting.

Dosage

Topical ointments contain up to 10% Chamomile. The product is also sold as bath salts and powders For internal use, purchase a commercial brand of Chamomile tea and follow the manufacturer's directions, or steep two to three teaspoons of dried Chamomile flowers in a cup of boiling water for 10 minutes. One teaspoon of dried flowers equals one gram of drug. The recommended dose of Chamomile is 10 to 15 grams.

Cranberry

Overview

This high vitamin C and anti-oxidant rich fruit is grown in the U.S. and has been used in the past to fight scurvy. The bright red berries traditionally found alongside turkey dinner are great all year round. The plant is a close relative of the blueberry.

Benefits

The anti-adhesive and bacteria-blocking action of cranberries make them ideal in preventing urinary tract and bladder infections. Cranberry juice is a well-known defense against these frustrating infections. In the case of sexually active women with recurring UTI's, this potent juice may be able to reduce reoccurrences by as much as 50%. The berries seem to be equally effective in either juice or tablet form. It is also famed to help prevent kidney stones, to keep blood toxin-free, and to prevent gum disease.

Considerations

Cranberry juice and tablets seem to be safe for pregnant and breast-feeding women. Don't replace antibiotic treatment with cranberry juice, but rather take it after you finish your treatment to avoid a recurrence. People with a history of kidney stones should consult their doctor before taking cranberry tablets as it has not been well studied. By stimulating the kidneys, cranberry may reduce the effectiveness of any drugs you are taking (i.e. antidepressants, painkillers, alkaline drugs).

Side Effects

None have been recorded.

Dosage

Drink 300 to 400 ml of cranberry extract, or take a 400 mg tablet – all twice a day. If you prefer juice, you can drink eight to 16 ounces a day for effectiveness.

Echinacea

Overview

Echinacea is one of the most popular over-the-counter herbs, the botanical names are *Echinacea purpurea, E. angustifolia,* and *E. pallida.* The plant is native to the Great Plains and southern United States; cultivated both there and in Europe. It is a purple "coneflower."

Benefits

Echinacea is the primary respiratory remedy in Germany for mild infections. The herb is an immune booster, and can either stave off or treat infections such as the flu. Powdered root of the plant can be used (alone or in combination with other herbs) to treat external open wounds. It may also help celiac disease, diverticulitis, chronic fatigue syndrome, bronchitis, ear infections, laryngitis, and cystitis.

Considerations

It loses effectiveness if taken year-round. Some herbalists recommend taking echinacea for two to three weeks, then resting for a week or two. Experts in Germany recommend not exceeding eight straight weeks of treatment. People with autoimmune deficiencies should seek a doctor's opinion before self-treating with echinacea. Also, people taking chemotherapy drugs, cisplatin, Cyclophosphamide, Docetaxel, Fluorouracil, Methotrexate, Paclitaxel should speak to a doctor to understand drug interactions. Echinacea may decrease the effectiveness of econazole.

Side Effects

People with allergy to plants in the daisy family should avoid echinacea. The herb might cause increased urination and minor gastrointestinal symptoms, but they are very uncommon.

Dosage

It's best to start taking the herb right at the beginning of your cold, when symptoms are mild to stave off full infection. Take a three to four ml dose of tincture, or a 300 mg tablet three times a day. You can actually take this in double dose, or even every two hours on the first signs of infection, then reduce dose. Echinacea juice can be taken at two to three milliliters, three times a day.

Evening Primrose

Overview

 A native of North America, this herb yields just leaves in its first year and yellow flowers with seeds in its second year. The second year is key, because it's the small reddish seeds that elicit the oil and thus the plant's medicinal effects. The oil is 60 to 80% linoleic acid, and eight to 15% gammalinolenic acid (GLA). The latter is one of the omega-6 fatty acids, and is used by the body to fight inflammation. Other than these, it contains a host of phytochemicals and nutrients.

Benefits

 It is often used to help relieve the effects of eczema: the skin itchiness, flaking, and inflammation. It's also taken for premenstrual syndrome. Its anti-inflammatory effects have made it useful in the treatment of rheumatoid arthritis as well. Some experts suggest taking evening primrose oil for a month or so to treat skin inflammation rather than starting a course of steroid medication. It helps to reduce hypertension and aids in weight loss.

Considerations

 This oil should not be used during pregnancy. Evening primrose oil promotes estrogen production, thus women who have breast cancer diagnosed as related to estrogen levels, should avoid or limit their intake. Those with a history of seizures or seizure disorders shouldn't take the oil. If taking blood pressure medications, check with a doctor first.

Side Effects

 There is little evidence of side effects or health problems with this herb, when taken at recommended levels. Very high doses can lead to nausea, upset stomach, seizures, and headache.

Dosage

 It's mainly taken in pill form. Look at the ingredients and choose the type with at minimum 40 mg of GLA per 500 mg of evening primrose oil. Daily dosage is about two to three grams of oil. But up to 360 mg of GLA may be needed if you are aiming to treat arthritis and very bad eczema, and researchers often use three to six grams of oil a day to achieve this level. Alternatively, you can take one teaspoon. of the plant with one cup of water.

Garlic

Overview

In the U.S. about 250 million pounds of Garlic is used in cooking every year. The smelly herb is part of the onion, chives, and leek family. Everyone knows what it looks like, but what they may not is that it's been used for medicinal purposes for thousands of years. "Allicin" is the central compound, and is widely thought to be the source of Garlic's health benefits. When you crush or cut cloves, it releases allicin. Another compound, "ajoene," appears responsible for reducing blood clots. It is easily one of the most studied herbs.

Benefits

This is what Garlic can do: reduce LDL cholesterol while boosting the "good" HDL cholesterol. This can take two to four months to show. It can also help lower triglycerides and blood pressure. This can take anywhere from one to six months. Garlic can help with circulation and enhance fibrinolysis, the process of removing blood clots. Germany has approved it as a dietary approach to managing cholesterol and ensuring the arteries stay clean. Garlic fights infections (external and internal). May help coughs (and other lung/throat infections), asthma, fevers, fungal infections, ear and sinus infections, and gastric upsets.

Considerations

Contraindictions have been seen in patients taking anticoagulants, hypoglycemic drugs, those with allergies, and pregnant women. It can increase the anti-inflammatory actions of Aspirin and interact with Warfarin. Due to its antihypertensive actions, it can increase the potency of drugs taken for hypertension, but if taken with diuretics it can actually result in hypertension or diuresis. People with gastrointestinal irritation should use caution.

Side Effects

Mainly the odor. Ew! It can cause occasional heartburn and gastrointestinal problems, or increase the body's number of white blood cells. May cause eruptions on the skin. Excessive amounts can lead to bleeding problems. Mostly, however, Garlic is very safe.

Dosage

Cooking Garlic will reduce its effectiveness by eliminating certain compounds. Either eat Garlic cloves, anywhere from one to five cloves a day, or you can take about four grams of minced Garlic a day. Try enteric-coated pills for the best results, as they preserve these active compounds. Pills are also odorless, and you need about 4,000 mg a day.

Ginkgo Biloba

Overview

One of the most thoroughly researched herbs; from the leaf of the Ginkgo tree. The tree, notably, is the oldest species in the world that survived the Ice Age. In traditional Chinese medicine, the seeds are used in asthma and other respiratory conditions.

Benefits

Ginkgo stimulates circulation, particularly in the brain. May help heart disease, angina, stroke, clogged arteries, depression, dementia, Alzheimer's disease, Raynaud's disease, Parkinson's disease, tinnitus. It is known to improve cognitive function and memory in all ages, especially the elderly. It is known to possibly help with impaired circulation in the legs. Ginkgo is reported to improve sexual function in both men and women. (Note: may take one to three months to see results.)

Considerations

Do not take Ginkgo if you are on blood thinning agents (anticoagulants) such as Warfarin or heparin, Aspirin, or non-steroidal anti-inflammatory drugs, or antidepressant drugs such as phenelzine sulfate or tranylcypromine. Do not take more than 240 mg of concentrated extract per day. Depressed patients should avoid combining St. John's Wort with Ginkgo. Don't use it if you have bleeding disorders, diabetes, epilepsy, or are undergoing surgery within two weeks.

Side Effects

There are rarely any side effects to Ginkgo. In studies, adverse effects included headaches, dizziness, and allergic skin reactions. There is a bit of concern that the herb can invoke seizures – those at risk of them should avoid Ginkgo.

Dosage

Ginkgo comes in many forms, including capsules, tablets, and extracts. The standard dose is 120 mg per day (up to 160 mg), split into three 40 mg doses. Look for an extract at least 24% "Ginkgo flavone glycosides" and six percent "terpene lactones."

Ginseng

Overview

From the root of one of three different plants, *Panax quinquefolius* (American Ginseng), *P. Ginseng* (Asian Ginseng), and *Eleutherococcus senticosus* (Siberian Ginseng). It serves as an "adaptogen," that helps boost the body's energy.

Benefits

Ginseng boosts energy and mood, and although it hasn't been completely proven, this could be a great herb for people with stressful lives. It is said to fight cancer, fibromyalgia, chronic fatigue syndrome, heart disease, impotence, stress, muscle soreness, low immunity, and depression. May improve stamina, and brain function.

Considerations

Do not take Ginseng if you have ischemic or vascular heart disease, thyroid disease, diabetes, or migraine. Consult your doctor first if you have a heart condition, high blood pressure, or an anxiety disorder. Theoretically, it could disrupt any antipsychotic or immunosuppressant drugs being taken.

Side Effects

May cause insomnia, nervousness or headaches. Mostly, it is very safe. Research continues in this area. Some believe there is a greater risk of hypertension if prolonged use of Ginseng is combined with daily caffeine intake. Cut down on coffee if taking this herb.

Dosage

A typical dose is one to two grams daily of raw Ginseng root or 100 to 200 mg of standardized extracts. (Commercial strengths vary; follow manufacturer's instructions). Note: Quality of products available varies; seek out a trusted supplier.

Green Tea

Overview

Only in the past decade, or so have scientists really started to look at the health benefits of green tea, an ancient drink. The preparation and harvesting is what makes all the difference. The unfermented form becomes green tea, which is becoming quite a popular social beverage as well as a medicinal one. It is chalked full of polyphenols, which have a slew of medicinal properties.

Benefits

This herb helps prevent and treat atherosclerosis, high cholesterol, tooth decay, and leukoplakia. It also is thought to have some cancer-preventative benefits as well, and might help hepatitis, osteoporosis, and atherosclerosis. It has great antioxidant and polyphenol content and is a good general health booster.

Considerations

This tea may also block iron absorption, so if you suffer from a deficiency, you may want to avoid green tea unless advised by your physician. It may create adverse effects with people taking any MAO inhibitors or Warfarin.

Side Effects

While green tea contains half as much caffeine as coffee, it can still create nervousness and insomnia in high doses so it's best not to drink it before bedtime. It may have averse effects if you take contraceptives, antipsychotic drugs, Clozaril, and quinolones, but these are all theoretical.

Dosage

It is suspected that strong, bitter concoctions of tea are needed for the best effects, but it isn't certain how much is necessary for benefits to be reaped. It is suggested to be between three and 10 cups a day of one teaspoon dried green tea leaves to one cup of hot water, steeped only three minutes. This should provide you with 240 to 320 mg of polyphenols, which are the active medicinal ingredients in the tea. There are also pills whose typical dosage is 100 to 150 mg three times a day, but they are not as well documented as the tea.

Hawthorn

Overview

This tree, native to Europe, springs white blossoms and bright red berries in the summertime. Hawthorn is the source of many phytochemicals, which have health-promoting properties – including flavonoids, which hunt free radicals and reduce inflammation. They also give the berries the reddish-blue hue. Experts don't concur on which part of the plant is most beneficial to medicine, but the berries (fresh or dried), flowers, and leaves have all been alluded to.

Benefits

Hawthorn is believed to alleviate congestive heart failure in the early stages. It may improve blood circulation, increase the strength of heart muscles, and help reduce blood pressure by widening or "dilating" the blood vessels. It appears able to help patients with angina or heart failure, reduce blood pressure while increasing their capacity to exercise. It may also strengthen collagen, which makes up arteries and blood vessels. Essentially, any time heart muscle has deteriorated, Hawthorn may help. It can't reverse damage, but it can strengthen the heart and help with it vital function.

Considerations

The plant is a very safe herb, even over prolonged periods of time. It is of course never meant to be a substitute for medical intervention in the case of heart problems, but can complement a doctor's guidelines. This herb will not take action right away; it's been known to take six weeks before improvements are noticeable. Use caution if taking Calcium channel blockers, any central nervous system depressants, nitrates, or Lanoxin.

Side Effects

Some adverse reactions include fatigue, sweating, rash on the hands, nausea, and stomach upsets. Slightly worse effects can include headache, palpitations, dizziness, vertigo, nosebleeds, insomnia, and circulatory problems.

Dosage

The herb is sold in dried form in pills, fluid extract, solid extract, or tinctures. The most you should ever take is 900 mg a day, but doses can range as small as 160 mg a day. You don't take it all at once either, but rather two or three times a day to reach that number. It can also be used to make tea: drop a teaspoon into about a cup of boiled water for 15 minutes. Strain and drink. Alternatively, add one teaspoon of crushed Hawthorn berries to a half-cup of cold water. Let stand overnight, then boil it in the morning, strain, and drink a teaspoon at a time. Take capsules with food or a tincture about 15 minutes before a meal.

Licorice (Glycyrrhiza glabra)

Overview

Licorice is a shrub that has been used medicinally for centuries. It has also been heavily researched and studied. The key therapeutic element of Licorice is glycyrrhizin, which is found in the rhizome (part of the root structure). Licorice also contains flavonoids and phytoestrogens that may be significant. In addition to its medicinal properties, Licorice is often added to medications for its taste.

Benefits

Licorice is an anti-inflammatory. The evidence suggests it might help relieve peptic ulcers and hepatitis. It may help soothes coughs and asthma as well as boost the immune system. Also, it is thought to relieve chronic fatigue syndrome and fibromyalgia, shingles, and eczema, and soothe PMS and menopausal symptoms in women.

Considerations

Take Licorice orally as a medicine under a doctor's supervision. Do not take Licorice if you are on medication for high blood pressure or diuretics, or taking steroids. Avoid this kind of Licorice if you have high blood pressure, glaucoma, diabetes, or diseases of the heart, liver, or kidneys. Women who are pregnant or breast-feeding should not use Licorice. Further, if you are taking Licorice as medicine, avoid eating Licorice candies and other food products at the same time.

Side Effects

Licorice can raise blood pressure (while you are taking it). If you will be taking Licorice for four weeks or more, get tested. High or prolonged doses of Licorice can result in diverse side effects, including headache, swelling, stiffness, shortness of breath, upper abdominal pain, and lethargy.

Dosage

Licorice is sold in a range of formats, including wafer, tincture, tablet, lozenge, liquid, dried herb/tea, cream, and capsule. A quality product will be standardized to contain 22% glycyrrhizinic acid or glycyrrhizin. A typical dose of whole Licorice is five to 15 grams a day. But the actual dosage will depend on your condition. Consult a trained medical professional. Licorice cream can be applied twice a day to affected areas of eczema, psoriasis, or herpes.

Peppermint

Overview

Peppermint has a host of uses in the medicine world, much to do with its main ingredient, menthol. It is known as a soothing, numbing, calming agent. Commercially it's used in tea, toothpaste, gum, and other products because of these effects. The plant grows two feet tall and blooms in the height of summer sprouting small purple flower heads. It's found all over the world.

Benefits

Peppermint can soothe upset stomachs and aid digestion. For tension headaches, it can be applied to the head to reduce symptoms. It helps soothe and relieve itching and irritations on the skin – things such as hives and poison ivy. For the intestinal tract and the stomach, its calming effect relaxes muscles, helping the flow of bile. This means it may be effective for irritable bowel syndrome. It can help relieve indigestion, gas, and bloating too. Its decongestant effect produced by menthol can thin mucous and help with the common cold and flu. For sore throats and coughs, it can soothe and calm the area.

Considerations

Because it relaxes the sphincter muscle, it shouldn't be used by those who have been diagnosed with gastoesophageal reflux disease (it may worsen heartburn and indigestion). It's a good idea to avoid using peppermint on the skin if you are using other topical ointments for cancer.

Side Effects

Side effects are rare for the most part. If taking pills with peppermint oil, you may get skin rash or muscle tremors. The oil needs to be taken in small amounts – and always diluted or taken in capsule form, because it can cause (albeit rarely) slowed heart rate, cramping, diarrhea, and drowsiness.

Dosage

Peppermint tea is prepared from dried leaves of the plant. Such teas are widely available commercially. A tincture that contains one part peppermint oil and nine parts pure grain alcohol (ethanol) can be made and applied lightly to the forehead for headaches. Any creams should have between one percent and 16% menthol. Use cream no more than three times a day. For irritable bowel, stomach problems, or gallstones, take one to two "enteric-coated" pills three times a day (between meals). There should be 0.2 ml of oil per pill.

Psyllium

Overview

Psyllium is the main ingredient of such commercial laxatives as Metamucil. It is a potent source of fiber. The seeds are used in traditional medicine and the seed *husks* are used for constipation. It's sometimes referred to as "Ispaghula."

Benefits

Psyllium is a superior laxative because the gel inside psyllium seeds is not digested. Instead it swells up and provides lubrication when combined with water. It is highly effective for chronic constipation, simple constipation, relieving diarrhea, and hemorrhoids, and even abdominal pain. It might also help with weight loss, as eating psyllium makes you feel "full" and therefore stops you from overeating. What else? It may reduce cholesterol levels in patients who have mild to moderate hypercholesterolemia, ulcerative colitis, and hypertension.

Considerations

If you have been prescribed drugs to treat a condition, it might be wise to avoid psyllium because soluble fibers may hinder your body's ability to absorb drugs – these include antibiotics, antidiabetes drugs, carbamazepine, Digoxin, Lithium, Warfarin, and possibly *every drug that is taken orally*. Pregnant women, diabetics, and people with symptoms of an obstructed bowel should consult a doctor before taking psyllium.

Side Effects

Psyllium may cause temporary bloating and gas. To avoid this, increase your dose of psyllium slowly over a week's time. You must drink plenty of water, because psyllium absorbs it and thus can cause mild dehydration. Occasionally it can cause an allergic reaction – in this case, visit your doctor immediately.

Dosage

The typical dose of psyllium for constipation and diarrhea is one to three teaspoons of powder dissolved in water. For irritable bowel syndrome, gallstones, or hemorrhoids take only one teaspoon. These doses are all just once a day.

Vitamins

Beta-Carotene

This is actually a natural chemical, but we'll plunk it in here because of its relationship to vitamin A: the body can transform it. It is also similar to both vitamin E and C because it is an antioxidant. Beta-carotene is the best way to get vitamin A because your body only transforms it when it needs it. Best way to get this chemical is through such yellow and orange vegetables as carrots, yams, and squash, and such dark green veggies as spinach, broccoli, and green peppers. There's conflicting research here in terms of whether beta-carotene can help slow cataracts from forming, prevent macular degeneration (eyes), protect against cancer, and heart disease, boost immune function in HIV patients, protect against sunburn, and help fight Parkinson's disease, rheumatoid arthritis, and hypertension. There is no firm evidence it works in any of these.

Niacin (vitamin B-3)

This vitamin is either Niacin or nicotinic acid. Vitamin B-3 plays an active role in several important bodily functions, especially in maintaining healthy skin and a working gastrointestinal tract and nervous system. Most notably, Niacin metabolizes fats and when used medicinally it can lower the levels of LDL cholesterol while raising HDL levels. It can help widen blood vessels too, which means it's valuable as a circulatory aid. Although linked to the nervous system, it is not conclusive that Niacin can help with the treatment of mental disorders (although doctors have tried). You can find vitamin B-3 in fish, beef, pork, dairy, whole wheat, potatoes, corn, broccoli, carrots, and tomatoes. It can be lost if food is boiled, though. Niacin and Niacinamide are both available as supplements, mainly involved in lowering cholesterol.

Vitamin C

It's possible up to 40% of people in the U.S. don't take in enough vitamin C, an essential nutrient that fights illness and bacteria, helps maintain eyesight, and may aid asthmatics, hypertensive patients, and autistic people. It's a strong antioxidant that keeps you healthy and quickens your body's ability to shake off bacterial invasions, such as the common cold. Food sources go well beyond orange juice to red chili peppers, sweet peppers, parsley, broccoli, kale, cabbage, strawberries, watercress, and citrus fruits. Eating fresh will ensure you get the maximum effect.

Vitamin E

This vitamin is an antioxidant that roams around in the body's fat and oils to fight free radicals. It has shown some usefulness in treating pregnancy complications, side effects of antipyschotic drugs, boosting the body's immune system, improving fertility in men, slowing the progression of Alzheimer's, and even helping prevent cancer (particularly in the prostate). It may lead to blood-thinning problems if used in conjuction with a few herbs (notably Garlic and Ginkgo biloba). In food, you can find vitamin E in seeds, nuts, whole grains, and polyunsaturated vegetable oils. It's of course available in therapeutic doses.

Fish Oil/Omega-3 Fatty Acids

Fish oil is becoming a tremendously popular supplement, as it is full of vitamin D and omega-3 fatty acids, both needed by the body. Cod liver oil is the most common source of fish oil, but you can also try salmon, mackerel or halibut oils and all those from cold water fish (and they may be safer than cod). The therapeutic possibilities of fish oil are not small. For the heart and circulatory system, there's evidence it helps prevent heart disease, lower LDL cholesterol levels, and even helps treat hypertension. To a lesser-known degree, fish oil may help with all these conditions: rheumatoid arthritis, osteoporosis, menstrual pain, lupus, psoriasis, Raynaud's phenomenon, bipolar disorder. Very preliminary, but still notable evidence has found that is may help treat depression, kidney stones, chronic fatigue syndrome, allergies, gout, and migraines. Is it any wonder this supplement, which is safe, is gaining popularity? (*Flaxseed oil is another good source of omega-3.*)

NOTES

Avoid the

Harmful Side Effects

of Today's Commonly
Prescribed Drugs

BRAND-NAME
DRUG INDEX

NOTES

217 - See Aspirin
692 - See Aspirin

A

A&D w/Prednisolone - See Prednisolone
Accolate - See Anti-Leukotriene Family
Accuneb - See Albuterol
Accupril - See ACE Inhibitors
Accuretic - See ACE Inhibitors
ACE Inhibitors
Acebutolol
Acediur [CD] - See ACE Inhibitors
Acetic Acid
Acetylsalicylic Acid - See Aspirin
Aches-N-Pain - See Propionic Acid
Achromycin - See Tetracycline Antibiotic Family
Acrocidine - See Tetracycline Antibiotic Family
Actiprofen - See Propionic Acid
Actiq - See Fentanyl
Actisite - See Tetracycline Antibiotic Family
Activella - See Estrogens
Actron - See Propionic Acid
Acular - See Acetic Acid
Adalat - See Nifedipine
Adoxia - See Tetracycline Antibiotic Family
Advicor - See Extended Release Niacin/Lovastatin
Advil - See Propionic Acid
AeroBid - See Flunisolide
AeroBid-M - See Flunisolide
Aeroseb-Dex - See Dexamethasone
Aggrenox - See Aspirin
Airet - See Albuterol
Ak-Cide - See Prednisolone
Ak-Dex - See Dexamethasone
AK-Mycin - See Macrolide Antibiotic Family
Akne-Mycin - See Macrolide Antibiotic Family
Ak-Pred - See Prednisolone
Ak-Tate - See Prednisolone
Ak-Trol - See Dexamethasone
Albert Furosemide - See Furosemide
Albuterol
Aldactazide [CD] - See Thiazide Diuretics Family

Aldochlor [CD] - See Thiazide Diuretics Family
Aldoril - See Thiazide Diuretics Family
Aleve - See Propionic Acid
Alka-Seltzer - See Aspirin
Alora - See Estrogens
Altace - See ACE Inhibitors
Alti-Captopril - See ACE Inhibitors
Alti-Fluoxetine - See Fluoxetine
Alti-Morphine - See Morphine
Alti-Nadol - See Nadolol
Alti-Pindol - See Pindolol
Alti-Salbutamol - See Albuterol
Alti-Thyroxine - See Levothyroxine
Alti-Valproic - See Valproic Acid
Alzapam - See Lorazepam
Amantadine
Amersol - See Propionic Acid
A-Methapred - See Methylprednisolone
Amlodipine
Anacin - See Aspirin
Analgesic Pain Reliever - See Aspirin
Ancasal - See Aspirin
Angipec - See Isosorbide Dinitrate
Ansaid - See Propionic Acid
Antadine - See Amantadine
Anti-Alzheimer's Drug Family
Anti-Leukotriene Family
APC - See Aspirin
Apo-Acebutolol - See Acebutolol
Apo-Amilzide - See Thiazide Diuretics Family
APO-ASA - See Aspirin
Apo-Atenolol - See Atenolol
Apo-Beclomethasone-AQ - See Beclomethasone
Apo-Capto - See ACE Inhibitors
Apo-Cephalex - See Cephalosporin Antibiotic Family
Apo-Chlorthalidone - See Thiazide Diuretics Family
Apo-clonazepam - See Clonazepam
Apo-Clonidine - See Clonidine
Apo-Diazepam - See Diazepam
Apo-Diclo - See Acetic Acid
Apo-Divalproic - See Valproic Acid
Apo-Doxy - See Tetracycline Antibiotic Family

Apo-Erythro Base -
    See Macrolide Antibiotic Family
Apo-Fluoxetine - See Fluoxetine
Apo-Furosemide - See Furosemide
Apo-Hydro - See Thiazide Diuretics Family
Apo-Ibuprofen - See Propionic Acid
Apo-Indomethacin - See Acetic Acid
Apo-ISDN - See Isosorbide Dinitrate
Apo-Levocarb - See Levodopa
Apo-Lorazepam - See Lorazepam
Apo-Metformin - See Metformin
Apo-Methazide [CD] -
    See Thiazide Diuretics Family
Apo-Metoprolol - See Metoprolol
Apo-Nadol - See Nadolol
Apo-Nifed - See Nifedipine
Apo-Oflox -
    See Fluoroquinolone Antibiotic Family
Apo-Pindol - See Pindolol
Apo-Prednisone - See Prednisone
Apo-Propranolol - See Propranolol
Apo-Quinidine - See Quinidine
Apo-Sulfamethoxazole -
    See Sulfonamide Antibiotic Family
Apo-Sulfatrim [CD] -
    See Sulfonamide Antibiotic Family
Apo-Sulin - See Acetic Acid
Apo-Tetra - See Tetracycline Antibiotic Family
Apo-Timolol - See Timolol
Apo-Timop - See Timolol
Apo-Triazide [CD] - See Thiazide Diuretics Family
Apo-Valproic - See Valproic Acid
Apo-Verap - See Verapamil
Apresazide [CD] - See Thiazide Diuretics Family
Apresoline-Esidrix [CD] -
    See Thiazide Diuretics Family
Aquatensen - See Thiazide Diuretics Family
ARBs (Angiotensin II Receptor
    Antagonist Family)
Aricept - See Anti-Alzheimer's Drug Family
Armour Thyroid - See Levothyroxine
Arthritis Foundation Pain Reliever -
    See Propionic Acid
Arthritis Pain Formula - See Aspirin
Arthrotec - See Acetic Acid

ASA - See Aspirin
ASA Enseals - See Aspirin
Asasantine - See Aspirin
Ascriptin - See Aspirin
Aspergum - See Aspirin
Aspirin
Aspred-C - See Prednisone
Asprimox - See Aspirin
Astramorph - See Morphine
Astrin - See Aspirin
Atacand - See ARBs
Atacand HCT [CD] - See Thiazide Diuretics Family
Atemperator - See Valproic Acid
Atenolol
Athrombin-K - See Warfarin
Ativan - See Lorazepam
Atorvastatin
Atridox - See Tetracycline Antibiotic Family
Aureomycin - See Tetracycline Antibiotic Family
Avalide [CD] - See ARBs
Avalide [CD] - See Thiazide Diuretics Family
Avandamet - See Metformin
Avapro - See ARBs
Avelox - See Fluoroquinolone Antibiotic Family
Avinza - See Morphine
Axotol - See Aspirin
Azdone - See Aspirin
Azithromycin - See Macrolide Antibiotic Family
Azo Gantanol [CD] -
    See Sulfonamide Antibiotic Family
Azo Gantrisin -
    See Sulfonamide Antibiotic Family

B

Bactrim [CD] - See Sulfonamide Antibiotic Family
Baldex - See Dexamethasone
Bayer - See Aspirin
Bayer Select - See Propionic Acid
BC Powder - See Aspirin
Beclodisk - See Beclomethasone
Becloforte - See Beclomethasone

Beclomethasone

Beclovent - See Beclomethasone

Beclovent Rotacaps - See Beclomethasone

Beclovent Rotahaler - See Beclomethasone

Beconase AQ Nasal Spray - See Beclomethasone

Beconase Nasal Inhaler - See Beclomethasone

Benazepril - See ACE Inhibitors

Bendopa - See Levodopa

Bensylate - See Benztropine

*Benzamycin [CD] -
    See Macrolide Antibiotic Family*

Benztropine

Betachron - See Propranolol

Betaloc - See Metropolol

Betaxolol

*Bethaprim [CD] -
    See Sulfonamide Antibiotic Family*

Betimol - See Timolol

Betoptic - See Betaxolol

Betoptic-Pilo [CD] - See Betaxolol

Betoptic-S - See Betaxolol

Bextra - See COX II Inhibitor Family

Biaxin - See Macrolide Antibiotic Family

Biodopa - See Levodopa

Biquin Durules - See Quinidine

Blephamide - See Prednisolone

Blocadren - See Timolol

Bristacycline - See Tetracycline Antibiotic Family

Bronalide - See Flunisolide

Buffaprin - See Aspirin

Bufferin - See Aspirin

C

C2 Buffered - See Aspirin

Calan - See Verapamil

Cama Arthritis Pain Reliever - See Aspirin

Candesartan - See ARBs

Capoten - See ACE Inhibitors

Capotopril - See ACE Inhibitors

Capozide [CD] - See ACE Inhibitors

Capozide [CD] - See Thiazide Diuretics Family

Carbolith - See Lithium

Cardioprin - See Aspirin

Cardioquin - See Quinidine

Carfin - See Warfarin

Carisoprodol Compound - See Aspirin

Carteolol

Cartrol - See Carteolol

Carvedilol

Cataflam - See Acetic Acid

Catapres - See Clonidine

Ceclor - See Cephalosporin Antibiotic Family

Cedocard-SR - See Isosorbide Dinitrate

Cefaclor - See Cephalosporin Antibiotic Family

Cefadroxil - See Cephalosporin Antibiotic Family

Cefanex - See Cephalosporin Antibiotic Family

Cefixime - See Cephalosporin Antibiotic Family

Cefprozil - See Cephalosporin Antibiotic Family

Ceftin - See Cephalosporin Antibiotic Family

*Ceftriaxone -
    See Cephalosporin Antibiotic Family*

*Cefuroxime -
    See Cephalosporin Antibiotic Family*

Cefzil - See Cephalosporin Antibiotic Family

Celebrex - See COX II Inhibitor Family

Celecoxib - See COX II Inhibitor Family

Celexa - See Citalopram

*Cephalexin -
    See Cephalosporin Antibiotic Family*

Cephalosporin Antibiotic Family

Ceporex - See Cephalosporin Antibiotic Family

C.E.S. - See Estrogens

*Chibroxin -
    See Fluoroquinolone Antibiotic Family*

Chlorothiazide - See Thiazide Diuretics Family

Chlorotrianisene - See Estrogens

Chlorthalidone - See Thiazide Diuretics Family

Cin-Quin - See Quinidine

Cipro - See Fluoroquinolone Antibiotic Family

*Ciprofloxacin -
    See Fluoroquinolone Antibiotic Family*

Citalopram

Clarithromycin - See Macrolide Antibiotic Family

Climacteron - See Estrogens

Climara - See Estrogens

Climestrone - See Estrogens

Clinoril - See Acetic Acid

Clonazepam

Clonidine

CoAdvil - See Propionic Acid

Co-Betaloc [CD] - See Metropolol

Co-Betaloc [CD] - See Thiazide Diuretics Family

Codeine

Cogentin - See Benztropine

Cognex - See Anti-Alzheimer's Drug Family

Colesevelam

Coloxan - See Fluoroquinolone Antibiotic Family

Combipres [CD] - See Clonidine

Combipres [CD] - See Thiazide Diuretics Family

Combivent - See Albuterol

Comoxol [CD] -
   See Sulfonamide Antibiotic Family

Congest - See Estrogens

Conjugated estrogens - See Estrogens

Contimycin - See Tetracycline Antibiotic Family

Cope - See Aspirin

Coradur - See Isosorbide Dinitrate

Coreg - See Carvedilol

Corgard - See Nadolol

Coricidin - See Aspirin

Corobid - See Nitroglycerin

Coronex - See Isosorbide Dinitrate

Cortalone - See Prednisolone

Coryphen - See Aspirin

Coryphen-Codeine - See Aspirin

Corzide [CD] - See Nadolol

Cosopt [CD] - See Timolol

Cotrim [CD] - See Sulfonamide Antibiotic Family

Coumadin - See Warfarin

Covera-HS - See Verapamil

COX II Inhibitor Family

Cozaar - See ARBs

C-Solve 2 - See Macrolide Antibiotic Family

Cyclinex - See Tetracycline Antibiotic Family

Cyclopar - See Tetracycline Antibiotic Family

Cyclosporine

D

Dalalone - See Dexamethasone

Dalalone DP - See Dexamethasone

Dalalone LA - See Dexamethasone

Darvon Compound - See Aspirin

Daypro - See Propionic Acid

Decaderm - See Dexamethasone

Decadron - See Dexamethasone

Decadron dose pack - See Dexamethasone

Decadron Nasal Spray - See Dexamethasone

Decadron Phosphate Ophtalmic -
   See Dexamethasone

Decadron Phosphate Respihaler -
   See Dexamethasone

Decadron Phosphate Turbinaire -
   See Dexamethasone

Decadron w/Xylocaine - See Dexamethasone

Decadron-LA - See Dexamethasone

Decaject - See Dexamethasone

Decaject LA - See Dexamethasone

Decaspray - See Dexamethasone

Deenar - See Dexamethasone

Delestrogen - See Estrogens

Delta-Cortef - See Prednisolone

Deltasone - See Prednisone

Demi-Regroton [CD] -
   See Thiazide Diuretics Family

Deone-LA - See Dexamethasone

Depa - See Valproic Acid

Depakene - See Valproic Acid

Depakote (divalproex sodium) -
   See Valproic Acid

Depmedalone-40 - See Methylprednisolone

Depmedalone-80 - See Methylprednisolone

Depo-Estradiol - See Estrogens

DepoMedrol - See Methylprednisolone

Deponit - - See Nitroglycerin

Deronil - See Dexamethasone

Detensol - See Propranolol

Dex-4 - See Dexamethasone

Dexacen-4 - See Dexamethasone

Dexacen-LA-8 - See Dexamethasone

Dexacidin - See Dexamethasone

Dexacort - See Dexamethasone

Dexamethasone

Dexamethasone - See Dexamethasone

Dexasone - See Dexamethasone

Dexasone-LA - See Dexamethasone

Dexo-LA - See Dexamethasone

Dexon - See Dexamethasone

Dexone-4 - See Dexamethasone

Dexone-E - See Dexamethasone

Dexone-LA - See Dexamethasone

Dexsone - See Dexamethasone

Dexsone-E - See Dexamethasone

Dexsone-LA - See Dexamethasone

Dezone - See Dexamethasone

Diachlor - See Thiazide Diuretics Family

Diaqua - See Thiazide Diuretics Family

Diastat - See Diazepam

Diazemuls - See Diazepam

Diazepam

Diazide [CD] - See Thiazide Diuretics Family

Diclofenac - See Acetic Acid

Digitaline - See Digoxin

Digitek - See Digoxin

Digoxin

Dilatrate-SR - See Isosorbide Dinitrate

Dilatrend - See Carvedilol

Dimetapp - See Propionic Acid

Diovan - See ARBs

Diskhaler - See Albuterol

Diucardin - See Thiazide Diuretics Family

Diuchlor H - See Thiazide Diuretics Family

Diulo - See Thiazide Diuretics Family

Diupres [CD] - See Thiazide Diuretics Family

Diurese - See Thiazide Diuretics Family

Diurigen - See Thiazide Diuretics Family

Diuril - See Thiazide Diuretics Family

Dixarit - See Clonidine

Dizac - See Diazepam

Dologesic - See Propionic Acid

Dom-Divalproex - See Valproic Acid

Dom-Lorazepam - See Lorazepam

Dom-Metformin - See Metformin

Dom-Pindolol - See Pindolol

Dom-Timolol - See Timolol

Donepezil - See Anti-Alzheimer's Drug Family

Dopar - See Levodopa

Doryx - See Tetracycline Antibiotic Family

Doxy Caps - See Tetracycline Antibiotic Family

Doxychel - See Tetracycline Antibiotic Family

Doxcin - See Tetracycline Antibiotic Family

Doxycycline - See Tetracycline Antibiotic Family

Doxy-Lemmon -
    See Tetracycline Antibiotic Family

Dristan - See Aspirin

Dristan - See Propionic Acid -

Duapred - See Prednisolone

Duo-dezone - See Dexamethasone

Duraclon - See Clonidine

Duragesic - See Fentanyl

Duralith

Duramorph - See Morphine

Duraquin - See Quinidine

Duretic - See Thiazide Diuretics Family

Duricef - See Cephalosporin Antibiotic Family

DV - See Estrogens

E

E.E.S. - See Macrolide Antibiotic Family

Easprin - See Aspirin

Econopred Opththalmic - See Prednisolone

Ecotrin - See Aspirin

Effexor - See Venlafaxine

Elan - See Isosorbide Mononitrate

Elantan - See Isosorbide Mononitrate

Eltroxin - See Levothyroxine

Emgel - See Macrolide Antibiotic Family

Empirin - See Aspirin

E-Mycin - See Macrolide Antibiotic Family

Enalapril - See ACE Inhibitors

Endocet [CD] - See Oxycodone

Endodan [CD] - See Oxycodone

Enduron - See Thiazide Diuretics Family

Enpak Refill - See Methylprednisolone

E-Pam - See Diazepam

Epimorph - See Morphine

Epival - See Valproic Acid

Eprosartan - See ARBs

Erybid - See Macrolide Antibiotic Family

ERYC - See Macrolide Antibiotic Family

Erycette - See Macrolide Antibiotic Family

Eryderm - See Macrolide Antibiotic Family

Erygel - See Macrolide Antibiotic Family

Erymax - See Macrolide Antibiotic Family

EryPed - See Macrolide Antibiotic Family

Eryphar - See Macrolide Antibiotic Family

Ery-Tab - See Macrolide Antibiotic Family

Erythrocin - See Macrolide Antibiotic Family

Erythromid - See Macrolide Antibiotic Family

Erythromycin - See Macrolide Antibiotic Family

Escitalopram - See Citalopram

Esclim - See Estrogens

Esidrex - See Thiazide Diuretics Family

Eskalith - See Lithium

E-Solve 2 - See Macrolide Antibiotic Family

Esterified estrogens - See Estrogens

Estinyl - See Estrogens

Estradiol - See Estrogens

Estriol - See Estrogens

Estrogens

Estrone - See Estrogens

Estropipate - See Estrogens

Ethril - See Macrolide Antibiotic Family

Etodolac - See Acetic Acid

ETS-2% - See Macrolide Antibiotic Family

Eucardic - See Carvedilol

Euthroid - See Levothyroxine

Euthyrox - See Levothyroxine

Excedrin - See Aspirin

Excedrin IB - See Propionic Acid

Exelon - See Anti-Alzheimer's Drug Family

Extended Release Niacin/Lovastatin

Ezide - See Thiazide Diuretics Family

F

Femhrt - See Estrogens

Femogen - See Estrogens

Femogex - See Estrogens

Fenoprofen - See Propionic Acid

Fentanyl

Fernisolone-P - See Prednisolone

Fiorinal - See Aspirin

Floxin - See Fluoroquinolone Antibiotic Family

Flunisolide

Fluoroquinolone Antibiotic Family

Fluoxetine

Flurbiprofen - See Propionic Acid

Fluvastatin

Fluvoxamine

Fosinopril - See ACE Inhibitors

Froben - See Propionic Acid

Fumide MD - See Furosemide

Furocot - See Furosemide

Furomide MD - See Furosemide

Furose - See Furosemide

Furosemide

Furosemide-10 - See Furosemide

Furoside - See Furosemide

G

Galantamine - See Anti-Alzheimer's Drug Family

Gammacorten - See Dexamethasone

Gantanol - See Sulfonamide Antibiotic Family

Gatifloxacin -
     See Fluoroquinolone Antibiotic Family

Gen-Acebutolol - See Acebutolol

Genacote - See Aspirin

Gen-Fluoxetine - See Fluoxetine

Gen-Nabumetone - See Acetic Acid

Gen-Nifedipine - See Nifedipine

Genpril - See Propionic Acid

Genprin - See Aspirin

Glucophage - See Metformin

Glucovance - See Metformin

Glycon - See Metformin
Goody's Headache Powder - See Aspirin
Guildprofen - See Propionic Acid
Gynetone - See Estrogens
Gynodiol - See Estrogens
Gynogen LA - See Estrogens

H

H.H.R. - See Thiazide Diuretics Family
Halprin - See Aspirin
Haltran - See Propionic Acid
Hexadrol - See Dexamethasone
H-H-R - See Thiazide Diuretics Family
Humalog - See Insulin
Humulin - See Insulin
Hydelta-TBA - See Prednisolone
Hydrochlorothiazide -
    See Thiazide Diuretics Family
HydroDiuril - See Thiazide Diuretics Family
Hydroflumethiazide -
    See Thiazide Diuretics Family
Hydromal - See Thiazide Diuretics Family
Hydro-Par - See Thiazide Diuretics Family
Hydropres - See Thiazide Diuretics Family
Hydroserpine [CD] - See Thiazide Diuretics
    Family
Hydro-T - See Thiazide Diuretics Family
Hydro-Z-50 - See Thiazide Diuretics Family
Hygroton - See Thiazide Diuretics Family
Hylidone - See Thiazide Diuretics Family
Hyzaar [CD] - See ARBs
Hyzaar [CD] - See Thiazide Diuretics Family

I

Ibu - See Propionic Acid
Ibuprohm - See Propionic Acid
Iletin - See Insulin
Ilosone - See Macrolide Antibiotic Family
Ilotycin - See Macrolide Antibiotic Family
Imdur - See Isosorbide Mononitrate

Imitrex - See Sumatriptan
Indameth - See Acetic Acid
Inderal - See Propranolol
Inderide [CD] - See Propranolol
Inderide [CD] - See Thiazide Diuretics Family
Indocid - See Acetic Acid
Indomethacin - See Acetic Acid
Inflamase - See Prednisolone
Inflamase Forte - See Prednisolone
Infumorph - See Morphine
Initard - See Insulin
Innopran XL - See Propranolol
Innovar - See Fentanyl
Insulatard - See Insulin
Insulin
Insulin aspart - See Insulin
Insulin Human - See Insulin
Insulin-Toronto - See Insulin
Ipran - See Propranolol
Irbesartan - See ARBs
Ismelin-Esidrex [CD] -
    See Thiazide Diuretics Family
Ismo - See Isosorbide Mononitrate
Iso-BID - See Isosorbide Dinitrate
Isochron - See Isosorbide Dinitrate
Isonate - See Isosorbide Dinitrate
Isoptin - See Verapamil
Isopto Cetapred - See Prednisolone
Isordil - See Isosorbide Dinitrate
Isordil Tembids - See Isosorbide Dinitrate
Isordil Titradose - See Isosorbide Dinitrate
Isosorbide Dinitrate
Isosorbide Mononitrate
Isotrate Timecelles - See Isosorbide Dinitrate

K

Kadian - See Morphine
Keflet - See Cephalosporin Antibiotic Family
Keflex - See Cephalosporin Antibiotic Family
Keftab - See Cephalosporin Antibiotic Family
Kefurox - See Cephalosporin Antibiotic Family

Kerlone - See Betaxolol
Ketoprofen - See Propionic Acid
Ketorolac - See Acetic Acid
Key-Pred - See Prednisolone
Klonopin - See Clonazepam
Kydeltrasol - See Prednisolone

L

Lanoxicaps - See Digoxin
Lanoxin - See Digoxin
Lantus - See Insulin
Larodopa - See Levodopa
Lasaject - See Furosemide
Lasimide - See Furosemide
Lasix - See Furosemide
Lasix Special - See Furosemide
Lemtrex - See Tetracycline Antibiotic Family
Lente - See Insulin
Lente Iletin - See Insulin
Lescol - See Fluvastatin
Levaquin - See Fluoroquinolone Antibiotic
    Family
Levodopa
Levofloxacin -
    See Fluoroquinolone Antibiotic Family
Levo-T - See Levothyroxine
Levotabs - See Levothyroxine
Levothroid - See Levothyroxine
Levothyroxine
Levoxine - See Levothyroxine
Levoxyl - See Levothyroxine
Lexxel [CD] - See ACE Inhibitors
Lin-Fosinopril - See ACE Inhibitors
Lipitor - See Atorvastatin
Liquid Pred - See Prednisone
Lisinopril - See ACE Inhibitors
Liskonium - See Lithium
Lithane - See Lithium
Lithium
Lithizine - See Lithium
Lithobid - See Lithium
Lithonate - See Lithium

Lithotabs - See Lithium
Lo-Aqua - See Furosemide
Lodine - See Acetic Acid
Logimax [CD] - See Metropolol
Lomefloxacin -
    See Fluoroquinolone Antibiotic Family
Lopressor - See Metropolol
Lopressor HCT - See Thiazide Diuretics Family
Lorabid - See Cephalosporin Antibiotic Family
Loracarbef -
    See Cephalosporin Antibiotic Family
Loraz - See Lorazepam
Lorazepam
Lortab ASA - See Aspirin
Losartan - See ARBs
Lotensin - See ACE Inhibitors
Lotrel - See ACE Inhibitors
Lotrel [CD] - See Amlodipine
Lovastatin -
    See Extended Release Niacin/Lovastatin
L-Thyroxine - See Levothyroxine
Luramide - See Furosemide
Luvox - See Fluvoxamine

M

M Dopazide [CD] - See Thiazide Diuretics Family
M.O.S. - See Morphine
Macrolide Antibiotic Family
Marazide II - See Thiazide Diuretics Family
Marnal - See Aspirin
Mar-Pred 40 - See Methylprednisolone
Maxaquin -
    See Fluoroquinolone Antibiotic Family
Maxidex - See Dexamethasone
Maxzide [CD] - See Thiazide Diuretics Family
Measurin - See Aspirin
Med-Acebutolol - See Acebutolol
Med-Beclomethasone-AQ - See Beclomethasone
Med-clonazepam - See Clonazepam
Med-Fluoxetine - See Fluoxetine
Medicycline - See Tetracycline Antibiotic Family
Medipren - See Propionic Acid

Medi-Profen - See Propionic Acid

Medrol - See Methylprednisolone

Medrol Acne Lotion - See Methylprednisolone

Medrol Enpak - See Methylprednisolone

Medrol Veriderm Cream -
   See Methylprednisolone

Menest - See Estrogens

Menotab - See Estrogens

Menotab-M - See Estrogens

Menrium - See Estrogens

Meprolone - See Methylprednisolone

M-Eslon - See Morphine

Metaglip - See Metformin

Metahydrin - See Thiazide Diuretics Family

Metformin

Methyclothiazide - See Thiazide Diuretics Family

Methylprednisolone

Methysergide

Meticortelone - See Prednisolone

Meticorten - See Prednisone

Meti-Derm - See Prednisolone

Metimyd - See Prednisolone

Metolazone - See Thiazide Diuretics Family

Metoprolol

Metreton - See Prednisolone

Meval - See Diazepam

Micardis - See ARBs

Microx - See Thiazide Diuretics Family

Microzide - See Thiazide Diuretics Family

Mictrin - See Thiazide Diuretics Family

Midol - See Aspirin

Midol IB - See Propionic Acid

Milprem - See Estrogens

Minestrin - See Estrogens

Minims Prednisolone - See Prednisolone

Minitran Transdermal Delivery System -
   See Nitroglycerin

Mixtard - See Insulin

Moduret [CD] - See Thiazide Diuretics Family

Moduretic [CD] - See Thiazide Diuretics Family

Monitan - See Acebutolol

Monoket - See Isosorbide Mononitrate

Monopril - See ACE Inhibitors

Montelukast - See Anti-Leukotriene Family

Morphine

Morphitec - See Morphine

Motrin - See Propionic Acid

Moxifloxacin -
   See Fluoroquinolone Antibiotic Family

MS Contin - See Morphine

MS-IR - See Morphine

MS-Nabumetone - See Acetic Acid

Mydrapred - See Prednisolone

Mykrox - See Thiazide Diuretics Family

Mymethasone - See Dexamethasone

Myproic - See Valproic Acid

Myrosemide - See Furosemide

Mysteclin-F [CD] -
   See Tetracycline Antibiotic Family

N

Nabumetone - See Acetic Acid

Nadolol

Nalfon - See Propionic Acid

Naprelan - See Propionic Acid

Naprosyn - See Propionic Acid

Naproxen - See Propionic Acid

Naqua - See Thiazide Diuretics Family

Naquival [CD] - See Thiazide Diuretics Family

Nasalide - See Flunisolide

Nasarel - See Flunisolide

Natisedine - See Quinidine

Nativelle - See Digoxin

Natrimax - See Thiazide Diuretics Family

Naxen - See Propionic Acid

Neo-Codema - See Thiazide Diuretics Family

Neodecadron Eye-Ear - See Dexamethasone

Neodexair - See Dexamethasone

Neo-Medrol Acne Lotion -
   See Methylprednisolone

Neo-Medrol Veriderm - See Methylprednisolone

Neomycin-Dex - See Dexamethasone

Neo-Prox - See Propionic Acid

Neoral - See Cyclosporine

Neo-Tetrine - See Tetracycline Antibiotic Family

Niacin - See Extended Release Niacin/Lovastatin

Nicobid - See Extended Release
   Niacin/Lovastatin

Nifedipine

Niscort - See Prednisolone

Nitrek - See Nitroglycerin

Nitro Transdermal System - See Nitroglycerin

Nitro-Bid - See Nitroglycerin

Nitrocap TD - See Nitroglycerin

Nitrocine Timecaps - See Nitroglycerin

Nitrocine Transdermal - See Nitroglycerin

Nitrodisc - See Nitroglycerin

Nitro-Dur - See Nitroglycerin

Nitro-Dur II - See Nitroglycerin

Nitrogard - See Nitroglycerin

Nitrogard-SR - See Nitroglycerin

Nitroglycerin

Nitroglyn - See Nitroglycerin

Nitrol - See Nitroglycerin

Nitrol TSAR Kit - See Nitroglycerin

Nitrolin - See Nitroglycerin

Nitrolingual Spray - See Nitroglycerin

Nitrong - See Nitroglycerin

Nitrong SR - See Nitroglycerin

Nitroquick - See Nitroglycerin

Nitrospan - See Nitroglycerin

Nitrostabilin - See Nitroglycerin

Nitrostat - See Nitroglycerin

Nonsteroidal Anti-inflammatory Drugs -
   See Propionic Acid

Norfloxacin -
   See Fluoroquinolone Antibiotic Family

Norgesic - See Aspirin

Normozide [CD] - See Thiazide Diuretics Family

Noroxin - See Fluoroquinolone Antibiotic Family

Nor-Pred - See Prednisolone

Nor-Tet - See Tetracycline Antibiotic Family

Norvasc - See Amlodipine

Nova-Pred - See Prednisolone

Novasen - See Aspirin

Novoprednisolone - See Prednisolone

Novo-Clonidine - See Clonidine

Novo-Atenolol - See Atenolol

Novo-Betaxolol - See Betaxolol

Novo-Captopril - See ACE Inhibitors

Novo-clonazepam - See Clonazepam

Novo-Difenac - See Acetic Acid

NovoDigoxin - See Digoxin

Novo-Dipam - See Diazepam

Novo-Divalproex - See Valproic Acid

Novo-Doparil [CD] - See Thiazide Diuretics
   Family

Novo-Doxylin - See Tetracycline Antibiotic Family

Novo-Hydrazide - See Thiazide Diuretics Family

Novo-Lexin - See Cephalosporin Antibiotic
   Family

Novolin - See Insulin

Novolin-Lente - See Insulin

NovolinPen - See Insulin

Novolinset - See Insulin

NovoLog - See Insulin

Novo-Lorazepam - See Lorazepam

Novo-Metformin - See Metformin

Novo-methacin - See Acetic Acid

Novo-Metoprolol - See Metropolol

Novo-Nabumetone - See Acetic Acid

Novo-Nabumetone - See Acetic Acid

Novo-Nadolol - See Nadolol

Novo-Naprox - See Propionic Acid

Novo-Nifedin - See Nifedipine

Novo-Pindol - See Pindolol

Novo-Pranol - See Propranolol

Novoprednisone - See Prednisone

Novo-Profen - See Propionic Acid

Novo-Quinidin - See Quinidine

Novo-Rythro - See Macrolide Antibiotic Family

Novo-Salmol - See Albuterol

Novo-Semide - See Furosemide

Novo-Sorbide - See Isosorbide Dinitrate

Novosoxazole -
   See Sulfonamide Antibiotic Family

Novo-Spirozine [CD] -
   See Thiazide Diuretics Family

Novo-Sundac - See Acetic Acid

Novo-Tetra - See Tetracycline Antibiotic Family

Novothalidone - See Thiazide Diuretics Family

Novo-Timolol - See Timolol

Novo-Tolmetin - See Acetic Acid

Novo-Triamzide [CD] -

See Thiazide Diuretics Family

Novo-Trimel [CD] -
See Sulfonamide Antibiotic Family

Novo-valproic - See Valproic Acid

Novo-Veramil - See Verapamil

NPH - See Insulin

NSAIDs - See Propionic Acid

NTS Transdermal Patch - See Nitroglycerin

Nu-Atenolol - See Atenolol

Nu-Beclomethasone - See Beclomethasone

Nu-Capto - See ACE Inhibitors

Nu-Cephalex -
See Cephalosporin Antibiotic Family

Nu-Clonidine - See Clonidine

Nu-Cotrimox - See Sulfonamide Antibiotic Family

Nu-Diclo - See Acetic Acid

Nu-Flunisolide - See Flunisolide

Nu-Indo - See Acetic Acid

Nu-Loraz - See Lorazepam

Nu-Metop - See Metropolol

Nu-Nabumetone - See Acetic Acid

Nu-Nabumetone - See Acetic Acid

Nu-Naprox - See Propionic Acid

Nu-Nifed - See Nifedipine

Nu-Pindol - See Pindolol

Nupren - See Propionic Acid

Nu-Tetra - See Tetracycline Antibiotic Family

Nu-Valproic - See Valproic Acid

Nu-Verap - See Verapamil

O

Occupress - See Carteolol

Ocufen - See Propionic Acid

Ocuflox - See Fluoroquinolone Antibiotic Family

Ocupress - See Carteolol

Ocu-Trol - See Dexamethasone

Ofloxacin -
See Fluoroquinolone Antibiotic Family

OMS Concentrate - See Morphine

Opium Tincture - See Morphine

Opththo-Tate - See Prednisolone

Optimyd - See Prednisolone

Oradexon - See Dexamethasone

Oralet - See Fentanyl

Oramorph - See Morphine

Orasone - See Prednisone

Oretic - See Thiazide Diuretics Family

Oreticyl [CD] - See Thiazide Diuretics Family

Orphenadrine - See Aspirin

Orudis - See Propionic Acid

Oruvail - See Propionic Acid

Otobione - See Prednisolone

Oxaprozin - See Propionic Acid

Oxycocet [CD] - See Oxycodone

Oxycodan [CD] - See Oxycodone

Oxycodone

OxyContin - See Oxycodone

P

Panasol-S - See Prednisone

Panmycin - See Tetracycline Antibiotic Family

PAP w/Codeine - See Aspirin

Paracort - See Prednisone

Paregoric - See Morphine

Paroxetine

Paxil - See Paroxetine

PCE - See Macrolide Antibiotic Family

Pediaject - See Prednisolone

Pediamycin - See Macrolide Antibiotic Family

Pediapred - See Prednisolone

PediaProfen - See Propionic Acid

Pediazole [CD] - See Macrolide Antibiotic Family

Pediazole [CD] -
See Sulfonamide Antibiotic Family

Percocet [CD] - See Oxycodone

Percodan [CD] - See Oxycodone

Phenaphen - See Aspirin

Pindolol

PMS Dopazide [CD] -
See Thiazide Diuretics Family

PMS Propranolol - See Propranolol

PMS-Atenolol - See Atenolol

PMS-Dexamethasone - See Dexamethasone

PMS-Erythromycin -

See Macrolide Antibiotic Family

PMS-Estradiol - See Estrogens

PMS-Loraz - See Lorazepam

PMS-Metformin - See Metformin

PMS-Salbutamol - See Albuterol

Polypred - See Prednisolone

Pred Forte - See Prednisolone

Pred Mild - See Prednisolone

Predcor - See Prednisolone

PreDep 40 - See Methylprednisolone

Pre-Dep 80 - See Methylprednisolone

Pred-G - See Prednisolone

Prednicen-M - See Prednisone

Prednisolone

Prednisone

Prednisone Intensol - See Prednisone

Prelone - See Prednisolone

Premarin - See Estrogens

Premphase - See Estrogens

Prempro (low-dose) - See Estrogens

Prevpac [CD] - See Macrolide Antibiotic Family

Prinivil - See ACE Inhibitors

Prinzide [CD] - See ACE Inhibitors

Prinzide [CD] - See Thiazide Diuretics Family

Procardia - See Nifedipine

Progynon Pellet - See Estrogens

Proloid - See Levothyroxine

Prolopa [CD] - See Levodopa

Propaderm - See Beclomethasone

Propaderm-C - See Beclomethasone

Propoxyphene Compound - See Aspirin

Propranolol

Propionic Acid

Proreg - See Carvedilol

Protamine - See Insulin

Protrin [CD] - See Sulfonamide Antibiotic Family

Proventil (HFA, Inhaler, Repetabs, Tablets) -
See Albuterol

Prozac - See Fluoxetine

PSP-IV - See Prednisolone

Q

Q-Pam - See Diazepam

Quinaglute Dura-Tabs - See Quinidine

Quinapril - See ACE Inhibitors

Quinate - See Quinidine

Quinatime - See Quinidine

Quinestrol - See Estrogens

Quinidex Extentabs - See Quinidine

Quinidine

Quinobarb - See Quinidine

Quinora - See Quinidine

Quin-Release - See Quinidine

Quixin - See Fluoroquinolone Antibiotic Family

QVAR - See Beclomethasone

R

Ramace - See ACE Inhibitors

Ramipril - See ACE Inhibitors

Ratio-Nadol - See Nadolol

Regroton [CD] - See Thiazide Diuretics Family

Regular Insulin - See Insulin

Regular Purified Pork Insulin - See Insulin

Reminyl - See Anti-Alzheimer's Drug Family

Retet - See Tetracycline Antibiotic Family

Rhinalar - See Flunisolide

Rhodis - See Propionic Acid

Rhoproic - See Valproic Acid

Rhotral - See Acebutolol

Rhoxal-clonazepam - See Clonazepam

Rhoxal-Nabumetone - See Acetic Acid

Riphen-10 - See Aspirin

Rival - See Diazepam

Riva-Metformin - See Metformin

Rivastigimine - See Anti-Alzheimer's Drug Family

Rivotril - See Clonazepam

RMS Uniserts - See Morphine

Robaxisal - See Aspirin

Robimycin - See Macrolide Antibiotic Family

Robitet - See Tetracycline Antibiotic Family

Rocephin - See Cephalosporin Antibiotic Family

Rofecoxib - See COX II Inhibitor Family

Ro-Semide - See Furosemide

Rotahaler - See Albuterol

Roubac [CD] - See Sulfonamide Antibiotic Family

Roxanol - See Morphine

Roxicet - See Oxycodone

Roxicodone - See Oxycodone

Roxilox - See Oxycodone

Roxipirin [CD] - See Oxycodone

Roxiprin - See Aspirin

Rufen - See Propionic Acid

S

Salbutamol - See Albuterol

Saluron - See Thiazide Diuretics Family

Sandimmune - See Cyclosporine

SangCya - See Cyclosporine

Sangstat - See Cyclosporine

Sans-Acne - See Macrolide Antibiotic Family

Sansert - See Methysergide

Sarafem - See Fluoxetine

Savacort - See Prednisolone

Sectral - See Acebutolol

Semilente - See Insulin

Septra [CD] - See Sulfonamide Antibiotic Family

Ser-Ap-Es [CD] - See Thiazide Diuretics Family

Serpasil-Esidrex [CD] -
    See Thiazide Diuretics Family

Sertraline

Sildenafil - See Sildenafil Citrate

Sildenafil Citrate

Sinemet [CD] - See Levodopa

Sinemet CR [CD] - See Levodopa

Singulair - See Anti-Leukotriene Family

SK-65 - See Aspirin

SK-Chlorothiazide - See Thiazide Diuretics Family

SK-Dexamethasone - See Dexamethasone

SK-Digoxin - See Digoxin

SK-Erythromycin -
    See Macrolide Antibiotic Family

SK-Furosemide - See Furosemide

SK-Hydrochlorothiazide -

*   See Thiazide Diuretics Family*

SK-Oxycodone - See Oxycodone

SK-Prednisone - See Prednisone

SK-Quinidine Sulfate - See Quinidine

SK-Soxazole - See Sulfonamide Antibiotic Family

SK-Tetracycline -
    See Tetracycline Antibiotic Family

Slo-Niacin - See Extended Release
    Niacin/Lovastatin

Sofarin - See Warfarin

Sofracort - See Dexamethasone

Solu-Medrol - See Methylprednisolone

Solurex - See Dexamethasone

Solurex-LA - See Dexamethasone

Soma - See Aspirin

Sorbitrate - See Isosorbide Dinitrate

Sorbitrate-SA - See Isosorbide Dinitrate

Sparfloxacin -
    See Fluoroquinolone Antibiotic Family

Spersadex - See Dexamethasone

Statex - See Morphine

Statican - See Macrolide Antibiotic Family

Sterane - See Prednisolone

Sterapred - See Prednisone

Sterapred-DS - See Prednisone

Stievamycin - See Macrolide Antibiotic Family

Sublimaze - See Fentanyl

Sulfalar - See Sulfonamide Antibiotic Family

Sulfamethoxazole -
    See Sulfonamide Antibiotic Family

Sulfatrim - See Sulfonamide Antibiotic Family

Sulfisoxazole - See Sulfonamide Antibiotic
    Family

Sulfonamide Antibiotic Family

Sulindac - See Acetic Acid

Sumatriptan

Sumycin - See Tetracycline Antibiotic Family

Supasa - See Aspirin

Superior Pain Medication - See Propionic Acid

Supeudol - See Oxycodone

Suprax - See Cephalosporin Antibiotic Family

Supreme Pain Medication - See Propionic Acid

Supres [CD] - See Thiazide Diuretics Family

Symadine - See Amantadine

Symmetrel - See Amantadine

Synalgos - See Aspirin

Syn-Captopril - See ACE Inhibitors

Synflex - See Propionic Acid

Syn-Nadol - See Nadolol

Syn-Pindolol - See Pindolol

Synthroid - See Levothyroxine

Synthrox - See Levothyroxine

Syroxine - See Levothyroxine

T

Tab-Profen - See Propionic Acid

TACE - See Estrogens

Tacrine - See Anti-Alzheimer's Drug Family

Talwin Compound - See Aspirin

Tarka [CD] - See Verapamil

TBA Pred - See Prednisolone

Tecnal Tablet - See Aspirin

Teline - See Tetracycline Antibiotic Family

Telmisartan - See ARBs

Tenoretic [CD] - See Atenolol

Tenoretic [CD] - See Thiazide Diuretics Family

Tenormin - See Atenolol

Tequin - See Fluoroquinolone Antibiotic Family

Tetra-C - See Tetracycline Antibiotic Family

Tetracap - See Tetracycline Antibiotic Family

Tetra-Con - See Tetracycline Antibiotic Family

Tetracycline Antibiotic Family

Tetracyn - See Tetracycline Antibiotic Family

Tetralan - See Tetracycline Antibiotic Family

Tetram - See Tetracycline Antibiotic Family

Tetrex-F - See Tetracycline Antibiotic Family

Teveten - See ARBs

Thalitone - See Thiazide Diuretics Family

Thiuretic - See Thiazide Diuretics Family

Thiazide Diuretics Family

Thyroid USP - See Levothyroxine

Thyrolar - See Levothyroxine

Timolide [CD] - See Thiazide Diuretics Family

Timolide [CD] - See Timolol

Timolol

Timoptic - See Timolol

Tobradex - See Dexamethasone

Tolectin - See Acetic Acid

Tolectin 600 - See Acetic Acid

Tolectin DS - See Acetic Acid

Tolmetin - See Acetic Acid

Toprol - See Metropolol

T-Quil - See Diazepam

Trandate HCT [CD] -
*   See Thiazide Diuretics Family*

Transderm-Nitro - See Nitroglycerin

Trates S.R. - See Nitroglycerin

Triaphen-10 - See Aspirin

Trichlormethiazide -
*   See Thiazide Diuretics Family*

Tridil - See Nitroglycerin

Tropicycline - See Tetracycline Antibiotic Family

Trovafloxacin -
*   See Fluoroquinolone Antibiotic Family*

Trovan - See Fluoroquinolone Antibiotic Family

Trovan/Zithromax Compliance Pak -
*   See Fluoroquinolone Antibiotic Family*

T-stat - See Macrolide Antibiotic Family

Turbinaire - See Dexamethasone

Tylox [CD] - See Oxycodone

U

Ultracef - See Cephalosporin Antibiotic Family

Ultralente - See Insulin

Unipres [CD] - See Thiazide Diuretics Family

Uniretic [CD] - See Thiazide Diuretics Family

Unithroid - See Levothyroxine

Uridon - See Thiazide Diuretics Family

Uritol - See Furosemide

Uro Gantanol [CD] -
*   See Sulfonamide Antibiotic Family*

Uroplus - See Sulfonamide Antibiotic Family

Urozide - See Thiazide Diuretics Family

V

Vagila - See Sulfonamide Antibiotic Family

Vagitrol - See Sulfonamide Antibiotic Family

Valcaps - See Diazepam

Valdecoxib - See COX II Inhibitor Family

Valergen-10 - See Estrogens

Valium - See Diazepam

Valproic - See Valproic Acid

Valproic Acid

Valrelease - See Diazepam

Valsartan - See ARBs

Vancenase AQ Nasal Spray -
   See Beclomethasone

Vancenase Nasal Inhaler - See Beclomethasone

Vanceril - See Beclomethasone

Vanquish - See Aspirin

Vaseretic [CD] - See ACE Inhibitors

Vaseretic [CD] - See Thiazide Diuretics Family

Vasocidin - See Prednisolone

Vasotec - See ACE Inhibitors

Vazepam - See Diazepam

Velosulin - See Insulin

Venlafaxine

Ventodisk Rotacaps - See Albuterol

"Ventolin (HFA, Inhaler, Nebules, Rotacaps,
   Syrup, Tablets) - See Albuterol"

Verapamil

Verelan - See Verapamil

Verin - See Aspirin

Viagra - See Sildenafil Citrate

Vibramycin - See Tetracycline Antibiotic Family

Vibra-Tabs - See Tetracycline Antibiotic Family

Vioxx - See COX II Inhibitor Family

Viskazide [CD] - See Pindolol

Viskazide [CD] - See Thiazide Diuretics Family

Visken - See Pindolol

Vivelle - See Estrogens

Vivelle-Dot - See Estrogens

Vivol - See Diazepam

Volmax (Sustained Release Tablets,
   Timed-Release Tablets) - See Albuterol

Voltaren - See Acetic Acid

V-Throid - See Levothyroxine

W

Warfarin

Warnerin - See Warfarin

Welchol - See Colesevelam

Wesprin - See Aspirin

White Premarin - See Estrogens

Winpred - See Prednisone

Wyamycin - See Macrolide Antibiotic Family

X

Xalacom - See Timolol

Z

Zafirlukast - See Anti-Leukotriene Family

Zagam - See Fluoroquinolone Antibiotic Family

Zaroxolyn - See Thiazide Diuretics Family

Zendole - See Acetic Acid

Zestoretic [CD] - See ACE Inhibitors

Zestoretic [CD] - See Thiazide Diuretics Family

Zestril - See ACE Inhibitors

Zetran - See Diazepam

Ziac [CD] - See Thiazide Diuretics Family

Zide - See Thiazide Diuretics Family

Zileuton - See Anti-Leukotriene Family

Zinacef - See Cephalosporin Antibiotic Family

Zithromax - See Macrolide Antibiotic Family

Zoloft - See Sertraline

Zorprin - See Aspirin

Zyflo - See Anti-Leukotriene Family

NOTES

Avoid the
*Harmful
Side Effects*
of Today's Commonly
Prescribed Drugs

APPENDICES

NOTES

COMMON
MEDICATION
CATEGORIES

Acne and Skin Disorders

When oils produced under the surface of the skin cannot escape through hair follicles, what results is acne. It is a sebaceous gland disorder that can affect adults at any age. Along with topical and antibiotic solutions, there are more powerful drugs, such as Accutane/Isotretinoin and Soriatane/Acitretin, to combat this and other skin disorders.

Addiction

People who are addicted to alcohol or narcotics often experience psychological and physical effects of dependency and suffer extreme reactions upon withdrawal. Orlaa/Levomethadyl is an example of drugs that help addicts fight their addiction.

AIDS/HIV

The human immunodeficiency virus (HIV) causes the acquired immunodeficiency syndrome (AIDS), which attacks infection-fighting white blood cells. AIDS victims are susceptible to various infections. The disease can only be contracted though exposure to bodily fluids, including, but not limited to, blood and semen. Several drug therapies, such as Agenerase/Amprenavir, Norvir/Ritonavir, Serostim, T-Factor, Videx/Didanosine, Viramune/Nevirapine, Zerit/Stavudine and Ziagen/Abacavir Sulfate, slow the progress of the disease.

Allergies

Millions of Americans suffer from reactions to allergens in food, plants and animals. Most allergy sufferers experience mild bouts of sneezing and watery eyes, but some experience more severe attacks, going into the potentially dangerous state of anaphylactic shock. Chocolate may trigger severe stomach irritation if you are taking some of the more popularly prescribed histamine blockers. There are many, many drugs to prevent and treat allergy symptoms, including: Diphenhydramine (Benadryl); Chlorpheniramine (Chlor-Trimeton); Clarinex/Desloratadine; Claritin/Loratadine; Hismanal/Astemizole; and Seldane.

Alzheimer's or Dementia

The causes of Alzheimer's are not known, but the neurological disorder attacks brain cells, leading to slow and often unnoticed loss of memory and difficulty performing daily activities. Scientists suspect amyloid plaque build-ups in the brain lead to the degeneration. Drugs taken to suspend Alzheimer's and dementia include AN-1792 and Exelon/Rivastigmine.

Anemia

Anemia can result from excessive bleeding or iron and vitamin deficiencies that lead to a reduction of red blood cells or hemoglobin. If you are anemic, your blood lacks oxygen and you may feel tired or, in extreme cases, suffer a stroke or heart attack. Possible treatments include blood transfusion, iron and vitamin supplements, or drugs that stimulate the production of red blood cells, such as Procrit.

Artery Blockages

Patients whose blood clots too easily are candidates for stroke. Blood thinning drugs and anticoagulants act to prevent blood clots and blockages of arteries. Some of these drugs, like Aspirin, reduce the stickiness of blood platelets. Other anticoagulant drugs impede blood-clotting factors. These medications can lose effectiveness and/or encourage blood clots when combined with liver, certain cooking oils, or leafy greens. Common types of these drugs include Heparin, Abbokinase/Urokinase, Arixtra/Fondaparinux Sodium, Coumadin/Warfarin, Factor VIII/Antihemophilic Factor (AHF), Innohep/Tinzaparin, Sodium Lovenox/Enoxaparin Sodium, Plavix/Clopidogrel Bisulfate, and Refludan/Lepirudin.

Arthritis

Tens of millions of Americans are afflicted with arthritis of some type, experiencing painful and debilitation joint inflammation. There is an array of over-the-counter and prescription drugs available to alleviate this suffering, including: Arava/Leflunomide; Bextra/Valdecoxib; Celebrex/Celecoxib; Chondroitin; Enbrel/Etanercept; Kineret/Anakinra; Naproxen; Remicade/Infliximab; Ridaura/Auranofin; and Vioxx/Rofecoxib.

Asthma

The incidence of asthma in society is on the rise. Asthmatics suffer a narrowing and/or spasm of the airways in the lungs, which is caused by an acute sensitivity to air quality, dust, cold climate, etc. Attacks can be minor or life threatening. Therefore, the following types of emergency inhalers and drugs must be accessible to asthmatics in case of a sudden attack: Accolate/Zafirlukast; Advair Diskus; Flovent/Fluticasone; Proventil/Warrick's albuterol; Serevent/Salmeterol Xinafoate; Singulair/Montelukast; Terbutaline/Brethaire; Theophylline; and Vanceril.

Bacterial Infections

Bacterial infections require antibiotic drugs to fight them effectively. There are several classes of antibiotics to attack certain types of bacteria, including tetracycline, sulfonamides, quinolone, penicillin, and macrolides. Unfortunately, each of these is becoming increasingly ineffective due to over-prescription by doctors. Some popular antibiotics are: Avelox/Moxifloxacin Hydrochloride; Biaxin/Clarithromycin; Cipro/Ciprofloxacin; Cleocin/Clindamycin; Doxycycline; Erythromycin; Floxin/Ofloxacin; Gentamicin; Levaquin/Levofloxacin; Minocin/Minocycline Hydrochloride; Tequin/Gatifloxacin; Trimethoprim; Trovan/Trovafloxacin; Xigris/Drotrecogin Alfa; Zithromax/Azithromycin; and Zyvox/Linezolid.

Some antibiotics decrease the synthesis of vitamin K by the bacteria normally found in our intestines. Vitamin K is important for normal blood clotting.

Birth Control Pills

Taking these drugs with a diet already low in vitamin B6 or folate can lead to deficiencies in these important nutrients. Some popular brands are Alesse, Levlen, Norinyl, Ortho-Cyclen and Triphasil.

Blood Clots

Patients whose blood clots too easily are candidates for stroke. Blood thinning drugs and anticoagulants act to prevent blood clots and blockages of arteries. Some of these drugs, like Aspirin, reduce the stickiness of blood platelets. Other anticoagulant drugs impede blood-clotting factors. These medications can lose effectiveness and/or encourage blood clots when combined with liver, certain cooking oils, or leafy greens. Common types of these drugs include Heparin, Abbokinase/Urokinase, Arixtra/Fondaparinux Sodium, Coumadin/Warfarin, Factor VIII/Antihemophilic Factor (AHF), Innohep/Tinzaparin, Sodium Lovenox/Enoxaparin Sodium, Plavix/Clopidogrel Bisulfate and Refludan/Lepirudin.

Blood Transfusion

Recipients of organ transplantation or blood transfusions run the risk of their body rejecting the foreign tissue type. Immunosuppressant drugs help the body avoid rejection of the new organ by suppressing the immune system. Some of these lifesaving drugs are Rapamune/Sirolimus, SangCya & Neoral, Simulect/Basiliximab, and Zenapax/Daclizumab.

Cancer

Cancer is a condition that can strike any part of the body, causing cells to grow in an irregular fashion. A normal and healthy cell inflicted with cancer exhibits abnormal growth when a carcinogen (pesticide, tobacco, sunlight, etc.) alters its genetic material. People with poor immune systems are unable to destroy these cancerous cells, which then multiply and expand to other parts of the body, eventually requiring treatment. Treatments include surgical removal of the affected area, chemotherapy and radiation, depending on the stage of development. Some examples of specific drugs used during cancer treatments and recovery are: Aloe Therapy; Altretamine/Hexalen; Camptosar/Irinotecan Hydrochloride; Chemotherapy/Alkylating Agents; Cytosar-U/Cytarabine; Eloxatin/Oxaliplatin; GnRH-a Therapy; Herceptin/Trastuzumab; Hydrazine Sulfate; Lupron/Leuprolide; Neumega/Oprelvekin; Neupogen/Filgrastim; Nolvadex/Tamoxifen Citrate; Antineoplastic agents; Methotrexate; Platinol/Cisplatin; Proleukin/Aldesleukin; Radioactive Iodine (RAI); Taxol/Paclitaxel; Taxotere/Docetaxel; Trisenox/Arsenic Trioxide; and Xeloda/Capecitabine.

Common Cold

A variety of viruses can cause the common cold. In the winter, you will get influenza, and in the summer your cold is be caused by a rhinovirus. While there are no known remedies to prevent the common cold, there are several drugs that will offset the symptoms, including Aller Relief,

Chinese Herbal Remedy, Coricidin & Triple C, Cydec Drops, Hismanal/Astemizole, PPA/Phenylpropanolamine and Seldane.

Depression

One in 10 people you know will suffer severe depression at some time. Professional guidance and counseling from a medical expert can be coupled with the following drugs to help alleviate symptoms of depression and other emotional conditions: Ativan/Lorazepam; Clozaril/Clozapine; Droleptan; Effexor/Venlafaxine Hydrochloride; Geodon/Ziprasidone; Mellaril/Thioridazine Hydrochloride; Paxil/Paroxetine Hydrochloride; Prozac/Fluoxetine Hydrochloride; Remeron/Mirtazapine; Risperdal/Risperidone; Ritalin/Methylphenidate; Serentil/Mesoridazine; Seroquel/Quetiapine; Fumarate; Serzone/Nefazodone Hydrochloride; St. John's Wort/Hypericum Perforatum; Trilafon/Perphenazine; Wellbutrin/Bupropion Hydrochloride; Zoloft/Sertraline; Zyban/Bupropion Hydrochloride; and Zyprexa/Olanzapine.

The body creates compounds called monoamines, such as serotonin, dopamine or norepinephrine. Monoamine Oxidase (MAO) inhibitors decrease the body's use of these compounds. For instance, MAO that regulates serotonin is used to treat depression. While MAOs are quite effective, they can be dangerous if combined with the wrong foods, drugs, or supplements. For instance, when taken in combination with foods containing tyramine, the reaction can cause a dangerous rise in blood pressure, perhaps leading to death. Tyramine is a substance in some aged cheeses, beer, fermented soy products, Brewer's yeast, yeast extracts, Chianti wine, pickled herring, fava beans, etc. Pseudoephedrine is a stimulant drug in this category. Antidepressants in this family include Furazolidone/Furoxone, Isocarboxazid/Marplan, Phenelzine Sulfate/Nardil and Tranylcypromine Sulfate/Parnate.

Diabetes

Type I and Type II diabetes occur when the body fails to make Insulin, a hormone produced in the pancreas that regulates the body's blood sugar level. Some drugs for diabetics are: Actos/Pioglitazone Hydrochloride; Avandia/Rosiglitazone; Bicarbonate Glucophage/Metformin; and Rezulin/Troglitazone.

Dieting

Along with, or in place of, diet and exercise, Americans turn to diet drugs as a method of weight control. Many are unaware that these drugs can cause serious side effects, such as primary pulmonary hypertension, stroke or heart valve disorders. Drugs promoted as miracle weight loss agents include: Fen-Phen; Meridia/Sibutramine Hydrochloride; Pondimin; PPA/Phenylpropanolamine; and Redux.

Disease Vaccination

One of the greatest medical legacies of the 19th and 20th centuries, is the use of vaccines to prevent the occurrence of certain illnesses. Vaccines contain deactivated or partial components of the virus or bacteria, which act to ward off infection by triggering the body's natural defenses. There are approximately 25 vaccines available for preventing disease, including: Anthrax Vaccine; Hepatitis A Vaccine; Hepatitis B Vaccine; LYMErix/Lyme Disease Vaccine; Mumps-Measles-Rubella Vaccine; Polio Vaccine; Prevnar Meningitis Vaccine; RhoGAM; RotaShield; and Yellow Fever Vaccine.

Epilepsy

Irregular electrical impulses in the brain may be a sign of epilepsy. The cause of these seizures has not been determined, but drugs to control their development include: Depacon/Valproate Sodium; Dilantin/Phenytoin Sodium; Felbatol/Felbamate; Lamictal/Lamotrigine; Neurontin/Gabapentin; Tegretol/Carbamazepine; Topamax/Topiramate; and Zonegran/Zonisamide.

Erectile Dysfunction

Better known as impotence, erectile dysfunction (ED) refers to a man's inability to achieve or manage an erection, because the nerves that carry signals to and from his penis are damaged. Spinal cord injury or stroke, diabetes or its medications, antidepressants, heavy smoking or drinking, can all contribute to the disorder. There are drugs available for treating ED, including Cialis/Tadalafil, Uprima/Apomorphine, Viagra/Sildenafil Citrate, and ViraMax.

Fungal Infections

Fungi in the air around us can cause infections, ranging from minor to more severe (e.g. compromised immune system). Anti-fungal drugs to combat these infections include Lamictal/Lamotrigine, Lamisil/Terbinafine Hydrochloride, Miconazole, Nizoral/Ketoconazole, and Sporanox/Itraconazole.

Gout

Our bodies produce an organic acid called uric acid. The presence of increased uric acid in the body often results in gout, a condition that manifests as acute, chronic or deforming arthritis. About 95% of patients with this disorder are men over 30, with an association with obesity and heredity in some cases. The drug treatment of choice, which is to be accompanied by an anti-inflammatory drug such as Indomethecine, is Colchicine.

Heartburn

When acid escapes from your stomach and moves up to irritate the lining of your esophagus, you are experiencing heartburn or "acid reflux." The pain in your chest, neck or throat can be treated using prescription medications such as Propulsid/Cisapride Monohydrate or Reglan/Metoclopramide.

When acid escapes from your stomach and moves up to irritate the lining of your esophagus, you are experiencing heartburn or "acid reflux." The pain in your chest, neck or throat can be treated using prescription medications such as Propulsid/Cisapride Monohydrate or Reglan/Metoclopramide.

Long-term use of antacids may lead to certain nutrient deficiencies. This is because stomach acid is important in the digestion and/or absorption of nutrients. Older people produce less stomach acid, leading to low absorption of vitamin B_{12}. Regular use of antacids or acid blockers lowers vitamin B_{12} absorption even more. Vitamin B_{12} supplements may be required in this situation. Take antacids an hour after or in between meals. Avoid dairy foods – the protein they contain can increase acid in your stomach. If you are taking antacids as a Calcium supplement, avoid foods high in fiber (such as whole grains or dark green vegetables) or oxalates (tea), because they can bind with the Calcium and decrease absorption.

Heart Disease

Every year approximately one million people have heart attacks – half of which are fatal. We normally associate high cholesterol or high blood pressure with heart disease, but there are other factors that stop the flow of blood to the heart, leading to these disorders. Many heart-related conditions caused by diabetes, arterial disease, heart valve defects, high blood pressure or emphysema can weaken the heart's ability to pump sufficient volumes of blood to meet the oxygen needs of the body. The weakening of the heart muscle can lead to death. Combining digitalis drugs with a diet low in Potassium can cause Potassium deficiency and/or drug toxicity (high blood levels of digitalis). Natural methods to control heart damage include eating foods rich in antioxidants and Magnesium, limiting alcoholic intake, and getting plenty of fresh air, water and exercise. Some drugs to combat this heart disease are Bepridil, beta-blockers, Cordarone, Norpace/Disopyramide, Pacerone/Cordarone/Amiodarone Hydrochloride, Primacor/Milrinone, Quinidine/Quinidex, Tikosyn/Dofetilide and Vasotec/Enalapril.

Often prescribed for reducing blood pressure and heart disease, diuretics can cause increased excretion of urine and loss of minerals, such as Calcium, Magnesium or Potassium. Avoid salty foods and natural black Licorice, because they increase vitamin and mineral loss. Ask your doctor if you need supplements. Avoid large doses of vitamin D, because they can elevate blood pressure. Diuril, Lasix and Dyrenium are some commonly prescribed brands.

Hemophilia

Antihemophilic Factor (AHF) and Factor VIII are used in the treatment of hemophilia. These substances are made from donated blood. Drug makers have been accused of selling high-risk units of these drugs known to have been tainted with HIV or hepatitis C.

Hepatitis

Any inflammation of the liver caused by a viral infection can be classified as Hepatitis. Hep A is one of five human hepatitis viruses that infect the liver, causing illness. The other known types are B, C, D, and E. The contagious hepatitis infection has been known to lie dormant in a body for many years before coming to light. The condition may be acute or chronic, producing symptoms such as fever, jaundice, nausea and joint pain. Lamivudine is one drug used in to treatment of this disease.

High Cholesterol

Cholesterol is useful in producing hormones, vitamin D and bile acids, which digest fat in your body. Excess cholesterol, however, is deposited in your arteries, contributing to heart disease. Treatments that help to reduce cholesterol fall into five categories: resins, statins, Niacin, fibrates and probucol. Specific drugs are: Baycol/Cerivastatin; Crestor/Rosuvastatin; Gemfibrozil/Lopid; Lescol/Fluvastatin; Lipitor/Atorvastatin; Mevacor/Lovastatin; Pravachol/Pravastatin; Zetia/Ezetimibe; and Zocor/Simvastatin.

Antihyperlipemic drugs contain agents that lower blood cholesterol levels by reducing concentrations of lipids in the blood plasma. Cholestyramine/Questran is a drug commonly prescribed for this condition.

High/Low Blood Pressure

The measure of your blood circulating through your arteries is your "blood pressure." A person with chronically high blood pressure has hypertension; someone with low blood pressure has hypotension. Both conditions are dangerous. Any condition that dilates or contracts the arteries or affects their elasticity, or any disease of the heart that interferes with its pumping power, affects blood pressure. The most common treatments are diuretics, beta-blockers and ACE inhibitors. Medications for blood pressure can affect body levels of minerals, such as Potassium, Calcium and Zinc. For patients with diabetes, these drugs can cause problems in controlling blood sugar.

Drugs that maintain blood pressure within an average range, include the following: Accupril/Quinapril Hydrochloride; Altace/Ramipril; Cardizem/Diltiazem Hydrochloride;

Hexamethonium;   Lotensin/Benazepril   Hydrochloride;   Mavik/Trandolapril;
Monopril/Fosinopril   Sodium;   Posicor/Mibefradil;   Procardia   XL/Nifedipine;
Teveten/Eprosartan Mesylate; Univasc/Moexipril Hydrochloride; and Vasotec/Enalapril.

Combining certain blood pressure drugs with MSG (a common flavor enhancer) can cause flushing and feelings of tightness in the chest. Some brand-name examples are Lopressor, Zestril, Avapro, Vascor, and Lexxel.

Often prescribed for reducing blood pressure and heart disease, diuretics can cause increased excretion of urine and loss of minerals, such as Calcium, Magnesium or Potassium. Avoid salty foods and natural black Licorice, because they increase vitamin and mineral loss. Ask your doctor if you need supplements. Avoid large doses of vitamin D, because they can elevate blood pressure. Diuril, Lasix, and Dyrenium are some commonly prescribed brands.

Inflammation

Anti-inflammatory medication is prescribed to patients for a number of problems, such as chronic joint pain, headaches, and arthritis. These medications should be taken with food. Nonsteroidal anti-inflammatory drugs, such as ibuprofen and naproxen, can sometimes irritate the stomach lining. It's best to take them *with* food and to avoid alcohol and acidic foods. Long-term use may lead to stomach irritation and, eventually, ulcers. Drugs falling into this category include: Indomethacin; Flurbiprofen, Naproxen; and Sulindac.

Influenza

Influenza is the virus responsible for the A- or B-strand flu that gives us headaches, cough and runny nose, for a few days. Apart from receiving a flu vaccine, there are drugs on the market that have been developed to reduce flu symptoms. Relenza/Zanamivir is one of these types of drugs.

Irritable Bowel Syndrome

Emotional stress or poor diet can result in Irritable Bowel Syndrome. Sufferers of this disorder can experience symptoms such as excessive gas build-up, problems achieving bowel movement (constipation), loose stool (diarrhea), and/or bloating. IBS is not the same as colitis, mucous colitis, spastic colon, spastic bowel, or functional bowel disease, but may be incapacitating. There are several drugs that can combat associated symptoms, including Lotronex/Alosetron Hydrochloride and Zelnorm/Zelmac.

Laxatives, used to treat constipation, can cause vitamin deficiencies when combined with diets already low in vitamins A, D, E, or K. Certain laxatives cause stomach cramps when combined with milk.

Menopause

Women going through menopause experience a decrease in estrogen. Synthetic estrogen replacements have been around since the 1920s to help relieve menopausal symptoms. The use of hormone replacement therapy, commonly known as HRT, has long been touted as protection against osteoporosis and heart disease. Of late, researchers have suspected it also reduces the risk of Alzheimer's Disease. However, it was connected with the elevation of a patient's risk of endometrial or breast cancer. For this reason, doctors began to combine the hormone with progesterone. HRT is now given in formulations and dosage according to each individual patient's needs, but only amidst great controversy about its risks and benefits. Drugs used during the HRT process include Estrogen, Premarin, Prempro/Premphase, and Progestin.

Mental Disease

If you suffer from depression, anxiety, or other mental health conditions, you might be prescribed psychotherapeutic drugs, such as Thorazine, Haldol, or Clozapine.

Multiple Sclerosis

Your body produces myelin – a protective coating on the nerves of your eye, brain and spinal cord – that helps transmit electrical impulses throughout your body. It is thought that the deterioration of myelin, and the subsequent attack of antibodies on the electrical impulses, results in Multiple Sclerosis (MS). Drugs that help reduce the symptoms associated with this crippling disease include Avonex/Interferon and Novantrone/Mitoxantrone Hydrochloride.

Narcolepsy

Tens of thousands of Americans suffer this sleep disorder, which leaves them excessively tired, suddenly paralyzed, and sometimes even experiencing vivid dreams or hallucinations. A variation of the sleep disorder, hypersomnia, which makes people sleep more than they normally would, narcolepsy is thought to be caused by drug use, anemia, MS, depression, hypothyroidism or liver failure. Whatever its cause, it can put a patient in danger, unless they are taking a medication to curb its effects, such as Xyrem.

Neuropathic Pain

Anticonvulsant drugs control seizures and manage neuropathic pain, especially when the pain is lancinating or burning. Some drugs include Phenytoin/Dilantin, Phenobarbital, Primidone, Carbamazepine/Tegretol, Valproate Sodium/Depracon, and Clonazepam.

Nutritional Supplements

Dietary supplements – such as minerals, vitamins, herb or other botanical or amino acids – are readily available on the market as "cure-all" products. These are some of the more popular ones: Aller Relief Chinese Herbal Remedy; Anso Comfort Capsules; aristolochic acid; black cohosh; caffeine; chaparral/larrea tridentata; colloidal silver; comfrey; DHEA/Dehydroepiandrosterone; echinacea; Fat Trapper; germander/teucrium genus; germanium; Ginseng; hydrazine sulfate; jin bu huan; Kava Kava; Lipokinetix; lobelia/lobelia inflata; PC-Spes; shark cartilage; and willow bark/salix species.

In order to supplement your dietary intake, you might be taking water-soluble or fat-soluble vitamins. However, excessive amounts of these supplements can create harmful effects. Some vitamins with adverse reactions, when taken in excess, include Niacin/Nicotinic Acid/Nicotinamide, Prolongevity vitamin D Supplements, vitamin A, and vitamin C.

Organ Transplantation

Recipients of organ transplantation or blood transfusions run the risk of their body rejecting the foreign tissue type. Immunosuppressant drugs help the body avoid rejection of the new organ by suppressing the immune system. Some of these lifesaving drugs are Rapamune/Sirolimus, SangCya & Neoral, Simulect/Basiliximab, and Zenapax/Daclizumab.

Osteoporosis

A lack of sufficient Calcium in your diet may lead to a decrease in bone density. Osteoporosis can strike anyone, although it occurs more commonly among the elderly and puts them at increased risk of injury. Drugs to help prevent this debilitating disease include Alendronate or Ipriflavone.

Pain

Taking Pain medications on an empty stomach can cause stomach bleeding. When you experience pain, it is sensed by receptors located within your body. These receptors send signals through the nerves into the brain, which triggers a response. Combining Aspirin, and other over-the-counter pain medicines, with a diet low in vitamin C, can lead to vitamin C deficiency.

Depending on the type of pain you have, there are several analgesics or pain killers that will medicate you: Cafergot/Ergotamine; tartrate and caffeine; Dixon's Acetaminophen Tablets; Duract; Duragesic Patch; Imitrex/Sumatriptan Succinate; Lioresal; Intrathecal (Baclofen Injection); OxyContin/Oxycodone Hydrochloride; Parafon Forte/Chlorzoxazone; Pregabalin; Roxanol/Morphine Sulfate; Stadol/Butorphanol Tartrate; Tylenol; Ultram/Tramadol; Vicodin/Acetaminophen; and Hydrocodone Bitartrate.

Analgesics relieve pain, but often cause stomach irritation. Some examples are codeine, morphine, dextromethorphan, dextropropoxyphene, dihydrocodeine, diphenoxylate, ethlymorphine, pholcodine, propoxyphene, paracetamol, and tramadol.

General or local anesthesia is used to reduce or relieve pain, or to cause a loss of consciousness during surgery. Common anesthetics include: Inapsine/Droperidol; Propofol/Diprivan; and Raplon/Rapacuronium.

Parkinson's Disease

While anyone can contract Parkinson's Disease, one percent of all Americans over 65 suffer from it. The disease is caused by the reduction of dopamine, which facilitates muscle movement, in the brain. Sufferers experience tremors and the inability to move. Drugs to reduce the symptoms of the disease include Permax/Pergolide Mesylate and Tasmar/Tolcapone.

Performance-enhancing Supplements

Advocates for good health and fitness may take some of the many performance-enhancing supplements available on the market. Some of these include: Androstenedione; Butanediol or "BD;" Citrus Aurantium/Synephrine; Creatine; Ephedra; GBL/GHB; L-tryptophan; Tetrahydrogestrinone/THG; Tiratricol or TRIAC; and Yohimbe/Pausinystalia Yohimbe.

Pregnancy and Female Reproduction

Drugs used to prevent, or promote, a normal pregnancy include: Cytotec/Misoprostol; DES/Diethylstilbestrol; ED; Femodene; Gynecare Intergel; Marvelon; Mercilon; Minulet; Norplant Contraceptive; Oxytocin; Parlodel/Bromocriptine Mesylate; Prometrium/Progesterone; RU-486/Mifeprex; Tri-minulet; and Triadene.

Respiratory Syncytial Virus (RSV)

If you have a compromised immune system, you may be susceptible to Respiratory Syncytial Virus (RSV), a contagious infection affecting the lungs. Untreated, RSV can lead to pneumonia or more serious lung diseases. Synagis/Palivizumab and Virazole/Ribavirin are examples of drugs that help combat the virus.

Seizures

Anticonvulsant drugs control seizures and manage neuropathic pain, especially when the pain is lancinating or burning. Some drugs include Phenytoin/Dilantin, Phenobarbital, Primidone, Carbamazepine/Tegretol, Valproate Sodium/Depracon, and Clonazepam.

Spinal Cord Injury

Your spine controls your every movement. If it is compressed or severed during an accident, you may suffer severe damage to the cervical, thoracic, lumbar or sacral sections of your spine, resulting in numbness, loss of capacity, or even paralysis. While there is no current cure for spinal cord injury, there is a drug that helps promote the regeneration and healing of the spine and prevents further damage – Adcon-L.

Stroke

More than half a million Americans suffer a stroke each year; more than a quarter of this number consequently die or suffer severe brain damage. The disease occurs when the blood supply to the brain is interrupted, or when a ruptured blood vessel floods the brain with blood. A tissue plasminogen activator (TPA) can prevent some of the adverse impacts of a stroke, if administered within the first three hours and if there is no bleeding in the brain. These wonder drugs include Aptiganel/Cerestat or TPA.

Thyroid Disorders

Located in the neck, the thyroid gland produces, stores and releases hormones that control your body. If your thyroid gland produces too little hormone, you suffer hypothyroidism, experiencing symptoms such as fatigue, forgetfulness, depression, dry skin, or weight gain. If the gland produces too much of the hormone, you have hyperthyroidism, experiencing irritability or weight loss. This type of disorder is five times more likely to occur in women than men. Medications taken for thyroid disorders can be less effective when combined with iodine-rich foods. Sufferers of either imbalance need to take hormone replacement therapies, such as Levothroid/Levothyroxine Sodium or Synthroid/Levothyroxine Sodium.

Tuberculosis

Tuberculosis (TB), while found mostly in developing countries, remains a threat to the entire world, as it reaches epidemic proportions on a global scale. It is a chronic or acute bacterial infection, which can be fatal if it progresses to organs and systems throughout the body. It primarily attacks the kidneys, bones, lymph nodes, and brain; people with weak immune systems are the most susceptible. Some examples of antibiotics used to treat tuberculosis include Pyrazinamide and Rifampin.

NOTES

NOTES

COMMON FOOD ADDITIVES AND THEIR SIDE EFFECTS

Though we ordinarily associate side effects with medicine, in reality there are products we eat every day—often without realizing—that can also cause reactions, some of them quite severe.

Additives are chemicals "added" to food products during manufacture, typically as artificial flavors, colors or preservatives. While some of these seem harmless, others are clearly not. The table below identifies the most hazardous additives and the potential side effects and/or health risks associated with them.

As a general rule, reading labels will alert you to the presence of any of these additives in foods. However, you should be aware that the herbicides and pesticides sprayed on crops before harvesting are not considered additives, because they are not used during the "production" phase, and therefore do not appear on ingredient lists.

Additive	Brands/Varieties/Synonyms	Adverse Effects
Aspartame	Brands: NutraSweet, Equal, Spoonful, Equal-Measure	At least 92 conditions have been reported to the FDA, including seizures, migraines, dizziness, nausea, depression, fatigue, anxiety, memory loss. Consuming the sweetener may trigger or worsen several serious conditions, such as brain tumors, multiple sclerosis, Parkinson's, Alzheimer's, and diabetes.
Glutamates	Formulations: Yeast extract, hydrolyzed protein, MSG (monosodium glutamate)	Symptoms of allergic reaction include dizziness, headache, facial pressure, sensation of warmth, chest pain. Other side effects include rash, asthma, seizures, brain damage, learning disorders, stroke, depression, anxiety. Possible link to ALS, Parkinson's and Alzheimer's disease.
Colorants	Artificial colors, often identified with the initials "FD&C" and a number, e.g., FD&C Yellow No. 5	A range of allergic reactions in sensitive people. Depends on colorant, but may include hives, eczema, swelling, hyperactivity. May weaken the immune system. Some dyes, once considered safe, were later found to be carcinogenic. Many colorants allowed in North America are banned in Europe.
Preservatives – Sulfites	Sulfur dioxide, sodium bisulfite, Potassium bisulfite, sodium sulfite, sodium metabisulfite, Potassium metabisulfite	Sulfites used to be sprayed on produce until it was found they brought on attacks in people with asthma. The FDA banned their use in fresh/raw foods, but they are still used in dried fruits and vegetables, trail mix, wine, beer, seafood, potato products, dehydrated soups, maraschino cherries, and some soft drinks. Sulfites destroy vitamin B1 in food and susceptible people may suffer asthma attacks, anaphylactic shock, nausea and/or diarrhea.
Preservatives – BHA and BHT	Butylated hydroxyanisole (BHA) and butylated hydroxytoluene (BHT)	BHA may damage liver and kidneys. BHT may be even more toxic than BHA, harming liver and kidneys, promoting cancer and birth defects. BHT is banned in the UK.
Preservatives – Nitrates and Nitrites	Sodium nitrite, sodium nitrate, Potassium nitrite, Potassium nitrate	Known carcinogens. At one point the FDA mandated for these to be phased out, but withdrew its edict when the meat industry claimed they had no alternative. (Vegetables grown with high-nitrogen fertilizers may be high in nitrates.)

DETOX/CLEANSING PROGRAM

Here in the 21st century we live surrounded by more toxins than ever before. We're exposed to thousands every year. They're in our food and water, the clothes we wear, the building and decorating materials in our houses, the air that we breathe. Products so common that we take them for granted—such as cosmetics, carpets, and dry cleaning fluid. And we come in intimate contact with them every day.

All of this puts a huge strain on our bodies' systems—specifically our digestive and perspiration systems, which bear the responsibility for ridding us of toxins. Over time we accumulate toxins in our bodies, and the consequences include weakened immune systems, hormonal or psychological problems, and/or different forms of cancer. Meanwhile, some people develop sensitivities and have allergic reactions to the chemical in question

The issue of dealing with toxins is challenging enough when you're healthy. It's more problematic when you're unwell. Of all the times, that is when you most need healthy food, air and water—and are most susceptible to the chemicals in your surroundings.

In recent years a new field—"bioecologic medicine"—has grown up around the issue of toxins and pollutants in our world. The general consensus is that the prudent response to toxic bioaccumulation is periodic detoxification—that is, cleansing diets—plus the occasional juice or water fast. By eliminating chemical-laden meats, fats, alcohol, caffeine, refined foods and other chemicals you revitalize your body's systems. As an added bonus, spend a week on a detox diet and you will lose weight and boost your energy levels.

A word of caution: Depending on your condition and medication a detox diet may or may not be for you. Consult your physician before attempting this treatment.

What's Involved? The Four Rs

The detox program we present here is dependent on four critical components, which we've coined as the "Four Rs." They are:

1. Rid Your Diet of Vices and Your Body of Toxins
2. Return to Nature
3. Restore Your Vitamin/Mineral Balance
4. Relax

Our four Rs work together to help you cleanse your body and start anew. Following the guidelines of just one, two, or three of the components means your detox program is incomplete. Make a commitment to all four components for optimal results. Since our program is only seven days long, this is a commitment you can really make.

Rid Your Diet of Vices and Your Body of Toxins

We don't want to mislead you into thinking that this program is a piece of cake, because that piece of cake is exactly what you're going to have to give up for seven days. To detoxify your body, you *will* need to give up some foods. But let us reiterate here—you only have to give up your vices for a week to see the benefits of detoxification. You can do this!

During the week you commit to your detox program, you will need to take a break from caffeine, alcohol, sugar, refined grains, and most meats. While you're in detox mode, think about quitting smoking for good at the same time. Detoxification will actually help curb your cravings for nicotine, as well as sweets, white flours, coffee and alcohol.

The first day or two may be difficult—you could find yourself especially moody, or with a headache, or nausea as your body comes down from its sugar and caffeine high. We recommend that you start your program on a Friday or Saturday. That way you'll have the weekend to be at home and deal with the normal crankiness and fatigue that comes in the initial 48 hours of a detox program.

Drinking as much water as you can will help beat your cravings and limit the troublesome initial side effects of your detoxification program. If you feel under the weather when you begin, persevere! Your energy will increase as the program continues and your headache and nausea will pass.

Cut coffee, caffeinated tea, chocolate, sweets, desserts, potato chips, tortilla chips, cookies, crackers, white rice, white bread, bagels, donuts, muffins, beer, other alcoholic drinks, soda (diet and regular), cheese, potatoes, red meat, processed meats, and prepackaged foods from your diet altogether this week. It sounds radical—and it is. But it's well worth it!

Return to Nature

The foods you choose to eat during your one-week program are of critical importance to your detox success. You want to stay away from additives and preservatives, pesticides, and other chemicals, and overprocessed foods—in other words, you want to replace all the things you normally eat with natural foods.

This is the week to shop in the "organic" aisle of your local supermarket—or check out what the farmer's market or organic produce stores have to offer.

We've put together an alternating two day diet for you to follow during your detox program. On this plan, you'll feel full—not hungry—lose five to 10 pounds in a week, and improve your health.

Some tips for following the detox diet:

- If you're feeling hungry, drink a glass of water and snack on raw, organic vegetables and fruit.

- If you find that you're feeling headachy or nauseous, drink more water. The side effects you're feeling are likely due to dehydration, not hunger. The more water you drink, the better you'll feel.

- Steam a different variety of vegetables every day. Try to include at least three or four different vegetables in the mix. Not only will you ensure that your vitamin and mineral requirements are met by mixing things up, but you'll beat off the diet boredom blues with the variety.

- If you can't find organic vegetable broth where you shop, feel free to substitute the cooking water from your steamed vegetables. Add a little salt, pepper, rosemary and Garlic for extra flavor.

- Add some lemon juice to the water and herbal teas you drink. The flavor is nice and it boosts the detox process.

Restore Your Vitamin/Mineral Balance

This week, it's especially important to supplement your diet with vitamins and minerals. This will help you meet important nutritional needs, as well as assist the detoxification process itself.

Take a commercially prepared vitamin C supplement, a vitamin E supplement, a multivitamin, and a dose of omega-3 rich fish oil every morning with your two, eight-ounce glasses of water. Follow the manufacturer's directions, and speak to your pharmacist or natural foods store proprietor for a brand recommendation.

The powerful antioxidants these vitamins contain will kick your detox into high gear. Continue supplementing after the seven day period, to keep your body in top form.

Also think about adding a glass of water mixed with ground psyllium husk to your daily diet as well this week. Staying regular will mean that your body can efficiently flush the toxins and waste that are causing your health to deteriorate. If you don't want to take psyllium, we do not recommend that you take over-the-counter laxatives instead… they will just leave you dehydrated. Try instead a laxative herbal tea from your local herb market or natural foods store.

Relax

During your week-long detoxification, take some time for yourself! Now, make sure you understand that we don't mean sitting on the couch with a bag of chips when we say "relax"—look into a yoga class to try out three times this week, go on an half-hour to one-hour walk each evening, take a hot bath or hot shower—or jump in a sauna for a few minutes... the steam will help your skin detoxify, leaving you with a cleaner, healthier complexion.

Exercise is always important, but you don't want to be first in line for the spinning class this week. Your body will be undergoing some major changes, so you don't want to wear yourself out to the point of utter exhaustion. Now's the time to look into that T'ai Chi class at the local YMCA or buying those yoga/pilates DVDs you've had your eye on. Gentle, meditative movement is what exercise is all about during your detox.

Walking is a great way to claim some "me" time. Going for an evening—or morning, for that matter—stroll is fabulous for clearing your head, helping you focus, and finding some private time. Of course, we already know that benefits of walking as exercise!

Try to focus on your breathing, the way you walk, the way you interact with others, how you deal with stress... this week is all about you. Make it a positive week for your mind, body, and soul.

Your Seven Day Detox Meal Plan

	Friday, Sunday, Tuesday, Thursday	**Saturday, Monday, Wednesday**
Breakfast	Fresh fruit salad ½ cup steamed brown rice 2 8-ounce glasses spring water Green tea	Fresh fruit salad ½ cup cooked millet 2 8-ounce glasses spring water Green tea
Snack	Banana ½ cup organic yogurt 6-ounce glass organic vegetable juice 8-ounce glass spring water	Apple ½ cup organic yogurt 6 ounce glass organic vegetable juice 8 ounce glass spring water
Lunch	1 cup steamed vegetables Vegetable salad 8-ounce glass spring water	1 cup organic broth 8-ounce glass spring water Vegetable salad
Snack	10 natural almonds Chamomile tea Orange	10 natural almonds Chamomile tea Orange
Dinner	Small portion poached/steamed fish 1 cup of organic broth 2 8-ounce glasses spring water 1 cup steamed vegetables	Small portion poached/steamed/baked chicken 2 8-ounce glasses spring water 2 cups steamed vegetables
Snack	Dandelion tea 1 cup fresh vegetables	Dandelion tea Fresh fruit salad

NOTES

Avoid the
Harmful
Side Effects
of Today's Commonly
Prescribed Drugs

MEDICATION AND
SIDE EFFECTS DIARY

NOTES

PERSONAL
MEDICATION RECORD

Name _____   Phone number _____

Doctor's Name _____   Doctor's phone number _____

Pharmacy Name _____   Pharmacy Phone number _____

In case of emergency, contact_____   Phone number _____

Relationship of emergency contact _____

Other notes _____

_____

Medication

Name_____ Date Prescribed _____

Prescribed for the treatment of _____

Dosage (strength per pill. See bottle)_____Number of pills to take per day_____

I take a dose of _____ pills _____times a day at _____
                 (Number)   **(Number)**   **(Insert Times)**

If I miss a dose, I should_____

Other notes about taking this medication (Advice from doctor, pharmacist) _____

_____

_____

_____

_____

_____

Medication

Name_____ Date Prescribed _____

Prescribed for the treatment of _____

Dosage (strength per pill. See bottle)_____Number of pills to take per day_____

I take a dose of _____ pills _____times a day at _____
                  (Number)   (Number)   (Insert Times)

If I miss a dose, I should_____

Other notes about taking this medication (Advice from doctor, pharmacist) _____

_____

_____

_____

_____

Medication

Name_____ Date Prescribed _____

Prescribed for the treatment of _____

Dosage (strength per pill. See bottle)_____Number of pills to take per day_____

I take a dose of _____ pills _____times a day at _____
                  (Number)   (Number)   (Insert Times)

If I miss a dose, I should_____

Other notes about taking this medication (Advice from doctor, pharmacist) _____

_____

_____

_____

_____

Medication

Name_____ Date Prescribed _____

Prescribed for the treatment of _____

Dosage (strength per pill. See bottle)_____Number of pills to take per day_____

I take a dose of _____ pills _____times a day at _____
              (Number)   (Number)   (Insert Times)

If I miss a dose, I should_____

Other notes about taking this medication (Advice from doctor, pharmacist) _____

_____

_____

_____

_____

Medication

Name_____ Date Prescribed _____

Prescribed for the treatment of _____

Dosage (strength per pill. See bottle)_____Number of pills to take per day_____

I take a dose of _____ pills _____times a day at _____
              (Number)   (Number)   (Insert Times)

If I miss a dose, I should_____

Other notes about taking this medication (Advice from doctor, pharmacist) _____

_____

_____

_____

_____

Medication

Name_____ Date Prescribed _____

Prescribed for the treatment of _____

Dosage (strength per pill. See bottle)_____Number of pills to take per day_____

I take a dose of _____ pills _____times a day at _____
                    (Number)   (Number)   (Insert Times)

If I miss a dose, I should_____

Other notes about taking this medication (Advice from doctor, pharmacist) _____

_____

_____

_____

_____

Medication

Name_____ Date Prescribed _____

Prescribed for the treatment of _____

Dosage (strength per pill. See bottle)_____Number of pills to take per day_____

I take a dose of _____ pills _____times a day at _____
                    (Number)   (Number)   (Insert Times)

If I miss a dose, I should_____

Other notes about taking this medication (Advice from doctor, pharmacist) _____

_____

_____

_____

_____

Medication

Name_____ Date Prescribed _____

Prescribed for the treatment of _____

Dosage (strength per pill. See bottle)_____Number of pills to take per day_____

I take a dose of _____ pills _____times a day at _____
                    (Number)   (Number)   (Insert Times)

If I miss a dose, I should_____

Other notes about taking this medication (Advice from doctor, pharmacist) _____

_____

_____

_____

_____

Other notes (e.g., information on vitamin and herbal supplements)

_____

_____

_____

_____

_____

_____

_____

_____

_____

_____

_____

_____

Medication and Side Effects Diary (Page 1)

For the week starting_____ and ending_____

Monday

Check off the appropriate box when you take your medication.

Medication	Dosage	# Pills	Wake-Up	Breakfast	Lunch	Supper	Bedtime

Notes

Change in Condition _____

Side Effects _____

Other Comments _____

Tuesday

Check off the appropriate box when you take your medication.

Medication	Dosage	# Pills	Wake-Up	Breakfast	Lunch	Supper	Bedtime

Notes

Change in Condition _____

Side Effects _____

Other Comments _____

Medication and Side Effects Diary (Page 2)

For the week starting_____ and ending_____

Wednesday

Check off the appropriate box when you take your medication.

Medication	Dosage	# Pills	Wake-Up	Breakfast	Lunch	Supper	Bedtime

Notes

Change in Condition _____

Side Effects _____

Other Comments _____

Thursday

Check off the appropriate box when you take your medication.

Medication	Dosage	# Pills	Wake-Up	Breakfast	Lunch	Supper	Bedtime

Notes

Change in Condition _____

Side Effects _____

Other Comments _____

Medication and Side Effects Diary (Page 3)

For the week starting_____ and ending_____

Friday

Check off the appropriate box when you take your medication.

Medication	Dosage	# Pills	Wake-Up	Breakfast	Lunch	Supper	Bedtime

Notes

Change in Condition _____

Side Effects _____

Other Comments _____

Saturday

Check off the appropriate box when you take your medication.

Medication	Dosage	# Pills	Wake-Up	Breakfast	Lunch	Supper	Bedtime

Notes

Change in Condition _____

Side Effects _____

Other Comments _____

Medication and Side Effects Diary (Page 4)

For the week starting_____ and ending_____

Sunday

Check off the appropriate box when you take your medication.

Medication	Dosage	# Pills	Wake-Up	Breakfast	Lunch	Supper	Bedtime

Notes

Change in Condition _____

Side Effects _____

Other Comments _____

Comments – The Week In Review

_____

_____

_____

_____

_____

_____

_____

_____

_____

_____

_____